"*Keeping Faith in Rabbis* is a though[t] collection of essays on religious leader[s] —Adam Grant, Wharton Professor an[d] bestselling author of *Give and Take*

"This is the book we've been waiting for... This book pulls it all together with stories, arguments, the latest scholarship and common sense. If you are in the synagogue or rabbinic world, you need to read this... A great visionary and reflective work that will hopefully shape our understanding for many years to come."
—Rabbi Asher Lopatin, President of Yeshivat Chovevei Torah Rabbinical School

"*Keeping Faith in Rabbis* is like having coffee with 33 rabbis and lay leaders who speak to you as a trusted confidant. Before you get to the last drop, you've been challenged, and inspired to re-imagine the future of rabbinic leadership and education for our changing world."
—Cyd Weissman, Director of Innovation, Congregational Learning, The Jewish Education Project and Adjunct Lecturer Hebrew Union College-Jewish Institute of Religion

"The book explores many issues that face Christian pastors as much as they do rabbis... The issues are hauntingly similar... Here as elsewhere, significant conversation between Jews and Christians can be valuable for all."
—Professor Darrell Jodock, Martin E. Marty Regents Chair in Religion and the Academy, St. Olaf College

"*Keeping Faith in Rabbis* delivers even more than it promises. Through the conversation about raising up the rabbis of tomorrow, the essays in this volume put forth bold visions of what Jewish life in America could yet be. These are voices of leadership, unfettered."
—Professor Shaul Kelner, Professor of Sociology and Jewish Studies at Vanderbilt University

"Keeping Faith in Rabbis is an important contribution to the struggle for American Jewish continuity in the 21st Century. As our numbers continue to diminish, the need for quality rabbinic leadership grows. This volume highlights the importance of providing every tool necessary, including 'best practices' to the bedrock of our Jewish future, the rabbinate."
—Noah Alper, Author of *Business Mensch*, Founder of Noah's
    Bagels and Bread & Circus

"Keeping Faith in Rabbis delivers a frank, insightful and often sharply funny conversation about 21st Century American rabbinical education that leaves no Jewish sacred cows unslaughtered."
—Rabbi Daniel Landes, Director of Pardes Institute of Jewish
    Studies

"This remarkable collection of reflections conveys the inner, and sometimes highly personal thinking of seasoned rabbis. Rabbis will find these essays revelatory, inspiring, instructive and often surprising—as would anyone with interest in America's clergy today."
—Professor Steven M. Cohen, Hebrew Union College—Jewish
    Institute of Religion, Research Professor of Jewish Social Policy

"Rabbis and everyday Jews share their learning to show someone like me how my involvement is relevant to both me, the Jewish community and beyond... People together makes the world better than people apart."
—Jeff Rothpan , Comedy writer, Producer and Comedian

"The 21st Century will be a period of exciting, positive change in all forms of education. I share a passion for leading that evolution with Hayim Herring, Ellie Roscher, and the 33 contributing authors of this book. It's energizing to think about the possibilities."
—Scott Kinney, Capella University President

"With this collection, the good Rabbi Herring once again shows us he has his finger on the pulse of the Jewish community. Keep the faith...read the book."
—Craig Taubman, Musician and Founder of the Pico Union
    Project

"Rabbis remain central figures in contemporary Jewish life…This volume provides a wealth of thoughtful and often provocative insights into what it means to be a rabbi today and how our vision of and aspirations for the rabbinate translate into a host of new challenges and opportunities for rabbinic education."
—Dr. Jonathan Woocher, President of Lippman Kanfer Foundation for Living Torah

"Passionate, deeply personal, funny, erudite (though worn lightly), sometimes confessional, always thoughtful and reflective, the essays in *Keeping Faith in Rabbis* probe the changing demands on and possibilities for rabbinic leadership. Essential reading for everyone who cares about the future of Jewish life."
—Dr. Ronald Krebs, Associate Professor, Department of Political Science, University of Minnesota

"This is a wonderful collection of engaging essays written from a variety of perspectives. Anyone interested in the future of the rabbinate in America will be challenged and inspired by the wide range of thoughtful insights, personal anecdotes, and Torah wisdom found in this book."
—Hanna E. Bloomfield, MD, MPH, Associate Chief of Staff of Minneapolis VA Healthcare System and Professor of Medicine at the University of Minnesota

"Hayim Herring thinks radically, re-imagining the roles, leadership models, relationships and behaviors of successful religious institutions. The future of Jewish life and religion in America depends on our willingness to rethink old forms and structures."
—David M. Elcott, PhD, Taub Professor of Practice in Public Service and Leadership and Robert F. Wagner School of Public Service at New York University

"*Keeping Faith in Rabbis* offers a rare glimpse into the minds, hearts, souls and hands of our rabbis, and I, for one, am honored to have been offered this intimate, touching, and sometimes surprising, view…A must-read."
—Deborah Grayson Riegel, Coach and Author of
Oy Vey! Isn't a Strategy: 25 Solutions for Personal and Professional Success

Keeping Faith in Rabbis

A Community Conversation on Rabbinical Education

To Wes –

קיהדוככב

ויבי׳ג׳13

Lynne

December 2014

Keeping Faith in Rabbis

Avenida Books may be ordered through booksellers or by contacting:

Avenida Books

www.avenidabooks.com

Printed in the United States of America

Avenida Books

A^{|V}

Contents

Editor's Note: There is no universally accepted transliteration guideline for Hebrew, Aramaic or Yiddish. We have generally followed the user-friendly "Transliteration Guidelines and Master Word List" (edited December 27, 2013) used by the Union for Reform Judaism (URJ) for transliterations.

Introduction

By Rabbi Hayim Herring, PhD

When the opportunity to create a book about rabbis and rabbinical education presented itself, I signed on immediately. What intrigued me about building this book was the chance to invite more stakeholders into an ongoing, curated conversation about 21st Century rabbinical education—not only rabbis, but educators of current and future rabbis and caring, thoughtful lay leaders. And while rabbis are not the only ones who set the spiritual tone of the Jewish community, there is no denying that they are key influencers.

The invitation to create *Keeping Faith in Rabbis* came at a perfect time. The soil is ripe for a fruitful conversation. The recent Pew Study's *A Portrait of Jewish Americans* confirmed an enigma about 21st Century Jewish Americans. They are extremely proud to be Jewish, yet only about one-quarter report that religion is very important in their lives (compared with more than half of Americans overall). As the Pew Study also notes, while more than half of the overall American population reports attending religious services at least once or twice a month, only about 25% of American Jews do. How do we make sense of the reality that the people who brought a belief system of ethical monotheism to the ancient world now perceive that the Jewish religion lacks meaning for them in contemporary America?[1]

Simultaneously with the publication of the Pew Study, I received an alarming volume of calls from rabbis who, after lovingly serving

---

1   As the Pew Study notes, individuals who identify as Orthodox report levels of practice and belief that more closely resemble or exceed the general American population.

congregations, felt betrayed by board members who fired them. Lay leaders called expressing deep disappointment that their rabbis had not effectively transmitted the value of being involved in Jewish community to their children and grandchildren. Meanwhile, however, I had also met thriving rabbis who love their work and lay leaders who love their rabbis. Pockets of Jewish spiritual creativity were popping up in long existing congregations and exciting new corners. This book project was an opening to better understand this mixed landscape of Jewish religious.

We are living in a time of transition when *Keeping Faith in Rabbis* is needed. How do we train our rabbis to lead us today? Some aspects of Judaism will clearly endure through and after the transition. Shabbat will still happen over a twenty-five hour period between Friday and Saturday evening. Children will become *b'nai mitzvah* and people of all ages will continue to engage in Jewish studies. But best practices from yesterday may offer little guidance for tomorrow. For example, a reporter recently shared his mother's final moments of life on Twitter.[2] According to Jewish religious tradition, these sacred moments are supposed to be private, and not open to the universe. Some people were offended by his actions, while others were comforted because of their own current grief. What does Judaism have to say today about the creation or maintenance of sacred boundaries in age of radical transparency?

What does it mean for our communities to have four and soon likely five generations of individuals in large numbers? The issues that emerge from this reality range from ensuring that everyone has reasonable health care to providing opportunities across the generations to share skills and life wisdom. Religious communities have the opportunity to shape this new reality by posing some of the most deeply spiritual and existential questions.

We are in new terrain, but we are not the first generation to be here. Tracing the historical and cultural situations of Jewish communities throughout the ages and discerning how they adapted their insights to society can inspire us in forging our own new pathways. Exploring new situations in a religious community, led by rabbis who can guide

---

2   Scott Simon., "Scott Simon on Sharing His Mother's Final Moments on Twitter." NPR: *All Tech Considered.* www.npr.org/blogs. July 30, 2013, acquired August 18, 2014.

and hold new conversations, can give us the confidence to work our way through them.

Our complex times will continue to create disorder, which religious communities can help to restructure. For that to happen, we need rabbis who are willing to respond with spiritual authenticity on empirical data from reports like the Pew Study. This means rabbis thinking and working really differently than they do now. We need rabbis who are trained to act strategically and secure enough in their rabbinic selves to take the risks of wisely leading us through uncharted territory with capable partners.

The volume of essays that rabbis in the field, lay leaders and academics generously submitted to this project validated my belief that there is a great hunger to have a multi-vocal conversation. *Keeping Faith in Rabbis* adds to the existing discussions and significant experimentation happening in Jewish religious life in exciting ways. The corresponding *Keeping Faith in Rabbis* website with additional essays, interviews and resources will help spur it further. We hope you will join us.[3]

My deep hope for *Keeping Faith in Rabbis* is that it will fuel continued conversations in person and online, through workshops, presentations and inclusive tables where decisions about rabbinical education are made. For those of us who care about Jewish communities and the potential impact that rabbis have, there is too much at stake to let the conversations be limited or dwindle.

My rabbinate thus far has encompassed three decades in one ZIP code through four iterations: congregational rabbi, federation senior professional, national foundation director and now author, consultant and organizational futurist. While my own rabbinate has taken me in and through places I never expected, and while my understanding of serving God and the Jewish people has evolved over the years, I have never wanted to do anything else. I have had my period doubts, but after each one, my resolve becomes deeper. Some of my rabbinical reiterations came through crisis, others through serendipity or Providence in the form of caring friends and

3   Find online conversation on Rabbi Hayim Herring's Facebook Page (www.facebook.com/ rabbihayimherring). Supported additionally on the book's website (www.ktfrabbi.avenidabooks. com) and Ellie Roscher's website (www.ellieroscher.com).

family members, and others through persistence and intention. What I have learned along the way is that having faith, *emunah*, means that even when you do not know how things are going to work out, you trust in God and the people you love that they will.

By extension, we do not know what we may look like as a Jewish community a century from now. But we can do what prior generations have always done: work hard and hold *emunah* that we will still be around having healthy debates about the nature and purpose of being Jewish. *Ani Maamin*—I believe and hope you will, too.

Speaking Torah:
From Stammering to Song

By Rabbi Sharon Cohen Anisfeld

Even the written Torah is meant to be spoken. Words lie inert on parchment or page until they are inflected and animated by our own speech, silence, and song. How much more so the oral Torah, centuries of commentary and conversation that become intelligible only when the dead voices preserved on the page are resurrected— mingling with the inquiring, insistent, *living* voices gathered around the table to learn.

In the context of early Chasidism, disciples would gather around the rebbe's table to hear their teacher "speak Torah." As Rabbi Arthur Green has written, "'Speaking Torah'—*zogn toyreh* in Yiddish—is a linguistic expression of Chasidism's most essential spiritual claim: the rebbe's speech is a continuation of the great font of revelation that opened up at Mount Sinai, 'a great voice that has not ceased.'"[1] For Green, the Chasidic notion of speaking Torah is the point of departure for an even more radical and egalitarian invitation—not only to contemporary rabbis but to all Jewish seekers—to participate in the ancient and enduring conversation that is nothing less than a continuation of the revelation at Sinai.

It is this invitation—to people of all ages, but especially to high school, college and graduate students who will help shape the Jewish future—that has been at the heart of my own rabbinate for nearly twenty-five years. How do we help people enter the richly

---

1   Arthur Green, with Ebn Leader, Ariel Evan Mayse, and Or N. Rose, *Speaking Torah: Spiritual Teachings from around the Maggid's Table.* (Woodstock: Jewish Lights Publishing, 2013) xiii.

layered textual tradition that is our legacy as contemporary Jews? How do we welcome people into the complexity, beauty, and depth of a conversation that has been carried on for millennia—not simply as passive observers, but as active and creative participants?

These questions have assumed even greater urgency and importance for me as I've become intimately involved with rabbinic education over the last decade. So much depends on our ability to help future rabbis become fluent in speaking Torah—and on their ability to invite others into the ongoing and unfolding conversation through which Torah is forever revealed and renewed.

What follows are personal reflections from my own life and rabbinic work about some of the demands and rewards of learning to speak Torah. Some of the challenges that I address are unprecedented and specific to Jewish life in North America at the start of the twenty-first century. Other challenges, I suspect, are more timeless and universal, and we do well to remember that we are not the first—or the last—generation to face them.

It is important to acknowledge that many of us—rabbis and rabbinical students alike—feel insecure about our own stumbling and stammering efforts at speaking Torah. Many of those in the communities we serve feel the same way, only more so. Too often, we are locked in a cycle of mutually reinforcing inadequacy in which we try to hide from each other all that we do not know. As we recommit ourselves to the task of speaking Torah, we can draw comfort and inspiration from the Torah's account of the first rabbi, "our rabbi," Moshe *Rabbeinu*, whose own path as a spiritual leader was a painstaking journey from stammering to song. As the philosopher Emmanuel Levinas writes, the Hebrew Bible, "is so suspicious of any rhetoric which never stammers that it has as its chief prophet a man [Moses] 'slow of speech and of tongue.'"[2]

Learning to speak Torah does not require having smooth and ready answers on our lips. It does demand having tongues that are willing to say "I don't know," ears that are inclined to listen, and hearts that long to open.

---

2   Emmanuel Levinas, "Revelation in the Jewish Tradition," *The Levinas Reader*, ed. Sean Hand (Oxford: Blackwell, 1989) 197.

* * *

Hebrew was my mother's native tongue, and she spoke it fluently until the age of five when she and her parents left Haifa and travelled to America by boat in 1938.

Of course, as new immigrants in the 1940's, my grandparents wanted nothing more than for their daughter to become fully Americanized. I imagine my mother learned English fairly quickly as a five-year old. I don't know how long it took for her to completely forget Hebrew, but I know that by the time I was growing up, she felt it was irretrievable, locked somewhere in the recesses of her own memory. She made some attempts at Hebrew study when I was a child, hoping there was a key that would open the gates and allow her native language to come flooding back to her, but it never did.

I didn't give it much thought at the time, but I suspect that my mother's story had something to do with my own passion for the study of the Hebrew language as a child, and later as a teenager and young adult. I was one of the few children in North America in the 1960's and early 1970's who actually enjoyed Hebrew School. And a few years later, before my junior year of high school, I spent the summer studying at a camp called International Torah Corps in Littleton, New Hampshire. It was there that I fell in love with the Hebrew root system and a little book called *How the Hebrew Language Grew.*

That summer, shortly after returning from camp, I was in the bathroom humming the melody to an old Israeli folk song called "*Shir Haemek.*" Suddenly, my mother called to me from down the hall.

"What is that song?" she asked with a note of urgent curiosity in her voice.

"It's an Israeli folk song we learned at camp."

There was a moment of quiet recognition, and then she said, "My mother used to sing that song to me as a lullaby when I was a little girl. I haven't heard it since then."

I can still feel the tug of tenderness that I felt in that moment—the sense of connection to my mother as a young girl, to the grandmother I never knew, and to the thread of Hebrew poetry and song that tied us together over vast distances of time and space.

* * *

About three decades later, I found myself sitting in a hotel room in Tzefat with a group of twenty-six North American Jewish teenagers—–a thoughtful, curious, passionate, and pluralistic cohort of seventeen year-olds who had been selected to participate in the Bronfman Youth Fellowships in Israel. It was late Shabbat afternoon, time for *S'udah Sh'lishit*, and we wanted to do some singing together. Because the program brings together a diverse group of fellows—from Reform, Conservative, Orthodox, Reconstructionist, Renewal, and non-affiliated backgrounds—finding a shared musical repertoire can be a challenge. In fact, simply singing together can be at least as difficult as bridging the more complex ideological differences that divide us.

After singing the few Hebrew songs that everyone knew—"*Hinei Mah Tov*," "*Oseh Shalom*," "*Eli, Eli*"—we cast about, searching for some common ground. After twenty minutes, we found it: old television commercial jingles, and Christmas carols.

There we were. A group of about thirty North American Jews, in a far-flung room in a small town in the North of Israel, singing TV commercials and Christmas carols together. Almost everyone—myself included—knew not only the melodies, but most of the words. It was funny, a little surreal, and more than a little sad. Don't get me wrong. I am not a cultural snob, and I do not believe that Jewish authenticity requires a renunciation of popular American culture or a retreat from the influence of other faith traditions. But I do believe that our own vocabulary—our reservoir of language that has Jewish resonance and depth—has become dangerously diminished.

I've come to think of my mother's early loss of her native tongue as a powerful metaphor for the North American Jewish experience in the middle of the twentieth century. Because of a confluence of forces—the pull of assimilation, the devastation of European Jewry, the pressures of American liberalism and capitalism—we are participants in a mass culture that has resulted in the dramatic loss of language, literature, and song that links us to our past, to our future, and to each other.

* * *

Rabbinic education in our generation is in no small measure about the retrieval of a rich, spiritually, culturally, and emotionally resonant Jewish language. It is about helping rabbis speak as insiders to the textual tradition so that they, in turn, can invite others to join the conversation. It is about helping rabbis learn to speak Torah.

This process, it should be noted, is very different from learning to speak *about* Torah. Speaking *about* Torah is an academic or anthropological exercise. Sources are held at a safe distance. The speaker, however articulate or astute, is a visitor, an observer, a critic, or a tour guide, at best. She stands outside looking in.

Speaking Torah is a more intimate act. It means letting words of Torah into our hearts, so that they might give voice to wisdom we didn't know we had. It means discovering language for longings we might otherwise have kept to—or from—ourselves. It entails all the risks and rewards of any real act of communication, as we try to speak honestly about what we know and what we don't know. It makes unexpected demands on us—as we listen carefully to the voices on the page and around the table and allow ourselves to be touched and inconvenienced by what we hear.

* * *

For aspiring rabbis, the process of learning to speak Hebrew is an essential step in learning to speak Torah.

Our students sense this. They understand that the Hebrew language is an indispensable key to the textual tradition. They want to be able to read our sacred sources in the original so that they can fully participate in the Jewish conversation with a sense of authenticity and nuanced appreciation—and so that they can invite others to enter it as well. They want their own access to Torah to be unmediated, so that they can engage in what Ruth Calderon has described as "reading barefoot."

Our students understand the importance of Hebrew to their own process of learning to speak Torah, and precisely because of this, their struggles around Hebrew language acquisition can carry enormous emotional weight. Especially for those who come to intensive Jewish learning later in life, or those who come with different learning styles, challenges, and disabilities—the study of Hebrew can be a painful and arduous process.

Needless to say, Hebrew is not the only doorway through which contemporary Jews may enter the Jewish conversation. Some people will find their way in through a powerful experience of community or a passionate engagement with Jewish politics. For others, the point of entry may not be biblical or rabbinic text, but a contemporary novel, a short story, a poem, a song, or a single word of prayer. For those drawn to classical text study, more and more sources have been made accessible through high quality translations.

But for rabbis in particular—for spiritual teachers who will themselves have to be thoughtful and inspiring translators, helping to transmit the textual tradition in ways that have relevance and resonance for our own time—we cannot relinquish the centrality of the Hebrew language.

Hebrew is, after all, not simply a doorway, but a deep well of memory and meaning, a vast reservoir that spans centuries, continents, and generations. The process of Hebrew language acquisition is much more than a technical undertaking for our students. It is, in some sense, a process of *t'shuvah*—that paradoxical process of return, in which we have to enter territory that is uncharted and unknown in order to find our way home.

Again, I return to the image of Moshe—and his feelings of inadequacy and shame about his own lack of fluency and facility with language. The midrash famously traces Moshe's "heaviness of tongue" to an encounter with Pharaoh in early childhood—in which he reaches for hot coals and brings them to his mouth, an encounter that left him with a speech defect but ultimately spared his life. But I can't help wondering whether Moshe's struggles with language were somehow in part the residue of ruptures in his own life, reflecting the ambiguity of his identity as a traveler between cultures. What was the language of the lullabies Moshe's mother sang to him when she nursed him as an infant? How did those melodies mingle with those that he learned from his adoptive mother, Pharaoh's daughter, as he grew up?

And, most importantly, what was it that enabled Moshe to find his own voice in the wilderness, leading—and finally—leaving the people of Israel with words that reverberate within and between us to this day?

* * *

There is an old Hebrew expression, *"Devarim sheyotzim min halev nichnasim el halev."* "Words that come from the heart enter the heart."

For our students, learning to speak Torah entails a rich journey into the textual tradition and into the Hebrew language. But it also entails a rigorous journey into unexplored regions of the heart. How can the Torah we transmit touch another soul if we do not first let it touch our own? Language, after all, is an expression of the deep human longing for connection, but our words can only be a bridge between us and another person if they are built on a foundation of trust. Whether standing on the bimah or sitting at a hospital bedside, our words will fall flat if we fail to speak honestly and from the heart.

This, too, is part of what our students must learn with and from each other around the tables of the *beit midrash*. This means taking the risk of sharing ideas, insights, and interpretations with people whose backgrounds and beliefs may be quite different from—and even at odds with—their own. But, even more significantly, it means taking the risk of sharing questions, being willing to explore places of uncertainty, confusion, and doubt. As my colleague Rabbi Ebn Leader has observed, when our students work together with a c*hevruta* (a study companion), "they learn to *not know* together." They learn to admit it when they do not understand what the text is saying. They learn to acknowledge it when they do not understand what another person is saying. They learn to become more comfortable with not having answers.

This is important practice for aspiring rabbis. In the words of *Pirkei Avot: Lamed leshoncha lomar eini yodeiah*—"Teach your tongue to say I don't know." If I have learned anything in the last twenty-five years of working as a rabbi, it is that I do not have answers to any of the most honest and serious questions that I've been asked. How could God let this happen? Do you believe that everything has a purpose? Why should I go on living? What do you think happens to us after we die? Do you think that God hears our prayers?

The experience of not-knowing, of accepting the limits of our ability to offer answers can be humbling and unsettling, but I believe it is actually the most solid ground we stand on as rabbis—the ground of our shared questions, the ground of our shared humanity as we encounter the endless mystery and complexity of life.

At different times and for different reasons, our efforts to speak Torah may leave us stumbling, stammering, and searching for words. In those moments, I return to this reflection on the limits of language by the great Hebrew poet, Haim Nahman Bialik:

> So much for the language of words. But, in addition, "there are yet to the Lord" languages without words: song, tears, and laughter. And the speaking creature has been found worthy of them all. These languages begin where words leave off, and their purpose is not to close but to open . . . Every creation of the spirit which lacks an echo of one of these three languages is not really alive, and it were best that it had never come into the world.[3]

* * *

Ultimately, of course, learning to speak Torah is not about speaking at all. It is about inclining our ears and our hearts—in every place, at every moment, with every person we encounter—to "the great voice that has not ceased." If we want to learn to speak Torah we must begin—again and again—by listening.

In a world that values noise, we have to teach the importance of quiet. In a world that values speed, we have to teach patience. In a world that values knowledge, we have to teach the importance of admitting what we do not know. In a world that values power, we have to teach the important of accepting our limits.

The Chasidic master, the Sefat Emet (Rabbi Yehudah Leib Alter of Ger) offers the following commentary on the verse "If you listen, listen to the voice of the Lord your God . . .":[4]

> The Midrash comments: "Happy is the one whose listenings are to Me, hovering always at My doorways, door within door."

---

3   Haim Nahman Bialik, "Revealment and Concealment in Language," *Revealment and Concealment: Five Essays*, translated by Zali Gurevitch (IBIS Editions, 2000) 26.
4   Deuteronomy 28:1.

Listenings means that one should always be prepared to receive and listen closely to the word of God. The voice of that word is in every thing, since each was created by God's utterance and has the power of divine speech hidden within it . . . Inwardness goes on, deeper and deeper, truly beyond measure. This is the meaning of "My doorways." Never think that you have come to the truth; understand that you are always standing at the entrance. The word "doorway" (*delet*) is related to "poverty" or "humility" (*dalut*). This is the way you find door after door opening for you [by always knowing how little you have achieved thus far].[5]

Once again, the image of Moshe Rabbeinu comes to mind, this time, standing at the doorway, at the threshold of the Promised Land. Perhaps this is his last gift to us, his greatest teaching, his final song. Wherever we are, no matter how far we have come, we are always standing at the entrance, but we do not stand there alone.

Rabbi Sharon Cohen Anisfeld *has been dean of the Rabbinical School of Hebrew College since 2006. Prior to assuming this position, she served as an adjunct faculty member and dean of students at the Rabbinical School. Rabbi Cohen Anisfeld graduated from the Reconstructionist Rabbinical College in 1990, and subsequently spent 15 years working as a Hillel rabbi at Tufts, Yale and Harvard universities. She has been a summer faculty member for the Bronfman Youth Fellowships in Israel since 1993 and is co-editor of two volumes of women's writings on Passover,* "The Women's Seder Sourcebook: Rituals and Readings for Use at the Passover Seder" *and* "The Women's Passover Companion: Women's Reflections on the Festival of Freedom." *In 2011, 2012, and 2013, Cohen Anisfeld was named to* Newsweek *and* The Daily Beast'*s list of Top 50 Influential Rabbis in America.*

---

5   Rabbi Yehudah Leib Alter of Ger, *The Language of Truth: The Torah Commentary of the Sefat Emet*, translated and interpreted by Arthur Green (The Jewish Publication Society, 1998) 325.

The Loneliness of the Rabbi[1]

By Rabbi Harold M. Schulweis

I was not born a rabbi. My father was not a rabbi, nor was his father. A rabbi is not a rebbe, someone who inherits the status and mantle of his ancestry. I was born a layman, and as a layman I had felt from the start a certain mystique about the rabbi. Not merely the mystery in that the rabbi was invisible during the week and incomprehensible during the weekend, but a clear sense that the rabbi is different.

A rabbi is unlike a lawyer or a doctor or an engineer or a businessperson. A rabbi is different. Not that the rabbi is superior; in fact, the tradition makes it clear that the rabbi, like any righteous person, cannot exist on this earth and do good without transgressing. The rabbi is not infallible, as the folk saying that nine rabbis don't make a minyan, but that ten laymen do. Rabbis may try to convince the world that they are accessible, and may even swap jokes and make light banter. But I think that despite themselves, they are different. And if they don't think that they are different, they are seen as different. The rabbi is alone:

> I am lonely. Let me emphasize that by stating that I am lonely I do not intend to convey to you the impression that I am alone. I, thank God, do enjoy the love and friendship of many. I need people, talk, preach, argue, reason; I am surrounded by comrades and acquaintances. And yet, companionship and friendship do not alleviate the passional experience of

1   A version of this essay was previously published at www.vbs.org.

loneliness which drains me constantly. I am alone because at times I feel rejected and thrust away by everybody, not excluding my most intimate friends. The words of the psalmist, 'My father and my mother have forsaken me' quite often ring in my ears.[2]

This confession has often made me wonder in what sense loneliness is the fate of the rabbi's faith.

Why should the rabbi be lonely? The rabbi's study is lined with books, with texts, commentaries and responses. He or she is not alone. Still, there are times, more frequent in recent years than ever before, that new situations arise, more pressing than ever before. New challenges, new questions, new facts, which call for his decision and his judgment. And with all due respect to the companionship of books and the collegiality of his rabbinic peers and the institutions of his training, it is the rabbi who must decide. In this, the rabbi cannot overcome his or her sense of aloneness.

People come to the rabbi with personal situations about abortions, homosexuality, and divorce that are quite new and personal and which the ancient text do not satisfy. They do not satisfy because so much of the background, assumptions, presuppositions of the ancient and medieval world are not those of the rabbis who are called upon to rule and decide today.

Simply put, facts have changed, attitudes have changed, and values have changed. The congregation has changed and the rabbi has changed. For example, from the time that I was ordained at the Jewish Theological Seminary in 1950 to the present, the attitude toward women has changed radically.

Most of the time the rabbi may conduct him or herself like the Jewish priest. The rabbi wears vestments, officiates, conducts the ritual, and follows the codes. But the law is necessarily impersonal. The rabbi, like the judge, lives by the Book. The law cannot make exceptions. The law seeks to be unveiled. But more often now, the rabbi confronts individuals, with personal lives and unique situations which require more than following the law. And the rabbi experiences the loneliness of not knowing where and how to decide. At such times

_____

2   Rabbi Joseph B. Soloveitchik, *The Lonely Man of Faith*. (Jerusalem: Maggid Books & OU Press, 2011).

the rabbi feels closer to his or her prophetic ancestry than to his or her priestly ancestry.

Not even Moses, the prophet of prophets, is always sure of himself. Consider the episode of the five daughters of Zelophchad, who in the Book of Numbers 27, came to Moses to protest the law. In accordance with the tradition only men are eligible to inherit the property, the land from their father. In their case, their father Zelophchad left no sons, only daughters, and they have no inheritance in this. They challenged Moses: "Is it fair? Does not God have compassion for all? Give us a possession among the brothers of our father."[3]

Moses knew the tradition. He knew the law, but he heard the moral rightness of the women who complained to him. He was alone. Moses brought their complaint to God, because according to a rabbinic commentary in *Sifrei*,[4] "The daughters saw what Moses could not see." Finally, Moses ruled that women should indeed inherit the property from their fathers. On this verse[5] Rashi says, "Praised is the person with whom God concedes." Moses made the right decision.

Moses was alone. He had no precedent and the Midrash cites case after case in which Moses did not and could not consult with his colleagues, and who, even when the law was unambiguous but violated the conscience of Moses, rose alone to contradict the law and God. Alone, Moses broke the tablets of the law and God said, "You have done right to break them." Alone, Moses instituted a procedure that defied God's order, and he did not attack the enemies but negotiated with them. Alone, Moses rejected the visitation of the sins of the fathers upon the sons against the edict of the law. In case after case, God acknowledged the wisdom of Moses' lonely decision, and declared, "Moses, you have instructed Me, and I God will cancel My judgment and place in its stead yours."

The rabbi is sometimes a priest, and sometimes like Aaron, tempted to listen to the voice of the populous even as Aaron listened to the worshippers of the golden calf. Aaron rationalized his decision. He thought *"vox populi vox dei"*—the voice of the people is the voice of God. Perhaps he wanted to be accepted as one of the boys. Perhaps

---

3   Numbers 27:4.
4   *Sifrei B'midbar Piska* 134.
5   See Rashi on Numbers 27:7.

he could not stand loneliness. But Moses, the prophet, could not enjoy the comfort of populism. He knew that popularity is not the mark of the prophet. Moses and the prophets generally were lonely and reviled and certainly not understood by the people around them.

The Torah for the rabbi is not a Xeroxed text. The rabbi has before him a Torah consisting only of consonants. It is an unvocalized text. The Radbaz explains, "The Scroll is not vocalized to allow the wise to give his own voice to the text, his own vowels, his own interpretation." That is what keeps the Torah eternal and keeps the congregation alive. The rabbi must accept his or her loneliness. It does not mean that he or she does not have deep and close friends. Perhaps more opportunity for friendship is given than to the average individual. But it means that the rabbi has decisions to be made and positions to be taken that may strain the relationship between the self, friends, and congregation. In this, the rabbi is alone. The rabbi has only God to call upon, only God to wrestle with and in the course of the wrestling the rabbi will be vulnerable to lameness, that will remain for him or her forever.

What then, in honesty, should we say to rabbis? On the walls of Beit Hatfatsot, the museum of the Diaspora in Tel Aviv, may be found a statement by a great rabbi who knew loneliness. Israel Salanter said, "A rabbi whose community does not disagree with him is no rabbi. A rabbi who fears his community is no man."

Rabbis, you are the children of prophets. In you is the solace that comes from loyalty to the conscience that has led you to this sacred vocation. In you is the moral passion that kept the prophet alive, who when he confessed that he felt the derision against him, and was tempted not to mention God's name was overwhelmed by the word that was "in my heart as a burning fire shut up in my bones."[6]

You belong to a loving congregation with an understanding heart whom you have no reason to fear. For they understand that rabbis throughout the tradition have never simply lived by the book or the letter of the law. Only the simplistic view of Judaism can picture the rabbi as governing by quotation, or by putting his or her hand on the pulse of the people. It is a magnificent calling, the rabbinate. Be strong and be a blessing to us all.

---

6   Jeremiah 20:9.

Rabbi Harold M. Schulweis *is one of America's most imaginative and prolific rabbis. He continues to serve at Temple Valley Beth Shalom (VBS) in Encino, California where he has been a rabbi since 1970. He education is the product of a diverse array of schools, including Yeshiva College, with graduate studies in modern philosophical and theological thought at New York University, the Jewish Theological Seminary and the Pacific School of Religion, from which he received his Th.D. in Theology. He has lectured at CCNY, the University of Judaism and Hebrew Union College. Rabbi Schulweis is the originator of synagogue programs such as the Synagogue Chavurah Program, Para-Rabbinics, Outreach to Jews-by-Choice, Inclusion of the Developmentally Disabled (Shaare Tikvah and Chaverim) and the VBS Day School. He is the Founding Chairman of the Jewish Foundation for the Righteous, an organization that identifies and offers grants to those non-Jews who risked their lives to save Jews threatened by the agents of Nazi savagery and the Founder of Jewish World Watch, a synagogue-based organization dedicated to raising both awareness and funds to protest genocide in Darfur and alleviate the suffering of the victims of its unrest. Author of over a dozen popular, scholarly volumes and numerous articles, he was a 2008 recipient of the coveted National Jewish Book Award: Contemporary Jewish Life and Practice.*

In the Right Direction:
Hashpaah and Spiritual Life

By Rabbi Rachel Barenblat

On the morning of my ordination as a rabbi, I sat with the other *musmachim* in my cohort and listened to the founder of our rabbinic program speak. He's been asking us to call him Zaide for a while now, but most of us still think of him as Reb Zalman. The rest of the Jewish world calls him Rabbi Zalman Schachter-Shalomi.

He would speak again during our ordination ceremony to the assembled crowd of friends, family, teachers, and congregants. But these words were just for the ten of us. We sat in a circle and listened as he shared stories from his own rabbinic life. And then, toward the end of his remarks, he gave us a few pieces of advice.

"Stay in *chevruta*," he urged us. "Keep studying Torah." Or Hasidut or prayer or Talmud or whatever text contains the spiritual vitamins our souls most need. "Don't just study what you need to prepare for the Torah study on Shabbos. Study Torah *lishmah*," for its own sake.

"Be accountable to each other," he suggested. "Do your own *t'shuvah* work: daily, weekly, and monthly, not just annually. Find someone with whom each of you can be open and honest about the internal work you need to do. And take turns serving as listener for each other, so that you each have an opportunity to hear and to be heard, to facilitate forgiveness and to be forgiven.

"Daven," he reminded us. There's no substitute for staying in regular conversation with God.

"And please, do yourself a favor—stay in spiritual direction."

Spiritual direction—in Hebrew, *Hashpaah*, from the root which connotes *shefah*, divine abundance—is the practice of walking with and guiding people as they deepen their relationship with God.

Every ALEPH student is required to be in spiritual direction during our years in the program. Depending on who you ask, this is either a reflection of our neo-Chasidism (Chabad, the Chasidic lineage in which Reb Zalman was ordained as a young man, places great importance on spiritual direction) or a reflection of our deep ecumenism (spiritual direction as it's currently practiced owes a great deal to the Jesuits, who require it as part of their standard process of spiritual formation).

When I entered into the ALEPH rabbinic program, I knew that my learning would have two poles. My academic life would be supervised by a committee of mentors chaired by my Director of Studies; my spiritual life would be tended by my *mashpia(h)*, my new spiritual director. As it happened, the ALEPH *vaad* connected me with a *mashpiah* before assigning me my first Director of Studies. At the time I thought that was coincidental. Now I'm not so sure. Most of us who enter rabbinic school as adults, pursuing a second or third career, have some idea of how to learn. Tending to what grows in our own spiritual soil—that's where many of us need direction most.

By the end of my rabbinic school adventure, I was studying to become a *mashpiah* myself in order to more skillfully facilitate this process of spiritual unfolding for those whom I serve. I don't have many congregants who opt for regular *hashpaah* sessions, but I draw on the skills I learned in the ALEPH Hashpaah Training Program every single time I meet with a congregant or a seeker. In my life as a congregational rabbi I think back on those charges from Reb Zalman frequently. "Stay in *chevruta*. Study Torah *lishmah*. Daven with regularity. And don't drop the spiritual direction relationship." It's ironic, given that I'm a trained *mashpi'ah* myself, that his last suggestion is the most difficult for me to sustain.

I love studying in *chevruta*. Learning is always more fun (and more productive) with a partner. This year I'm meeting with a cohort of local Jewish clergy to read Heschel one morning a week, and translating and exploring the Degel Machaneh Ephraim with a rabbinic school friend over Skype a couple of times a month.

Sometimes I glean insights from those sessions which find their way into *divrei Torah*, but I'm not studying for the sake of writing my next sermon. Studying Torah, broadly conceived, is part of my spiritual practice. And taking the time to learn, despite job and parenthood, can also be a kind of self-care.

Maintaining a regular practice of *davenen* isn't so difficult—although my prayer life now looks very different from the one I sustained when I was a rabbinic student. For a while I blamed the changes on the vagaries of trying to balance my rabbinate with the necessity of providing childcare. Then my spiritual director urged me to broaden my sense of prayer and see the practices and paraphernalia of parenting as part of my prayer life rather than impediments to it. That suggestion reframed my experience and opened me up to God's presence in new ways.

These days I still don't usually settle in for long luxurious weekday *shacharit* sessions the way I used to, but I've gotten awfully good at singing *modah ani* in the shower, murmuring a quick *yotzer or* when I see the sun rise, and rattling off *Maariv* as I drive down darkening roads. Even when it isn't transcendent (or full- text), *davenen* nurtures my spiritual life.

Of Reb Zalman's exhortations, the one with which I struggle most is the gentle nudge that we should remain in spiritual direction. Even now, after nine years of lived experience showing me that *hashpaah* makes a difference in my life, I catch myself making excuses for why I don't have time to email my *mashpiah*.

I have too much to do. I haven't finished the lesson plan for next Monday's Hebrew school class. I have to leave work now and pick up my four-year-old son from preschool. Groceries. Laundry. Filing books away on my bookshelves. You name an excuse, and I've noticed it arising in me.

And that's part of how I know that Reb Zalman is right, and I need to keep doing it. It's so tempting to imagine that I'm finished, that I've worked out all of my stuff and nothing in my spiritual life merits examination. It's tempting to imagine that my relationship with God is rock-solid and will never waver. But when I discern the same challenges arising in my life in new forms year after year, I know I'm still in progress. As a sufferer of depression, I know that sometimes I need help to find God when S/He seems *nistar*, hidden away and beyond reach.

There's nothing wrong with continuing to explore the furthest reaches of my relationship with the Holy One of Blessing. How could that work ever be complete? It's not about the destination; it's about the journey. Maybe that's the direction in Spiritual Direction— not just the ways in which my *mashpiah* guides me, but also the ways in which she keeps me turning and re/turning to orient myself toward God again and again.

I've found other forms of self-care, of course. Long hot baths. Manicures and pedicures, gifts to my physical being which nonetheless nurture me spiritually. Naps, on the rare occasions when I can manage them. Speculative fiction novels on my Kindle to encourage me to enjoy a different kind of text from time to time.

But the deepest self-care practices I know are the ones which Reb Zalman urged on us on the morning of the magical day when I leaned back into the hands of my teachers and soaked up their words which left me changed.

If I'm seeking to open myself to become a channel of blessing and guidance for those whom I serve, I need to be attentive to the places where I might be stuck or snarled-up. I can't facilitate that flow of *shefah* for them unless it's also flowing for me.

Or, in more prosaic language, I can't take care of them if I'm not also taking care of myself. And one of the ways I do that is by sitting down regularly over Skype with my long-distance *mashpiah* and opening up for our conversation about whatever is live in my spiritual life at that moment. It's one of the best ways I know to keep my spiritual garden watered and pruned and growing, even when there are congregational hands tugging on every aspect of my energy and time. Even when the days are short and the ground is frozen and the demands pile up like the snow.

Rabbi Rachel Barenblat was ordained by ALEPH: the Alliance for Jewish Renewal in 2011. She holds an MFA from the Bennington Writing Seminars and is author of three book-length collections of poetry: 70 faces: Torah poems *(Phoenicia Publishing, 2011),* Waiting to Unfold *(Phoenicia, 2013), and the forthcoming* Open My Lips *(Ben Yehuda, 2014), as well as several chapbooks of poetry. A 2012 Rabbis Without Borders Fellow, she participated in a 2009 retreat for Emerging Jewish and Muslim Religious Leaders in 2009, and in 2014 will serve as faculty for that retreat. Since 2003 she has blogged as* The Velveteen Rabbi; *in 2008,* TIME *named her blog one of the top 25 sites on the Internet. She has been an off-and-on contributor to* Zeek *magazine, a Jewish journal of thought and culture, since 2005. She serves Congregation Beth Israel, a small Reform-affiliated congregation in western Massachusetts, where she lives with her husband Ethan Zuckerman and their son.*

The Accidental Social Activist

By Rabbi Harold J. Kravitz

I am proud to serve as Chair of the Board of MAZON: a Jewish Response to Hunger, an anti-hunger advocacy organization based in Los Angeles. Playing a leading role in working to eradicate hunger in the United States and Israel, it is supported by more than seven hundred synagogue partners and thousands of people in the Jewish community. As I reflect back on my early years of rabbinical school, there is nothing that would have suggested that social justice would become an important part of my rabbinate. My having come to this leadership role is a credit to the possibility that one's experience in rabbinical school can profoundly influence one's path, the course of one's Jewish life, and can ultimately have a significant civic impact.

I was accepted to rabbinical school at the Jewish Theological Seminary (JTS) in New York in 1987 and chose to start my education at what was then the West Coast branch of the Conservative Movement's Rabbinical School, The University of Judaism. The curriculum of neither campus was especially focused on teaching the value of social justice; though, one cannot be exposed to Jewish texts without imbibing the deep humanistic values of Judaism and the concern Judaism has for the most vulnerable elements of a society. Before my last two years of school, JTS had launched a *Vaad G'milut Chasadim* to organize student's participation in addressing the needs that were widespread in New York City at the time. Upon arriving, I was shocked to see the extent of poverty visible on the streets where it was quite common to see people begging for handouts.

The mid-1980's were a time of rapid growth of poverty in the United States in part because of decisions of the Reagan administration to dramatically reduce the role of the Federal government in maintaining the social safety network. In 1983, in New York City alone, a hundred emergency food programs opened to address the rapidly expanding needs as people's benefits were severely cut. It was in this context in 1985 that Leibel Fein launched MAZON after the Hebrew word meaning sustenance as a Jewish organization supporting the excellent work of organizations combating hunger for all people. Fein proposed that Jews celebrating lifecycle events donate three percent of what they would spend on their simchas to address hunger. MAZON would be a Jewish response to hunger, rather than a response to Jewish hunger, addressing the excesses sometimes evident in Jewish celebrations and reminding people of their broader social responsibilities as they were focusing on the blessings they were experiencing.

I arrived in New York City with my wife in 1985 to complete my rabbinical school education at JTS. I was not especially well informed of the broader social issues that contributed to the astounding number of hungry people we encountered on the streets begging for food. I signed up for one of the projects being sponsored by the *Vaad G'milut Chasadim* of JTS, founded to engage students in social activism. I volunteered at the food pantry operating at the Riverside Presbyterian Church, located across the street from JTS. That work helped me to feel that, in a small way, I was contributing to ameliorating the overwhelming suffering we encountered in the city each day.

While I was completing my studies at JTS, my wife Cindy Reich was working as the Principal of a Religious School at Temple Emanuel of Westchester. It was Cindy who first directed my attention to Leibel Fein's call in the pages of *Moment Magazine* in 1985 for the formation of MAZON: A Jewish Response to Hunger. Cindy encouraged her congregation to become an early partner. MAZON helped me learn more about the responsibility that Judaism places upon us to address the needs of all who are hungry.

After being ordained at JTS in 1987, I accepted the position as Assistant Rabbi at the Adath Jeshurun Congregation in Minneapolis. I was deeply impressed with the vibrancy of the congregation and needed to figure out what I could possibly contribute as a young rabbi. It was surprising to me how little focus there was at our synagogue on issues of social justice. Like New York, Minneapolis had also experienced a rapid growth of people in deep poverty that the community was now expected to support. When I arrived, Adath Jeshurun had only one modest project collecting food in a barrel by the entrance to our chapel for the St. Louis Park Emergency Project (STEP), the only food shelf in Minnesota that served kosher as well as non-kosher food.

In my first year at Adath Jeshurun, I assembled a small group of people to brainstorm how our synagogue could become more involved in addressing the issues of hunger and homelessness that were evident in the city of Minneapolis. I proposed reestablishing a social action committee at Adath that had previously existed only intermittently. We named our group the Chesed Committee, clearly reflecting my experience with the *Vaad G'milut Chasadim* at JTS. Like the Vaad, we decided that our Chesed Committee would serve as an umbrella organization to foster acts of Chesed (loving kindness) by our congregants in the various communities in which we participated.

Seeking activities that could engage Adath congregants, our Chesed Committee accepted an invitation extended to the community's synagogues by the Urban Affairs Committee of the JCRC to recruit congregants to an evening of service at one of several different projects serving the needs of hungry and homeless people in the city. We ended up sending volunteers to at least six different projects. Eventually, we developed groups of volunteers from our synagogue to volunteer with each of these programs under the banner of the Chesed Committee.

Our Chesed Committee is now well-established as the incubator of social justice activities of our synagogue. We successfully maintain a spectrum of responses to social needs from direct service in various feeding programs and shelters, to sponsoring long-term solutions such as transitional housing projects, to the even more fundamental work of supporting advocacy efforts seeking to change public policies that contribute to social injustice.

In that first year of forming our Chesed Committee, while we were figuring out the agenda and operation of our committee, I called my congregants' attention to the outstanding work being done by MAZON: A Jewish Response to Hunger. We proposed to our synagogue board that Adath Jeshurun become a congregational partner of MAZON, encouraging members to donate to MAZON when they were celebrating simchas.

Early in 1988, the Adath board affirmed our partnership with MAZON and launched what has proved to be a deep commitment to this cause by our congregation and by me personally. Over the years I have supported the work of MAZON in various ways, serving on a rabbinic cabinet and eventually on MAZON's Board and Executive Committee. In 2012, I was honored to become MAZON's Board Chair. I am especially appreciative that the leadership of our congregation, where I became Senior Rabbi in 1996, has been so supportive of my taking on this national role, seeing it as a credit to our congregation.

Among the first initiatives launched when I became Board Chair was the MAZON Advocacy Project. MAZON has long recognized that the issue of hunger cannot be solved only by direct service. To have a significant impact in addressing hungering, we must also advocate for public policies that will alleviate this persistent problem. In 2012, with the guidance of our superb CEO and President Abby Leibman, MAZON decided to strengthen our commitment to advocacy. We sharpened the focus of the approximately $4 million dollars in grants that MAZON now makes each to year to 300 anti-hunger organizations in the US and Israel to support their advocacy efforts. We have increased our impact on federal policy through the excellent efforts of a staff person engaged in Washington, DC. We are also exploring how MAZON might influence policy on a state level. We had long seen our synagogue partners as a source of financial support for our work combating hunger and as a vehicle for educating the Jewish community. What could result if synagogues were engaged more directly in social justice advocacy to eradicate hunger?

Samuel Chu, who serves as MAZON's national community organizer began a process of working with local synagogues, with our hunger grantees, and others to be our advocacy partners. In Minnesota we decided to work on an issue of school lunch. In 2008, at a Minnesota Hunger Summit sponsored by MAZON at the Adath Jeshurn, we learned that schools were struggling with parents who were not keeping up with payments of their children's school lunch account. Concerned about this revelation, Jessica Webster of Mid-Minnesota Legal Aid, a MAZON grantee organization that has done excellent work advocating for underprivileged people, began to investigate the issue. Her research has uncovered that as many as 15% of Minnesota school districts had actually adopted turn-away policies, and many more schools had adopted stigmatizing collection practices towards children whose parents were not current in their school lunch accounts. For four years Jessica sought to get a bill passed in Minnesota that no child would be turned away from school lunch. MAZON decided that this would be the right issue around which we could organize a coalition for hunger advocacy.

In 2012, we began our organizing at Adath Jeshurun by recruiting from the past and present leadership of our Chesed Committee to initiate this advocacy project. A past president of our congregation, who is a respected business lobbyist in Minnesota, offered her services pro-bono to advocate for a legislative fix to this problem for the 62,000 kids on reduced lunch in Minnesota who were most vulnerable. Over the last two years, MAZON built a coalition of forty-four organizations and more than 250 people, including local synagogue partners, anti-hunger organizations, other faith organizations, pediatricians, the unions representing the lunch room workers responsible for carrying out troubling school lunch policies and agricultural organizations to advocate for change. Our ability to build this coalition fairly quickly was aided by the many relationships that I have developed in our community in my twenty-seven years here as a rabbi and by the excellent reputation of MAZON. We determined that $3.35 million dollars a year in state funding could significantly reduce the problem of kids being stigmatized, if their parents had not maintained their school lunch accounts. In May of 2014, MAZON Advocacy Project in Minnesota (MAP-MN) proposed legislation that passed in an effort that included a unanimous bi-partisan vote in the MN House of Representatives. The MAZON Advocacy Project is organizing similar advocacy efforts in other states across the country with our synagogue and anti-hunger partners. MAZON is presently working to ramp up our advocacy activities in Israel in the coming year.

As I reflect on my own involvement in the work of social justice and anti-hunger advocacy, I very much attribute my experience at JTS working on hunger issues through the *Vaad Gemliut Chasadim* with having significantly influenced the path that my rabbinate has taken.

I did not aspire to become involved in social justice advocacy. In that sense I have very much been an accidental social activist drawn in to this work one step at a time. Each step of the way, working with thoughtful partners, helped to empower the next step. I witnessed how people determined to do good accomplish great things. It is exciting to contemplate the impact that our Jewish seminaries are having on those now receiving that education. One can never know for sure where those experiences and influences will lead, but there is much to be hopeful for as new generations come forward pursuing their interests and utilizing their gifts.

Rabbi Harold J. Kravitz holds the Max Newman Family Chair in Rabbinics at the Adath Jeshurun Congregation, Minnetonka, MN. He has served the congregation since 1987 after he was ordained by the Jewish Theological Seminary. Currently serves as Chair of the Board of MAZON: A Jewish Response to Hunger. He serves as an officer of the Rabbinical Assembly in the role of Secretary. He also serves on the RA's Va'ad Hakavod (Professional Ethics Committee), which he chaired for six years.

Right-Skilling:
Rabbis and the Rabbinic Role for a New Century

By Barak Richman & Daniel Libenson

In 2010, a collection of prominent physicians and medical educators formed a Lancet Commission to assess the current state of training healthcare professionals. Recognizing the lapse in time since the last major assessment of medical education, the famed Flexner Report published 100 years earlier, the Commission began *Health Professionals for a New Century* with the following observation:

> By the beginning of the 21st Century, however, all is not well... Professional education has not kept pace with [new] challenges, largely because of fragmented, outdated, and static curricula that produce ill-equipped graduates. The problems are systemic: mismatch of competencies to patient and population needs; poor teamwork; persistent gender stratification of professional status; narrow technical focus without broader contextual understanding; episodic encounters rather than continuous care; predominant hospital orientation at the expense of primary care; quantitative and qualitative imbalances in the professional labor market; and weak leadership to improve health-system performance. Laudable efforts to address these deficiencies have mostly floundered, partly because of the so-called tribalism of the professions—i.e., the tendency of the various professions to act in isolation from or even in competition with each other...

What is clearly needed is a thorough and authoritative re-examination of health professional education, matching the ambitious work of a century ago.[1]

As we reconsider the role and education of American rabbis for the century ahead, even a brief glance at this report's introduction, without any context, is striking. In spite of obvious differences, similar forces have put pressure on traditional approaches in both medical and rabbinic education, and as will become clear in the discussion that follows, the shortcomings in training today's healthcare workers are parallel in surprising ways to the shortcomings of training today's rabbis.

This chapter therefore piggybacks off research into educating physicians, gathering lessons from a thorough inquiry into a profession that has had to face a variety of disruptions to its traditional structure and professional roles. We approach this topic as neither rabbis nor physicians but as congregational lay leaders who have recently participated in rabbinic search processes and as professionals whose careers have had us delve into matters of professional education, community organization, and institutions that either embrace or resist innovation.[2] While we bring both some personal experiences and professional expertise to our inquiry, our purpose here is to learn from others.

The Challenge of Developing a 21st Century Healthcare Workforce

The Lancet Commission begins with the observation that "the context, content, and conditions of the social effort to educate competent, caring, and committed health professionals are rapidly changing across time and space." It chiefly observes that dramatic demographic and epidemiological transitions have produced more socially diverse patients than ever before, and at the same time, the rise of information technologies has empowered citizens to be active in how they consume health services and also proactive in

---

1   Frenk J, et al., "Health Professionals for a New Century: Transforming Education to Strengthen Health Systems in an Interdependent World," *The Lancet,* December 2010.
2   As it turns out, both of us happen to be lawyers, though we readily concede that the common lessons drawn here could easily apply to our own profession.

their interactions with the healthcare system. Health educational institutions have had serious difficulty responding to these marked social and technological changes, promoting the Commission to give a frank and critical assessment:

> Consequently, a slow-burning crisis is emerging in the mismatch of professional competencies to patient and population priorities because of fragmentary, outdated, and static curricula producing ill-equipped graduates from underfinanced institutions. In almost all countries, the education of health professionals has failed to overcome dysfunctional and inequitable health systems because of curricula rigidities, professional silos, static pedagogy (i.e. the science of teaching), insufficient adaptation to local contexts, and commercialism in the professions.

In short, a 21st Century healthcare professional must respond to a diverse, informed, and dynamic population, yet current educational institutions are severely ill suited to meet those challenges.

A pervasive theme throughout the Commission's report characterizing the current challenges is one of *mismatches*: the Commission reports that there is "a maldistribution of professionals," "glaring gaps and striking inequities" both within and between countries, and "skill-mix imbalances" in rich and poor countries alike. The problem is not necessarily one of constrained resources, but instead one of misdirecting resources. Health professionals are acquiring expensive skills that offer care to small populations while failing to acquire skills that produce significant benefits to large populations. They prepare for a career of giving directions to patients, rather than enabling patients to make good decisions on their own. And they are trained to work in expensive health systems, are unable to maneuver outside those costly frameworks, and are ill equipped to enable "patient management," which has become the gold standard for cost-effective care. As one leader of a prominent academic medical center lamented, "Practically everything about healthcare needs to change, from who delivers it, to how they are organized together, to how we finance it, to where it's provided."[3]

---

3   William L. Roper, on *The State of Things*, WUNC Radio, January 23, 2014.

One growingly popular response to the pervasive problem of mismatch is to pursue "right skilling," which simply means developing and employing professionals with the skills the health sector needs. For example, one report, produced from the Global Health Policy Summit that was organized by the World Economic Forum, identifies that the priority for rich and poor alike should be "to get the most out of human capital." Entitled *A Neglected Resource: Transforming Healthcare Through Human Capital*,[4] the report observes that "the global economic recession has created challenges in a way that has not been experienced since the Great Depression of the 1930s," and that continuing to misuse human capital is financially unsustainable.

The report strongly urges industry leaders to re-channel how the health sector invests in human capital. The health sector currently overinvests in complex skills that are costly to develop and utilize. It underinvests in more pervasively useful skills that have both widespread utility and are utilized more efficiently. The authors urge training professionals with skills that are less specialized and costly, and more widely applicable and rudimentary. Would a community be best served by investing a salary line in one doctor or in a team of nurse practitioners? This approach to right skilling, the report argues, not only would better equip professionals with the skills needed for 21st Century medicine, with greater financial sustainability, but it also fits a model in which patients are encouraged to assert greater autonomy and control over their healthcare. In other words, pursuing a system of "patient management" goes hand-in-hand with right skilling professionals and employing human capital most effectively and most efficiently. This collective approach has been depicted in schematic form by Clayton Christensen, perhaps this generation's leading scholar of innovation. Consistent with Christensen's observations of how disruptive innovation can upend entire industrial sectors, Christensen warns that the health sector's transformation relies on right skilling professionals and achieving more sustainable trajectories.

---

4   Victor J. Dzau, et al., A Neglected Resource: Transforming Healthcare Through Human Capital, Report of the Innovative Delivery Models Working Group 2012, World Economic Forum.

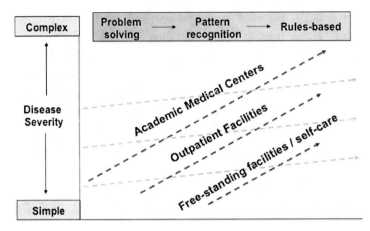

Adapted from Christensen, Bohmer, & Kenagy, Harvard Business Review (2000)

Transforming Healthcare Through Human Capital warns, however, that advancing this model of professional training and education will be difficult and disruptive: "In order to change the trajectories of health systems around the world, strong leadership and disruptive thinking will be required." It isn't likely that physicians will appreciate changes that make the healthcare system less dependent on them, relegate them to positions of less authority, or offer them less lucrative remuneration. Nonetheless, the authors observe that many leaders in medicine have already begun implementing this model:

> What is clear is that some individuals and organisations— imbued with an entrepreneurial spirit and a willingness to think creatively—have seized the opportunity. Unbounded by orthodoxy, they have found new ways to reach more patients, at lower cost, while also maintaining or raising quality and improving work attractiveness and professional motivation. They are proven examples that excellence in quality, efficiency and productivity is possible. These organisations succeed despite legacy health systems, not because of them; they stand out as isolated beacons within established systems.

The Lancet Commission put the urgency more starkly, concluding that "complacency will only perpetuate the ineffective application of 20th century educational strategies that are unfit to tackle 21st century challenges."

In sum, the need to reform the education and training of healthcare professionals is pressing, but the path ahead is daunting. Professional skills must better fit the needs of the population, with an emphasis on instilling skills that have greater applicability, are less costly to acquire, and follow a strategy of patient empowerment and self-management. The authors recognize that pursuing such a strategy requires major adjustments to well-established organizations, routines, and professional principles, but they urge the disruptive thinking and vigilant leadership that would enable the necessary reforms.

The Challenge of Developing a 21ˢᵗ Century American Rabbinate

Technological, demographic, and social changes have also altered the terrain for today's rabbis, and the Jewish world now experiences a mismatch between the skills Jewish communities need and the skills that rabbinic education provides.[5] Much like their physician counterparts, rabbis are acquiring expensive skills that fail to offer direct benefits to large populations, they prepare for a career of giving directions rather than enabling communities to make good decisions on their own, and they are trained to work in expensive environments that rely on diminishing financial resources. Yet 21ˢᵗ Century rabbis engage with a community that is more diverse, more independent, and more mobile than in previous generations, and thus are not a good match for rabbis with traditional training.

Nonetheless, many Jews who are synagogue members continue to cling to an idealized version of a rabbi, the image of which was developed in a very different time. This rabbi has known the family for decades, presided over multiple bar and bat mitzvahs, is certain to accompany those same children under the chuppah and perhaps even console them when their parents pass away. This vision of the family rabbi is not unlike the idealized vision of the house call-making family doctor of yesteryear. Yet many of the same powerful economic, social, and technological forces that have made the family doctor a thing of the past have also made the family rabbi an anachronism. These forces demand a new image of the rabbi's professional role and open the

---

5   Daniel Gordis presented a similar argument in *Requiem for a Movement*, available at http://jewishreviewofbooks.com/articles/566/requiem-for-a-movement.

door to considering new professional roles that might provide services that used to be in the sole purview of rabbis.

Religiosity. It seems that American Jews currently prefer expressions of their Jewishness that meaningfully differ from previous generations' expressions. The recent Pew Study of American Jews indicates that a large and growing percentage of American Jews identify as Jewish by culture or ethnicity, but not by religion. Yet the American rabbi's traditional role has been to offer spiritual, emotional, and educational leadership within a religious context, and synagogues—the primary employers of rabbis—continue primarily to be (and to be perceived as) places of religious worship. Twenty-first Century rabbis, other than those that serve highly religious and insular communities, will have to generate a broad appeal and offer services that stretch far beyond religious contexts.

Education. In 21st Century America, Jews have attained levels of secular education unimaginable to their ancestors. With greater secular education—and perhaps with the accompanying inculcation of liberal democratic sensibilities—comes greater emphasis on individualism and personal autonomy, an appetite for explanations and justifications for rules and conduct, and a general resistance to presumed authority. The 21st Century rabbi will need to adjust to both the blessings and the challenges of a highly literate, critically thinking, and intellectually demanding Jewish community.

In some respects, education has had predictable consequences. Just as it is the norm today for doctors to have highly educated patients, including those who (perhaps after having already done some Internet research) have developed views of what amounts to proper treatment, it is similarly the norm for rabbis to have individually-oriented and opinionated congregants. Just as physicians' instructions are less frequently accepted blindly and more frequently accepted only after thorough justifications, rabbis also are no longer the figures of authority who informed congregants what the rules were and instructed congregants what to do.

Rabbinic reasoning has always welcomed debate and disagreement, and in many respects a return by rabbis to their ancient rabbinic roots will be well suited for dialogue and deliberation rather than mere instructions. But some other features of the rabbinic role will likely adjust less gracefully. One might be the matter of pervasive use by rabbis of their honorific titles, as opposed to their names, a practice that judges, physicians, and some other status professions still cling to, but which serves to distance rabbis from their congregants. Another flows from the fact that the rabbi's role has often relied on having unusual access to certain materials or information—congregants, for example, were not well-versed in Jewish law or ancient Jewish transcripts—a kind of "secret knowledge" that was the hallmark of many ancient professions and guilds. But with excellent translations and other materials widely available, and with easy access to vast amounts of information, commentary, thought, and opinion on the Internet, rabbis no longer have the informational advantages that they once did.

Rabbis, like physicians, need to adjust to this democratization of information. In the extreme, both physicians and rabbis have been informational intermediaries whose role is being partially displaced by sites like WebMD and myjewishlearning.com. (In truth, the amount of Jewish material available on the Internet is staggering, yet it was not long ago that a person had only two routes to obtaining answers to substantive Jewish questions: spending time in a high-quality library or asking a rabbi.) We should expect only further disintermediation of professional knowledge. Physicians have made meaningful beginnings to accommodating patients who have acquired significant medical information on their own, and part of that transition has had physicians become co-discoverers more than repositories of information, and facilitators and curators of knowledge rather than presumed experts. To be sure, there are many congregants who will continue to expect rabbis to have informational expertise and moral authority, and perhaps an additional challenge for the 21st Century rabbi is to navigate multiple constituencies with different resources and demands. But there is little question that the degree and the nature of the education now enjoyed by American Jews, and their easy direct access to outstanding Jewish information, are presenting difficult challenges to the traditional paradigm.

Mobility. Twenty-first Century Americans—especially young ones—are substantially more mobile than they were in the past. The ideal of the American congregation is that of a stable community that stays connected to and invested in a single synagogue for many decades and perhaps generations, full of families who can be expected to be part of the community through multiple life-cycle events and throughout the childhoods of their children. But the 21st Century American Jewish community is highly mobile, easily moving to different regions and just as easily switching synagogues.

Mobility brings obvious challenges for any community institution that relies on local financial support. Mobility likely makes individuals more price sensitive and less committed to institutions that require legacy investments. Mobility also might undermine the strength of traditional rabbi-congregant relationships, which relied at least in part on deep understandings of family and community circumstances and a certainty of a long-term relationship ahead. Both the 21st Century rabbi and the 21st Century congregant must adapt to the reality that developing traditional rabbi-congregant relationships will be challenged by generational mobility.

The Digital Age. Though the digital age certainly has contributed to the widespread democratization of knowledge and to the population mobility, it also has had a meaningful impact on our social and community structures that traditional Jewish institutions have not yet fully realized. We communicate differently, relying less on sermons or mass gatherings. We develop social relationships differently, relying less on fraternal organizations, community centers, and youth groups. We also synthesize information differently, glued to smartphones and tweets.

Much ink has been spilled on how the digital age has forced changes upon education, politics, and the media, and Jewish leaders have similarly been probing at what the digital age has meant for the Jewish community. Rather than repeating that discourse, we merely observe that it is a technology that can potentially blindside traditional community structures, roles, and relationships.

Dwindling Resources. Although economic downturns are by no means uniquely 21st Century phenomena, the Great Recession was by far the worst economic downturn faced by the Jewish community since the bulk of today's communal infrastructure was built in the post-War years. In the 21st Century, Jewish institutions will not be able to rely on customary funding sources. Meanwhile, younger Jews display diminishing interest in traditional Jewish institutions. The foreseeable future will thus exhibit a declining desire of American Jews to pay—through membership dues, tuition, and charitable giving—what Jewish institutions have historically relied upon to function. Like healthcare professionals, Jewish leaders are confronted with new demands while also having to overcome the consequences of the Great Recession.

Towards the 21st Century American Rabbi

Some American professional education programs have markedly changed the nature of their curricula because of recent and rapid developments that often made the learning they offered obsolete. The Harvard Medical School engineered a dramatic change to its curriculum in 1985, underwent another major change in 2006, and is scheduled for yet another one in 2015. Harvard Business School also overhauled its curriculum in 2011, shifting from a case-study approach to one that emphasizes ethics and teamwork. Other areas of higher education are embarking on potentially dramatic strategic changes, in part necessitated by the challenge of online education. Thus, even within well-established professions, and even at age-old institutions, curricular change is possible when the demands for the profession similarly change.

Following the parallel lessons from medicine, we offer three primary recommendations. The first is to embrace the health sector's pursuit of right skilling. Given the increasingly limited resources of the organized Jewish community, we need to scrutinize critically the roles for which rabbis are truly necessary. Much like talented and appropriately expensive brain surgeons, rabbis should be used when their expertise is needed and when there are no substitutes. Otherwise, Jewish professionals with less elaborate and expensive training should have expanded roles in Jewish organizations. Professionals with master's degrees in Jewish education could play greater roles in fulfilling educational missions traditionally assumed by rabbis, social workers with a year of enhanced Jewish study could play larger roles in pastoral counseling, and community organizers could assume leadership of Jewish community organizations.

Even rabbis in more traditional roles need not require the extensive traditional training they now receive. For example, because information has become so much more widely available, including phenomenal audio and video lectures, courses, and books on the Internet, rabbis in some communities might serve congregants better as curators of the Jewish knowledge and experiences that are widely available, rather than themselves owning expertise in many fields. Congregants often need only an informed purchaser to help them navigate the instructional materials available online, rather than needing an actual instructor. Thus, rather than learning to be experts or even teachers themselves, rabbis might be trained to serve as concierges for their congregants. The Harvard Medical School pursued a similar strategy when it changed its curriculum in 1985, developing a "New Pathway" in light of the accelerating pace of medical discoveries, which aimed to adjust to the constantly changing status of medical knowledge; it became less important for medical students to learn information than to learn how to think, how to learn continually, and how to avoid becoming committed to an inadequate cognitive model of disease that was likely to change soon anyway. These concierges would not need five or six years of advanced study, but rather two or three years focused on their specific roles.

Jewish educational institutions should invest in developing less costly and extensive training programs, and Jewish organizations should seek to employ these right-skilled professionals in roles that traditionally have been occupied by rabbis. Many synagogues (especially small congregations) might benefit more from a rabbi (or Jewish professional with a different title) with skills that are tailored to the community's immediate needs, perhaps in leading prayer and offering rudimentary adult education, rather than one that has extensive graduate-level training—a rabbi more akin to a nurse practitioner than to the brain surgeon.

Our second recommendation is to encourage rabbis to reorganize themselves to accommodate for both the need for specialization and the economic necessity for right-skilling. One effective model pursued by physicians, as medical practice became more complex, was the multi-specialty physician practice, in which no one physician was individually expected to master all the fields necessary to serve patients. Rabbis too might find it infeasible to fulfill all the elements of the traditional relationship with the modern Jewish community and similarly might find attractive the many efficiencies that compelled physicians to specialize individually while offering a full range of services as a group.

Pursuing a group practice model might force a rethinking of the traditional rabbi-congregational relationship. Large congregations might be able to afford a large staff that captures all the necessary specialization, thus requiring little change, but a group practice approach would have a collection of rabbis serving a number of congregations. This approach might reflect the reality that it is increasingly difficult to find 300 families with sufficiently common needs and demands to sustain a mid-sized one-denomination synagogue. A rabbinic practice group would allow rabbis with different specialties to serve a number of congregations, and the model would allow multi-denominational congregations to exist without having to fight about what kind of rabbi to hire. The synagogues themselves would not have rabbis on their staffs, but rather their staffs would be made up of the "nurse practitioners" described above, and they would contract with a rabbinic practice group for a bundle of rabbinic services. The group's brilliant sermonizer might come to a given synagogue once a month, while the moving-life-cycle-event specialist can be on hand for every wedding and bar and bat mitzvah at multiple smaller synagogues, and can be on call for circumcisions and funerals. The great teacher can teach once a week at four or five different synagogues. Four (or more) synagogues could pay full-time salaries to a four-person rabbinic practice group and get outstanding rabbinical services in four different areas, rather than having to choose a rabbi who may be great at one thing but only mediocre at the other three.

If rabbis become specialized, then training of rabbis should also become more specialized. Rabbinic education could foster different specialties—pastoral care, education, prayer leadership, and public sermonizing, for example—while also preserving the opportunity for some rabbis to remain generalists. Presumably, some rabbis will find themselves in traditional rabbinic positions in relatively large single-denomination-based synagogues that are able to survive as such, but many others would play targeted roles and would require less expansive training. This would also mean that congregations would not be burdened by salary expectations that are appropriate for professionals expected to play leadership roles on multiple fronts.

A move towards reasonable specialization, with the efficiencies of collaboration, would offer some immediate rewards. It would open up advanced Jewish education, offering less expensive, less specialized degrees and training to a greater number of Jewish professionals with the skills that Jewish communities severely need. It would offer more affordable professionals and enable struggling Jewish organizations and congregations to benefit meaningfully from long-needed efficiencies, which is critical given the number of synagogues currently imploding under the weight of financial strain. And it might offer rabbis more professional satisfaction, allowing them to specialize in accordance with their skills and passions while also alleviating the pressures of having to serve a community alone.

There are certainly drawbacks as well. Something meaningful is lost when a rabbi is not squarely and exclusively associated with a congregation, and there might be a feeling of inadequacy when a congregation is served by a professional with more limited training than most current rabbis. By the same token, however, congregations might find that they are actually better served by devoted right-skilled professionals. These adaptations are unlikely to offer greater professional satisfaction to everyone considering a career in the rabbinate and are certain to deter some from becoming rabbis. But it is paramount that we construct a rabbinate that is attentive to the needs of Jewish communities, rather than attempting to construct communities in order to sustain the visions and demands of the rabbinate. Nonetheless, we are confident that there is sufficient commitment to serve Jewish communities among American Jews such that we will recruit talented individuals to assume these critical new roles. In any event, it is not helpful to pontificate only on the ideal rabbi, nor is it our agenda to praise or critique this new reality. Unless the traditional models somehow become both financially sustainable and adequate for modern demands, the training of rabbis must either prepare rabbis to confront and contribute to the new realities of Jewish life in America, or it ought to be training far fewer rabbis, as the numbers of jobs available for the old kind of rabbi are declining rapidly and will continue to do so.

Our third recommendation is to follow the medical world's focus on patient management—a strategy in which the focus is not the patient's specific interactions with healthcare professionals, but rather the patient's overall health needs. This approach has been proven not only to yield more cost effective care, but it also empowers patients, fosters autonomy and effective decision-making, and encourages self-management of health needs, thereby building greater patient dignity and improving patient quality of life. Rabbinic professionals, similarly, might produce better communities by seeking to foster self-management and self-sufficiency. Rather than placing centrality on individual interactions with religious professionals and religious institutions, Jewish clergy guide Jewish communities towards seeking and organizing their own Jewish experiences. And rather than constructing large organizations that place rabbinic professionals atop a religious hierarchy, Jewish professionals can foster organic, bottom-up expressions of Jewish practice through household or chavurot-based practices. This would make the community, not the professional, the locus of religious activity, and it is likely to foster more meaningful, gratifying, and self-sustaining religious experiences. Adapting Christensen's schema on the health sector to American Jewish communities might look something like the following:

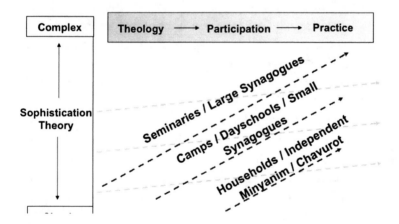

This connection between organizational innovation and the richness of religious self-sufficiency is not new. Clayton Christensen himself, who is attentive to organizational features across disciplines and contexts, has often parlayed his scholarly lessons to inform and explain his personal faith. A devout member of the Church of Jesus Christ of Latter Day Saints, Christensen has credited his church's organization for its vitality and the rewards it has provided him and his family: "because of the way the church is organized, it puts opportunities to help others in my path every day. It facilitates my efforts—and in some instances almost compels me—to practice Christianity daily, not just believe in it." Christensen offers a specific explanation of how organizational features translate into meaningful religious experiences:

> [T]he church helps me understand and practice the essence of Christianity. The mechanism by which the organization achieves this is to have no professional clergy. We don't hire ministers or priests to teach and care for us. This forces us to teach and care for each other—and in my view, this is the core of Christian living as Christ taught it. I actually have come to feel badly for my friends who belong to faiths in which professional clergy are employed—because they don't know how much joy they miss when they "outsource" the teaching and care of the members of their church to specially trained professionals.[6]

While some might take Christensen's suggestion to its logical extreme, that Jewish religious practice should be entirely without professionals, we merely heed his emphasis on how organizational features, including the role of professional clergy, can shape the meaning and content of a community's religious experience. Right skilling professionals, in both American industry and in American religious organizations, is both an economic imperative and a valuable strategy to organize meaningful religious life. At the very least, there are undeniably strong parallels between the success of organizing physicians around patient management and the potential of organizing clergy around the participatory model that Christensen describes.

Conclusion

Any professional education program must train professionals for the profession as it will be over the next forty years, not for the

---

6   Clayton Christensen, "Why I Belong and Why I Believe," *Clayton Christensen*, http://www.claytonchristensen.com/beliefs, accessed July 28, 2014.

profession as it was in the last forty. Rabbinical training is no different. In times of stability, this is relatively easy to do, bringing to mind a recent *New Yorker* cartoon in which a caveman tells his son, "When I was your age, things were exactly the way they are now." But in times of rapid Jewish change, such as our time, it is entirely unclear what the role of a rabbi will be (or ought to be) in four years, much less forty.

Perhaps we need fewer rabbis, perhaps we need more, and perhaps we need different kinds. Perhaps—following the advice that Jethro gave to Moses in the book of Exodus—rabbis might need to see themselves as part of a system of professionals that works together, rather than as figureheads atop discrete communities. It seems we have again become a "desert generation," living in a time of wandering, and our religious leaders accordingly will need to assess our changing needs and evolving community structures. At the very minimum, we need to educate rabbis to expect and embrace change, just as the medical profession is learning that doctors must be trained to do, and we need to design professional training in accordance with the needs of the population rabbis serve. We have no doubt that Jewish continuity will remain strong, but our promising future will be more indebted to our ability to manage change than to our commitment to ossified paradigms, including the roles and education of rabbis.

Daniel Libenson *is Founder and President of the Institute for the Next Jewish Future, an education and idea center dedicated to accelerating bold innovation in Jewish Life. He is also Founder and Executive Director of jU: Jewish U Chicago, a new campus organization focused on empowering students to build Jewish communities for themselves and their peers. Libenson previously served as Executive Director of the University of Chicago Hillel and as Director of New Initiatives at Harvard Hillel. He has received major awards for his innovative work, including the AVI CHAI Fellowship and Hillel International's Richard M. Joel Exemplar of Excellence award. Libenson has published articles on Jewish innovation, Jewish education, and the Jewish future in numerous newspapers, journals, and on-line publications. He has an A.B. degree from Harvard College and a J.D. degree from Harvard Law School. He lives in Chicago with his wife and two children.*

Barak Richman *is the Edgar P. and Elizabeth C. Bartlett Professor of Law and Business Administration at Duke University. Both an attorney and an institutional economist, his primary research focuses on how social relationships shape economic performance. His book* Stateless Commerce, *to be published by Harvard University Press in 2015, studies how ethnic merchants organize the diamond industry, and his research on health policy has examined the utilization of*

health insurance benefits, antitrust policy towards healthcare providers, and organizational innova-
tion in healthcare markets. Professor Richman's primary appointment is at Duke Law School,
where he won the Blueprint Award in 2005 and was named Teacher of the Year in 2010, and
he also is on Fuqua's Health Sector Management faculty and is a Senior Fellow at the Kenan
Institute for Ethics. He represented the NFL *Coaches Association in an amicus curiae brief in*
American Needle v. The Nat'l Football League, *which was argued before the U.S. Su-*
preme Court in January 2010, and again in Brady v. The Nat'l Football League *in 2011.*
His recent work challenging illegal practices by Rabbinical Associations was featured in the New
York Times.

A Letter to a New Reform Rabbi[1]

By Rami Shapiro

There are two kinds of Jews in America today: the minority who are involved in institutional Jewish life and the majority who are not. Those who are involved are by and large happy with their institutions. Those who are not involved are by and large unhappy with them. Involved Jews are active, passionate, loyal, and essential to the Jewish community. They are never to be disparaged or disrespected. Uninvolved Jews are also active, passionate, and loyal, just not about institutional Jewish things. These Jews, too, are never to be disparaged or disrespected.

In all likelihood you will work for the happy minority, who will ask you to make the happy happier while making the unhappy happy. Unfortunately for you, you can't do both.

During my first week at Hebrew Union College-Jewish Institute of Religion (HUC-JIR) in Jerusalem my class of '81 mates and I were told, "You have only one choice to make as a rabbi. Will you be a prophet or a clerk? Most of you will be clerks." The Jewish establishment values clerks, and is willing to pay them well. The Jewish establishment tends to hate prophets, and does what it can to ignore them.

Clerks comfort; prophets discomfort. Clerks legitimize; prophets challenge. Clerks maintain the decency of our lives; prophets reveal the brutality and emptiness at its core. Clerks say what others have said, and find meaning in being an echo rather than a voice; prophets speak what needs to be said so that others can find their own voices.

---

1   A version of this essay was previously published on *ReligionNext With Rabbi Rami*, July 2, 2012.

Clerks make nice; prophets make waves. Clerks warm hearts; prophets set them ablaze. All rabbis need to know how to be competent clerks. The great rabbis learn to be prophets as well.

Don't imagine that happy Jews want clerks and unhappy Jews want prophets. The fact is nobody wants prophets, and everyone wants the status quo. The involved Jews want it because the status quo is comforting. The uninvolved Jews want it because the status quo provides them with excuses for not being involved. And because they both want the status quo, they both want rabbis who support the status quo. They both want clerks. Therefore, it should be no surprise to you that you are being trained as a clerk. You are learning to teach what has already been taught; to repeat what has already been said, and to say what everyone expects to hear and therefore ignores. This wasn't how it used to be.

The way I see it, early rabbis were prophets rather than clerks. They based their authority on the conceit of the Two-fold Torah, Written and Oral, and insisted that the Oral trump the Written. They were literary anarchists wielding *g'matria*, *atbash*, and other swords of the imagination to create new Torah by deliberately misreading the old one, and, as the story of Akiva interpreting the crowns of the Hebrew letters admits, they knew exactly what they were doing.

The intrinsic chaos and anarchy of the rabbinic promise should have led to an ever-renewing Judaism, but over time the rabbis came to fear their own creation the way Rabbi Loew came to fear the Golem. Their Torah was too strong, wild, and uncontrollable. So they did what Rabbi Loew did: they turned *emet* into *met*, Truth into Death, by erasing the *aleph*—the creative chaos—at the head of the entire project.

As a result Judaism collapsed in on herself. The rabbinate, once the midwife of the new, became its mortal enemy. They turned what was a creative and redemptive wisdom into a fixed body of knowledge to be passed down rather than freed up. They took their Judaism of questions, doubt, and argument, and turned it into a system of answers, certainties, and rote. They stopped being prophets and started being clerks.

Clerks have two basic strategies when working with Jews: demand more or demand less. Neither one works very well. The more of the demand more strategy is halachah. Using halachah as our standard,

Reform Jews admit that Orthodoxy is the more authentic Judaism. For us, the demand more strategy fails for three reasons: it can demand too much, there is always more to demand, and Reform Jews don't want to be Orthodox Jews.

Take the so-called Cheeseburger Rebellion, for example. In the late 1990s the Reform leadership decided to promote traditional kashrut among the Reform laity. Not eco-kashrut, or some other invention linking diet to justice, but the very kashrut that Reform Jews rejected in 1885 with the Pittsburg Platform. What happened? The people rebelled. They refused to abandon their cheeseburgers, and they didn't care what God, Torah, and their rabbis had to say about it.

The same thing happened when the Reform leadership tried to promote the use of the *mikvah* among Jewish women. Rather than draw from tradition to invent an old/new spiritual practice based on the cycles of the moon, the body, and the alchemical potential for transformation that is what immersing oneself naked in a *mikvah* is all about, they just thought that liberal Jewish women would love an opportunity to cleanse themselves of the impurities of menstruation. This imitation of the past only served to enrage liberal Jews in the present, making it all the more difficult to create a new and vibrant Judaism for the future.

The alternative to demand more is to demand less. I grew up in an Orthodox world where the length of services was determined by the speed of the *davenen*. Shabbat and holy day services would go on for hours. Today's notion that Reform Jews can't gather for more than an hour without breaking for cake is demeaning. And the idea that rabbis shouldn't talk for more than ten minutes forces you to offer a message that isn't just simple, but simplistic. No wonder Jews avoid services! They aren't given enough time to be moved or enough wisdom to be enriched.

If demanding more always has you demanding too much, and if demanding less leaves you with nothing to offer, perhaps it is time to demand different.

There is only one reason for the Jewish people to survive, and that is to live Judaism. There is only one reason for Judaism to survive, and that is because it offers a path to life in a world obsessed with death. Resting on Shabbat matters because working sixty to eighty hours a week is killing us. Not shopping on Shabbat matters because consumerism is killing us. Pesach matters not because we *were* slaves to Egypt's Pharaoh, but because we *are* slaves to the Pharaohs of the military-industrial-financial-media complex.

Judaism matters only if it offers us a way to free ourselves from the killing machine of contemporary culture and to build a new world based on justice and compassion rather than greed and consumption. And you matter because you are a rabbi, and rabbis matter because they are the people who can free Judaism to be what it is meant to be—a vehicle for blessing all the families of the earth (Genesis 12:3).

My grandparents kept kosher because God demanded it. My parents kept kosher because Judaism demanded it. I keep kosher because life depends upon it. For me kashrut is about ethical consumption. It is about living in a way that enhances life. Kashrut is about caring for myself (*sh'mirat haguf*), for others (*ahavta l'reiacha kamocha*), for animals (*tzaar baalei chayim*), and for nature (*bal tashchit*) by linking diet, desire, and consumption to the highest ethical and ecological standards I can muster. Because I keep kosher I don't eat meat, and someday will stop eating fish, eggs, and dairy as well. Because I keep kosher I don't drive a gas-guzzling car, and someday will ride my bike to work. I do what I can to shrink my carbon footprint. I drink only fair trade coffee. Because I keep kosher I don't buy products produced in sweatshops (unless of course Apple makes them).

Kashrut helps me live my life in service to life. And what is true of kashrut can be true of every other aspect of Judaism. In a world obsessed with work, can you make Shabbat a day of play? In a world obsessed with pornography, can you revive the erotic through *Shir haShirim*? In a world obsessed with sex, can you reinvent love through *Tu b'Av*? In a world that has forgotten how to grieve, can you show people a way to a liberating grief through Tisha b'Av? Just look at the world, and imagine it different. Then make your Judaism a means to embody that different world. This is what the rabbi-as-prophet is called to do.

Unfortunately, this embodying of a better world through the practice of Judaism isn't what most rabbis are paid to do.

Reform rabbis are expected to play many roles that I believe we should look at critically and carefully. If you can hire a specialist to support you, you will not be expected to be the jack-of-all-trades.

Judge. Traditionally a rabbi rules on cases of Jewish law, but I have yet to meet a liberal Jew who lived her life according to Jewish law, or a Reform rabbi qualified to rule on Jewish law. If you want to be a Talmudic lawyer and judge, go to an Orthodox yeshiva. If you run into someone who needs a Talmudist, send him to a Talmudist.

Educator. If rabbis are supposed to be Jewish educators, why aren't we taught pedagogy, curriculum development, learning styles, new learning technologies, and how to work with special needs learners? If you want to be a top-notch Jewish educator, get a top-notch degree in Jewish education. Otherwise insist that your community hire the best professional Jewish educators they can find, and pay them what they are worth.

Psychologist. If you were having marital problems would you go to a rabbi or a licensed marriage counselor? The best thing you can do for people who come to you for counseling is to meet with them once, listen to them carefully, and then refer them to the appropriate specialist. Don't practice therapy without a license, and *s'michah* isn't that kind of license. If you want to practice therapy, become a therapist.

Celebrant. Officiating at life-cycle events can be fulfilling, but is this the reason you became a rabbi? After all, if officiating at life-cycle events is what you want to do with your life, you could have become a professional celebrant in a fraction of the time and at a fraction of the cost, and with a much larger client base. So enjoy this part of the job if you can, but don't make it the centerpiece of your rabbinate.

Announcer. Somebody has to welcome the congregation, read out the names on the Yahrzeit list, give a *brachah* for birthdays and anniversaries, or explain why we Jews who supported the efforts of African Americans to desegregate the buses in Montgomery must support the efforts of the Israeli government to segregate the buses in Jerusalem. But does this somebody have to be you? Did you spend five years of your life just to learn how to read responsively, or say, "We continue on page 1226" (is the *siddur* too long, or is it just me)? If you want to be Don Pardo, train as a voice actor.

The Jew. Some synagogues hire a rabbi to be The Jew the way Colonial Williamsburg hires an actor to be The Butter Churner. You can't stand in for the congregants. If your congregation doesn't want to be Jewish, leave before they cause you to feel the same way. This is the fastest path to rabbi burnout.

Fundraiser. Synagogues have real expenses, and no one should be embarrassed about asking for money. But are you really the best person to be the lead fundraiser? If serious funds need to be raised, get a professional with a solid track record of success to raise them. You might be asked to tag along to add gravitas, but leave the actual fundraising to the professionals.

CEO. Managing a small business takes real skills. I've taught these skills to senior executives of Fortune 500 companies, and I've ghost written a best selling book on the subject. I know what managers need to do, but I personally have no desire to do it. Nor was I taught this in rabbinical school. If you know how to manage, and want to be a manager, great, but you might be happier working for Wal-Mart. If you don't want to be a manager, hire someone who does.

Team Leader. If you're lucky you will work with cantors, educators, administrators, and other professionals who are as creative as you are. Be clear about your vision, enlist them to further it, and release them to manifest it. You want to work with people who understand your vision, and who can achieve it in ways you may not have imagined. Only clerks hire clones.

All of these things may be part of your job, just do your best to make them a small part. Otherwise you won't have the time or the energy for the real job. A rabbi's real job is to use Jewish traditions, texts, and teachings to help people create, articulate, and live deeply meaningful and purpose-filled lives. Notice that Judaism is a means not an end. Clerks make Judaism an end; prophets use it to achieve something greater than itself.

To do this job well you will need Torah, midrash, and mitzvot. By Torah I mean the entirety of Jewish literary creativity from *Taneah* and Talmud to Zohar and Tanya; from Rashi and Maimonides to the Besht and Buber; from Nachman of Breslav to Kafka of Prague; from Agnon to Jabes to Chabon. By midrash I mean the capacity to boldly and deliberately misread this Torah to create new meanings. If all you can do is repeat what long dead rabbis have said, refer your congregation to Wikipedia and sleep in on Shabbes. And by mitzvot I mean those traditional practices that can, when reworked in your hands, translate newly discovered meaning into purpose-filled living.

Are you learning how to be this kind of rabbi? Are you learning not only how to study Torah but also how to reveal Torah? Are you learning not only how to study midrash but also how to create it? Are you learning not only how to use mitzvot as they are, but how to shape them into what you need them to be? To borrow from Rabbi Abraham Isaac Kook, are you being taught how to "make the old, new; and the new holy?" Ask your professors for help. Some of them are prophets dying for the opportunity to share what they know. The best learning I did at HUC-JIR was after hours and under the table. Give your teachers the chance to teach, and there is no limit to what you can learn.

You are not only a rabbi. You may also be a friend, spouse, partner, parent, sibling, and child. Don't expect your congregants to honor your other roles. They like it when you praise family values, but they may not like it when you live them. Set boundaries and stick to them.

Make yourself unavailable. Schedule family time, personal time, and study time before you schedule time for anyone or anything else. Refuse to attend meetings unless your opinion and presence are absolutely necessary. The community belongs to the people, not to you. Let them work matters out for themselves. Care only about those things that are fundamental: your vision and your values. These are the things you will quit over, the things you are willing to be fired over. If these are threatened, be their champion. If they are not, stay home and read a book or plot a revolution or play with your kids. Don't work full-time work for part-time pay. If your community wants to hire you part-time, charge them by the quarter–hour like a lawyer using lawyerly rates. They will complain, but chances are they are lawyers themselves, so stick to your guns.

You know you are owned if there is some one or some group in your congregation to whom you cannot say, "No." Rabbis who are owned come to hate their jobs, their communities, and themselves. They are slaves preaching a tradition of liberation. The irony poisons them.

Stay free by being clear about what you will and will not do, and don't cave. Live debt-free as quickly as you can. Live well below your means so that you can survive financially if you decide that getting paid is no longer worth the cost. Cultivate a second career, something you might like doing if being a rabbi is no longer feeding you and those for whom you work.

I was a congregational rabbi for twenty years, and worked as a business consultant for fifteen of those years. I also wrote books and cultivated a national and eventually international speaking career. When I left congregational life, I had other skills to fall back on and a resume to back them up. The early rabbis didn't earn their living from Torah. Follow their example. Shammai was a general contractor. Go to night school and get an MA in Concrete Management.

I had five congregational rabbis in my youth, and not one touched me. They were interchangeable cogs in an institutional wheel that chewed them up and spit them out. They weren't memorable. I had five amazing rabbis in my adulthood: Mordecai Kaplan, Zalman Schachter–Shalomi, Eugene Mihaly, Ellis Rivkin, and Alvin Reines. Not all of these men were ordained, but they were rabbis nonetheless. I remember them because they touched and changed my life. I want to honor them by doing the same for others. So should you. The skills of a transformational rabbi are three: deep listening, bold reframing, and knowing how to make meaning in a way that creates purpose. You may not learn these at school. You will learn them by being transformed by someone who has them, and then hanging around those people long enough to learn the skills yourself.

Spinoza is one of my heroes. He wore a ring on which he personally engraved a thorny rose and the Latin inscription, *Caute*, "cautiously." His ring reminded him to be a thorn in the side of the establishment, but to prick cautiously. Thankfully, he didn't take his own advice. Neither should you. Know your vision and don't let others blind you to it. Know what you stand for, and be willing to be knocked down on account of it, and ready to stand back up because of it. Know why you became a rabbi, and settle for nothing less. Know who you are, and don't let others get you to be who you aren't. Be bold. Be a prophet. This may not be what Jews want, but it is what we need.

I have been a rabbi for over thirty years. I would not want to be anything else. I hope some day you will be able to say the same.

Rabbi Rami Shapiro *is an award–winning author of over two-dozen books on religion and spirituality. He received rabbinical ordination from the Hebrew Union College–Jewish Institute of Religion, and holds a Ph.D. from Union Graduate School. A congregational rabbi for twenty years, Rabbi Rami currently co–directs One River Wisdom School (oneriverwisdomschool.com), blogs at patheos.com, writes a regular column for* Spirituality and Health *magazine called* Roadside Assistance for the Spiritual Traveler, *and hosts the weekly Internet radio show,* How to be a Holy Rascal *on* Unity On-line Radio *(www.unity.fm/program/howtobeaholyrascal). His newest book is* Embracing the Divine Feminine: The Song of Songs Annotated and Explained *(SkyLight Paths). Rami can be reached via his website, rabbirami. com/.*

The Seminary and the Non-Pulpit Rabbinate

By Rabbi Ellen Flax

Since receiving my rabbinical ordination in 1997, I have been privileged to serve the Jewish community through what many might label a "non-traditional" rabbinate. Most of my work post-*s'michah* has been at foundations as a grant maker, providing necessary funds to non-profits in both the Jewish and secular communities. In addition, through the generosity of one such funder, I led the Schusterman Rabbinical Fellowship program, a joint program for rabbinical students from the Hebrew Union College-Jewish Institute of Religion (HUC) and the Jewish Theological Seminary of America (JTS).

I am very grateful for the education I received from HUC. My professors were dedicated to my growth both intellectually and spiritually. And I feel fortunate to have studied with an inspiring cohort of students who did and continue to support and challenge me in many ways.

As wonderful as my studies at HUC were, the program did fall short in one critical respect. The sad truth is that my five years of rabbinical school did little to prepare me for what was to become the day-to-day work of my rabbinate. That is not to say that my rabbinical school experience was not worthwhile, or that it wasn't religiously and intellectually stimulating, prompting personal and spiritual growth. Nor could I say that it did not provide a proper foundation to engage in certain aspects of traditional "classic" practical rabbinics such as conducting a wedding or funeral. But was it solid preparation for my personal rabbinate, which has been primarily non-pulpit? No, quite frankly, it was not.

When I entered rabbinical school in 1992, I wasn't quite sure what I was going to do upon ordination five years later. I had a strong inkling, however, that whatever my future held, it was not likely to be in a full-time pulpit position.

I did not follow a straight path to the seminary. I was raised in a large, traditional, non-egalitarian Conservative congregation. I walked away from shul life—despite thriving on Hebrew school and services—when my bat mitzvah was limited to reading haftarah on a Friday night, instead of chanting Torah on a Shabbat morning, like the boys in my class. At sixteen, I spent a summer on a kibbutz, and returned home with stronger Hebrew skills as well as a more nuanced and critical understanding of Israeli politics and policies. Seen as a potential recruit by several Jewish youth groups in my area that fall, I was promptly discouraged from joining—even though I strongly identified as a Zionist, my politics (for that time) were viewed as beyond the pale. At college, as a freshman, I tested out my campus Hillel, but finding the then-campus rabbi to be less-than-impressive and other extra-curricular activities to be more tempting, I stayed away. In my junior year, after studying and traveling through the (then Communist) Central and Eastern Europe, I realized that being Jewish meant a lot more to me than I previously acknowledged. Upon my return home, I started attending Shabbat services on a regular basis, and decided that finding an appropriate Jewish community after graduation was a top priority for me.

In Washington, D.C., as a new college graduate employed as a journalist, I was fortunate that such a Jewish community practically fell into my lap. As luck would have it, the (non-Jewish) friend-of-a-friend who found me an apartment in his (Jewish) girlfriend's building mentioned that there was a Jewish group that met right across the street from her, and said it might be a good fit for me. That first Saturday morning in my apartment, I walked out the door, across the street, and entered another portal, one that would totally change my life.

To say that that group, Fabrangen, was not your *zayde's* shul would be the understatement of the century. On that first Shabbat, a young African-American woman about my age wearing a t-shirt and sweatpants was leading services. While there were some chairs in the room, many sat on the floor on large pillows. Yes, there was a traditional Torah service (with both men and women having *aliyot* and reading from the scroll!) but it was what happened afterwards that was really different: they passed around a *Chumash*, and the congregants took turns reading the entire portion aloud, in English, paragraph by paragraph. Most astonishing, a lay person then gave a very short *d'var Torah*, followed by a more extensive public conversation about the *parshah*, with everyone contributing their two cents. I truly felt like my head was going to explode. I raised my hand to participate in that discussion, and for the next five-plus years before I went to rabbinical school, I continued to raise my hand to participate in this lay-run chavurah. Over time, I also served on the board of a region-wide Jewish adult-education organization, as well as in a leadership capacity at my local JCC.

Almost everything I ever needed to know about what makes a non-Orthodox Jewish congregation and community successful came from my time at Fabrangen. While there were several members with rabbinical ordination in the group, for the most part, the chavurah was powered by dedicated lay leaders. They led the services, chanted Torah, trained people to lead services and read Torah, organized and led adult education programs, organized shiva minyanim, and taught the children and trained the *b'nai mitzvah* students. No one cared if someone was single, married, divorced, widowed, gay, straight, with or without children, black, white, Latino, well-employed or under-employed. You were judged on your mensch-quotient, and whether you were willing to roll up your sleeves and become involved. Because the group's main expenses were rent and a part-time coordinator, dues were low—and when I, as a poorly paid entry-level employee couldn't afford even that amount, I paid what I could with no questions asked.

The rabbis I came to know through Fabrangen had a wide variety of day jobs including university professor, Hillel directors, day school teachers, and Jewish communal and non-profit workers. At the chavurah, however, they were rabbis in the most traditional sense—their role was that of teacher. They were sometimes asked to *posken*—to offer their interpretation about Jewish law—but given the non-Orthodox and completely democratic ethos of the community, the group as a whole made decisions about our Jewish practices.

Given my background, and my re-embrace of Jewish life and practice in a vibrant community without a standard rabbinical figure, it is not surprising that when I entered rabbinical school, I wasn't sure if I wanted to become a traditional rabbi—the leader of my own congregation serving as the primary service leader, meaning-maker, and ritual leader for other Jews. I knew first hand that lay people could do those tasks and create authentic community on their own terms without the benefit of formal programs or paid personnel.

To its credit HUC did try to acknowledge that the rabbinate came in a variety of shapes and flavors. There were the requisite programs featuring rabbis who had pursued alternative rabbinates as well as opportunities for students to get hospital chaplaincy training and pursue a career in the military. Students could also fulfill at least part of their practical work requirement in non-pulpit settings. But the overall thrust of the program—pedagogically, as well as culturally—centered on the assumption that we would serve in a congregation. More specifically, we would serve as an assistant rabbi in large congregation for a couple of years, likely holding a predominately youth-related portfolio, before heading off to run our own community. There was an acknowledgement that some—particularly older, second career students—would start at and potentially remain in smaller congregations in less ideal locations either due to market conditions (read: discrimination) or more optimistically, because they had a passion to serve smaller communities and really know their congregants, something that is impossible to do when one is serving a temple with 1,000 or more member units.

For most of my time at HUC, I felt like a fish out of water. Academically, things went very well for me. I entered school with a strong Judaic background, thanks to good Hebrew skills and years of living as an involved Jew in communities centered on Jewish texts and traditional practice; I ate it all up and wanted more. I had spent years as a reporter and editor, so writing and delivering sermons was not a stretch either.

Fitting in culturally, however, was a different matter. Some of the difference could be attributed to the fact that I did not grow up within the Reform movement. (I used to joke that because I was Reform-summer-camp-deprived as a child, I could not master, as an adult, some of the hand movements that accompany popular youth-movement songs.) At heart, I was a chavurah-nik, and had an alternate understanding and experience of religious community. For me, I was—and am—first of all a practicing Jew, and secondarily, a rabbi. I could not see how I could transmit Judaism to others unless I felt I was living a rich and authentic Jewish life. Consequently, it was of critical importance to me to find a good religious home, independent of my various and changing rabbinical school work settings that could sustain me for at least five years of graduate school. However, for some of my classmates, it was far more important to accumulate practical, traditional rabbinic experiences while in seminary than to merely live and participate in a religious community to fill or replenish one's own spiritual well. The rabbinic internships that were well paid and demanded over the standard twenty hours a week including most Shabbatot were highly coveted.

Another challenge I faced was that my work history was just plain wrong for the expected career path in rabbinical school. I had good job search and interview skills and a resume that was strong. I graduated with honors from a top university, had several career-oriented college internships followed by a solid employment history and lay leadership in the Jewish community. However, the fact that I had never been in a youth group, served as a summer camp counselor, or had otherwise done hands-on work with youth, was a definite deficit. Indeed, I knew that few congregations would consider hiring a rabbi without such experience. I tried to overcome this shortcoming by teaching Hebrew school, creating a confirmation class focused on identity formation across multiple religious and ethnic groups, and putting together family education programs at my out-of-town monthly pulpit. I also sought out additional youth work. Unfortunately, not once was I seriously considered for any job with a major youth programming component besides Hebrew school teacher; even securing a youth-group leader post was beyond my reach. Consequently, during rabbinical school, I was unable to gain the very experiences that would have enabled me to follow the traditional, and expected, rabbinic career path.

Periodically, I would question what I felt was an overemphasis on the importance of youth work, and not just for narrow parochial reasons. There was a general agreement at school, at least theoretically, that pediatric Judaism (a dumbed-down Judaism that may speak to kids but not to adults) should not set the tone of a synagogue, even though strong youth education programs are clearly extremely important. I knew from my own experience that there were countless adults out there who were seekers, who needed to be challenged and embraced. Would it be possible for us to create communities that put a greater emphasis on serving adults, I asked, on the theory that adults would be more likely to attend services, participate in the community, and indeed, bring their children, if their own needs were met? And what about all the childless adults, those whose children were grown, or who have never had children— should their needs also be put on the back burner? While there were some who were undoubtedly sympathetic to this line of thinking, at the end of the day, the fact that most synagogues were willing to put significant funds, and staff time, into youth programs, and not into adult-oriented programs, trumped any serious questioning of the larger system.

Realizing that I was unlikely to buck the system, and quite frankly, ambivalent about full-time congregational work, I knew I had to explore other options. While in school, as a self-supporting student on loans, I had done some editorial work in addition to the usual Hebrew school/student pulpit jobs to finance my education— indeed, as a former reporter for a national newspaper, I could command far more per hour for this kind of work than when I taught Hebrew school. One such project, documenting the implementation and impact of a national school reform effort that was supported by a leading foundation, led to other foundation-related work, including writing grant proposals.

Then, one day at school, at one of few career programs that we had featuring rabbis pursuing non-pulpit paths, I heard Rabbi Rachel Cowan describe her then-work at the Nathan Cummings Foundation as their inaugural Program Director for Jewish Life. I realized that foundation work might be a viable option for me, a path that could draw on a number of my strengths and interests. Fortunately, one such position opened up in New York shortly before ordination, and since then, I have spent most of my work life in the field.

HUC did prepare me well for the traditional rabbinical work I have done on top of my regular jobs—over the years, I have served several very small congregations on a part-time basis, and have worked as the rabbi at a series of nursing homes and assisted living facilities on Friday afternoon. These positions have involved leading services, teaching text, giving sermons, performing life cycle events, and pastoral counseling—all topics covered by an HUC education. But most of the skills I have needed for my bread-and-butter, nine-to-five work—writing, analyzing budgets, working with a board, working with a funder, fund raising, knowing how the nonprofit sector actually works, program evaluation, knowing how to gather a lot of information in a limited amount of time and translating that into something that can be acted upon, strategic planning, never mind deep knowledge of different giving areas, Jewish and secular—were not developed in rabbinical school. Some of these skills were honed while I was a reporter and most of the others were developed on the job. At key points in my career, I was able to take advantage of secular professional development opportunities, and I have benefited from participating in different peer-support networks, mostly those devoted to people in the philanthropy field. The bottom line has been that for most of my post-seminary career, I have primarily secured and maintained work as a result of my secular knowledge and skills, with my rabbinical degree seen as a pleasant bonus. My rabbinical studies have certainly helped me present things to others through a Jewish lens, and I'd like to think that my pastoral skills have facilitated my work with donors and lay leaders, but these rabbinic skills have certainly taken a back seat to the secular knowledge I need to know to do my job properly on a day-to-day basis and build a career.

To be fair, it would be unreasonable to expect HUC—or any seminary—to provide training to students in the full range of skills that they may need over the course of their careers. There are just too many skills, and they are just too varied, for any one institution to provide.

At the same time, the nature of the Jewish community is changing. There are fewer non-Orthodox Jews, and a smaller percentage of this group is electing to affiliate with a traditional synagogue. There is an increasing concentration of Jews in a smaller number of metropolitan areas, leading to the closure of synagogues in less populous areas. Congregations, even those affiliated with a movement, are willing to hire graduates of less-established seminaries who often command lower salaries as well as competition from Chabad, independent minyanim, and on-line/virtual communities. It is not unreasonable to suggest that the rabbinate, and the market for rabbis, is undergoing a significant shake up. Rabbinical schools have no choice but to respond to these trends.

The aforementioned Schusterman Rabbinical Fellowship Program attempted to address some of these gaps. Rabbi Hayim Herring led the shaping of the program. I helped, and then ran three cohorts of outstanding students through. The program, which included students from HUC and JTS, focused on the changing demography of the Jewish community, cutting-edge outreach efforts, and provided students with a range of management and leadership skills such as visioning and strategic planning. Most of the formal learning occurred over the course of several intensive retreats for each cohort, and featured speakers from across all the denominations and from both inside and beyond the Jewish community. Equally important was the informal learning that occurred throughout the school year and beyond the end of the program—many of the Fellows, eager to continue their cross-denominational conversations, organized on-going mutual support sessions even after ordination.

It appears that the schools themselves are responding to some of these challenges by presenting more non-pulpit options and increasing course offerings about the nonprofit sector and social entrepreneurship. While this is a good start, I am not sure that this goes far enough.

I think we have to accept the uncomfortable truth that there are likely to be far fewer good, full time, well paying jobs within the Jewish community appropriate for rabbis in the not-too-distant future, and that the whole paradigm for training tomorrow's rabbis will need to change as a result. We cannot expect prospective students to take on substantial debt, as many currently do, for an uncertain career path. Many rabbis will be forced to be fundraisers and social entrepreneurs to cover the costs of their efforts in the nonprofit world, whether they work at Hillels, at JCCs, or create their own programs and institutions. The seminaries would be well advised to ensure that their graduates have these skills. Those who want to engage in traditional rabbinic work may need, like many of their Orthodox brethren, to pursue secular work for most of their parnasah if they want to maintain a middle class lifestyle, with their congregational efforts limited to part time hours. At the same time, the seminaries, unable to provide all the skills that a future rabbi may need, should consider investing in additional career planning counselors and resources. This would enable students to draft individualized career paths that feature both rabbinic and secular work, and to craft a plan for acquiring appropriate secular skills at other institutions.

In short, I think far more future rabbinates will look like mine than what has been the norm in the past. Institutions that are training rabbis have no choice but to fully accept and adapt to this reality.

Although the seminary may not have prepared me for my day-to-day work, tasks, and duties, it certainly helped prepare me for my life's work: serving the Jewish people in whatever modest ways that I can, and doing what I hope is God's work on this earth. My rabbinical school studies helped guide me as I struggled—and continue to struggle—with questions about meaning and purpose, and God's role for us in this world. I hope I am a better professional, a better person, a better Jew, a better rabbi, a better teacher and a better guide for others as a result of this struggle.

Rabbi Ellen Flax is the director of The Hadassah Foundation, which invests in social change for girls and women in Israel and the United States. Previously, she ran the Schusterman Rabbinical Fellowship Program, which helped create a cadre of future religious leaders from both the Reform and Conservative movements who share a broad and dynamic vision for American Jewry. She has served as: a program consultant to STAR (Synagogues: Transformation and Renewal); a senior consultant to the Charles and Lynn Schusterman Family Foundation; a program officer for a large family foundation; and as the director of education and outreach for a public foundation. Before receiving rabbinical ordination from the Hebrew Union College-Jewish Institute of Religion, Ellen was a journalist, and worked for Education Week and the Associated Press.

Being a Rabbi

By *Rabbi Morley T. Feinstein*

The results of a computerized survey indicate the perfect rabbi preaches exactly fifteen minutes. He condemns sins but never upsets anyone. He works from 8:00 AM until midnight and is also a janitor. He makes $50 a week, wears good clothes, buys good books, drives a good car, and gives about $50 weekly to the poor. He is 28 years old and has preached 30 years. He has a burning desire to work with teenagers and spends all of his time with senior citizens. The perfect rabbi smiles all the time with a straight face because he has a sense of humor that keeps him seriously dedicated to his work. He makes 15 calls daily on congregation families, shut-ins and the hospitalized, and is always in his office when needed. If your rabbi does not measure up, simply send this letter to six other synagogues that are tired of their rabbi, too. Then bundle up your rabbi and send him to the synagogue on the top of the list. In one week, you will receive 1,643 rabbis and one of them will be perfect. Have faith in this procedure. One congregation broke the chain and got back the rabbi they fired 25 years ago.[1]

I am certainly glad I never read this bit of humor before I was ordained. Yet there is an element of truth in the humor. People expect that we rabbis (especially in congregations) are Jewish experts at everything; every question can be answered because we have an infinite amount of time to handle every event, meeting, committee,

---

1   Author unknown.

class, service, and program by using phone calls, email, letters, Facebook and Twitter to deal perfectly with every baby, toddler, child, teenager, college student, single, married, young, and old. And we learned everything we needed to know during our seminary education.

Rabbinic education creates authenticity in the rabbi. We learn in our Yeshivah Shel Matah to study, think, and dream, but we live in a world in which our actual training doesn't match the reality of our work. It doesn't provide a framework for the ways in which we act as rabbis in real life. There are too many situations that occur which remove us from the safety and comfort of our study. In only a few years I've had to deal with issues regarding a former employee, interacting with lawyers and human resource experts; the largest donor to our building project went bankrupt and instant job training on how to deal with financial emergency; a flooded preschool, repairing the facility while dealing with insurance claims, while at the same time creating a healthy environment for the little learners and teachers to remain in school; active shooter training, intruders, and other security issues; and the inevitable costs and responsibility of sustaining Jewish life and the livelihoods of over thirty-five employees. There may be ways to learn about these scenarios in theory, but there was little to no training for this in my rabbinic education.

Perhaps we ask too much of our teachers and faculty in our seminaries, for each school is a combination institution of higher learning and a trade tech. But we are not alone. There are similar issues whether one is a rabbi, lawyer, or physician. We learn theory in the ivory tower and then go on to practice. No one can actually teach us how to be at ease while inviting a family to consider a legacy gift to a synagogue or singing a *Mi Shebeirach* when the patient is on a ventilator. Many of the experiences we have shape our learning, and our hands on practice allows us to become better at what we do. Physicians have the pithy pedagogical statement, "See one, do one, teach one," which we might expand as rabbis to learn one, experience many, do one competently, continue to refine and to learn as we perform our mitzvot.

Along the way, I have learned that I do speak the mitzvot far louder than the words of my sermons. When I preached about homelessness in Indiana, and then urged my congregation to help with the founding of the South Bend Center for the Homeless, there was a connection between word and deed. When my sons became *b'nai mitzvah*, and each wanted to plant a tree as a mitzvah project, they were witnesses to our concern for the environment. We are living role models of Judaism: our children and congregants keep us under their watchful eyes. I can't speak about worker's rights without caring for every waiter, busboy, parking lot attendant, carwash jockey, or store clerk I meet. I can't talk about the holiness of our Sabbaths, festivals, and sacred times if I don't observe them. I can't profess concern for Israel without visiting there, learning about the land and the State and teaching about the importance of Israel to us as Jews. Rabbis cannot be hypocritical.

Our sources from the ancient past continue to speak to me about life in the present. I have learned to extract from our tradition and from my teaching the way to make our texts speak to modern life. Though few classes taught this leap they were invaluable. Each of us owns a modern little device that holds more technological power than the first spaceship, but the age old stories of our Biblical heroes and heroines, prophets and judges, the questions raised by the Talmudic rabbis about ethics and morality, of what is right and what is wrong, about how people are to deal with one another, maintain extraordinary relevance today. In one class, as we discussed matters of *lifnim m'shurat hadin*—going beyond the letter of the law—my adult students raised profound links to the ancient texts ranging from the daily news to sophisticated philosophical questions. Even more so, our younger students approaching bar or bat mitzvah and their Tichon High School years must learn how our ancient sources can speak to us each and every day.

It requires that we rabbis continue to put the fuel of knowledge in our spiritual tanks. Early on I learned the value of continued study and rabbinic camaraderie. Meeting colleagues over the ancient texts of our tradition, learning from them and with them, has given me the energy I try to bring back to the congregation. It authenticates us as rabbis. It reminds us of why we became Jewish role models and teachers. Study connects us to Hebrew and to the essence of our faith. It brings us close to the only people who truly understand what we do—other rabbis. From rabbinic gatherings, to my work in local, regional, and national associations as member and officer, to my fellowship at the

Shalom Hartman Institute in Jerusalem, I live by "Oh *chevruta* oh comradeship or the death of the spirit"[2] and "for The Torah is not learned alone but in pairs."[3]

Martin Buber was right: relationships matter. Rabbis uniquely enter the incredibly holy and personal space of individual lives and family processes. So much of what we do is never seen at all by the congregation—it happens in private, in the office, a living room or a hospital, without congregants or the leadership watching. It is in the inter personal relationship that we live our Torah. Every child has to feel that his bar mitzvah is the most important. Every bride has to feel that her wedding is going to be amazingly special. Every family member wants the rabbi's complete attention when his mother is ill. And every funeral is unique because a family's dynamics are incomparable. There are no cookie cutter recipes for such moments. A wise president once said, "Every bar mitzvah is the same and there's none like any other." We rabbis have to be fresh and inspiring and personal and warm to the limit of our abilities. And our presence at such moments can, in the eyes of the family, represent the totality of Jewish faith and tradition.

Not every moment, however, is easy, sweet, meaningful, and enjoyable. When tough moments do come, rabbis may receive criticism. We are in the public eye. Our decisions affect real lives at important symbolic moments. Whether fair or not, listening carefully, dealing with the critics kindly, and understanding the comments are essential. We may actually be the harshest critics of what we do when we fail. I have learned to have the highest expectations of myself because I can never know exactly what generates how a congregant may view his or her rabbi. We must remember that perception is reality. And we cannot shrink from facing that perception even when it may hurt. Apologizing maintains a balance in the relationship even when it is strained. I have visited people in their homes to apologize even if I felt wronged by gossip or innuendo, and being direct and honest when discussing matters with a family or someone who felt wronged has helped bring healing.

---

2   *Taanit* 23b.
3   *B'rachot* 63b.

We rabbis are privileged to teach God's Torah. We have to be God wrestlers ourselves, Yisrael, representatives of a people deeply bound to and engaged in a hearty and constructive dynamic with God. Some may think us odd to be believers when they themselves are not. Most have given up on their fourth grade concept of God but not refreshed themselves from the springs of our heritage with a new idea, a radically different concept. That's why I challenge every bar or bat mitzvah and confirmand to struggle with a personal and individual God concept. We rabbis must be God enthused, God intoxicated, God enveloped because if we are not, how can we possibly expect others to relate? And when we are personally challenged by the death of the young and the innocent, the suffering that has neither logic nor reason—that is when we must draw deep from the wells of our faith.

Our experiences as rabbis cause us heartache, as we deal and cope with other people's sadness. And sometimes that ache is ours as well, as we may really know who died tragically or who is grieving a serious loss. Rabbi Adin Steinsaltz asks, "What is a true Jewish leader?" The Torah defines leaders as "the heads of the thousands of Israel,"[4] which, according to Steinsaltz, defines their essence. "The Torah is thus telling us that a true leader is like a head which is the part of the body that knows what is happening in all of the other organs, and feels the pain of each and every one of them."[5] Steinsaltz notes that a true rabbi, as a leader, is supposed to sense the problems and feel the pains of everyone. That comes with great pressure on the individual rabbi and his or her family. Rabbis may need people to seek out to discuss their own difficulties and be open to conversations within their family as these situations arise. That's a life lesson, not a seminary lecture.

Most importantly, we have to place our family on our pedestal, always in front of our eyes, always before us, always before the consuming, demanding, energizing, crazy and sometimes ridiculous pressures we face. Family gives us our strength, our hope, our nourishment, and our love. Many synagogues have the words inscribed near the Holy Ark from Psalm 16:8, "I have set the Eternal always before me." Rabbis need to have the words inscribed on the walls of our offices, "I have

---

4   Numbers 1:15.
5   Adin.Steinsaltz, "Who Will Be Our Rabbis?" *The Times of Israel.* www.timesofisrael.com. Acquired December 27, 2013.

set my family always before my rabbinate." When we take care of those nearest and dearest to us, we can be genuine. If we don't, we can rightfully be called phonies. A congregation which cares for its rabbi and his or her family welfare ensures that the rabbi will be able to continue to give as much as possible back to the community. It's a relationship based on our covenant.

When Miriam and Aaron challenge Moses' leadership, they criticize his wife. Yet the Torah responds, "The man Moses was more humble than anyone on earth."[6] Nachmanides interprets this to say that Moses never quarreled, never expected anyone to hold him in esteem, and did not boast about his merits. Moses recognized his own faults, personal flaws, and limitations even though he was chosen by God for his holy task. We rabbis must follow the example of Moses as we remember our history, work each day in the midst of the community with its heartaches and joys, and always focus our eyes on the Yeshivah Shel Malah.

Rabbi Morley T. Feinstein is the Senior Rabbi of University Synagogue. He served previously as Rabbi of Temple Beth-El in South Bend, Indiana. Rabbi Feinstein has taught at the University of Notre Dame and Indiana University, and received the Sagamore of the Wabash honor from the Governor of Indiana for his numerous civic contributions. He continues to play local leadership roles in the Board of Rabbis of Southern California and at the national level through the Central Conference of American Rabbis (CCAR). He is also a Senior Rabbinic Fellow at the Shalom Hartman Institute in Jerusalem and received the degree of Doctor of Divinity from the Hebrew Union College-Jewish Institute of Religion. Rabbi Feinstein is the father of four children and is married to Prof. Margarete Myers Feinstein, a German historian.

---

6   Numbers 12:3.

Rabbi as *Madrichah Ruchanit*

By Rabbi Debra Rappaport

In Jerusalem circa 1998, taxi drivers would turn around and look at me with puzzled curiosity when I said I was exploring becoming a rabbi. It wasn't just that I was a woman, but also that what distinguished a rabbi from other Halakhic Jews was his role as a *posek*, the one who makes decisions for the community on issues of Jewish law. Based on my dress alone, I wasn't even part of a religious community as it was understood. I learned to describe my quest as becoming a *madrichah ruchanit*, a spiritual guide. I like the understanding of the role of rabbi as someone who accompanies and sometimes coaches fellow Jews on their journey through life.

What sort of rabbinic education is required to merit the honor of being a *madrichah ruchanit* on behalf of American Jews? Rabbinical education is bigger than rabbinical school. It is a foundation for lifelong learning. Fifteen years ago, when I was applying to rabbinical school, it was clear to me that I needed a lot more Jewish knowledge. When I reflect on the question today, I would say there are three tap roots that were the basis of my development as a rabbi. Taproots are the big fat roots that grow straight down when a plant is young. As the plant grows into a tree, fibrous roots grow horizontally in all directions, as wide as the tree is high, supplanting the need for the early taproots. Change and growth and pruning are all part of the rabbinic education process. A single deep root can't support a fully-grown tree—the root system needs breadth as well. My three taproots are my business background and training, what I learned in rabbinical school, and my inner work.

Rabbi David Zeller, *alav hashalom*, when I was learning with him at Yakar in Jerusalem, used to say, "I come from a family of Reform Jews and Orthodox Jungians." I related to that statement in the sense that I came from a family of Reform Jews who were Orthodox Business people. My parents, their parents, their friends, were all business people. Business was the language I absorbed at the dinner table, even as I was involved with Temple youth group and camp.

The language of the business world is of getting things done. In an ideal business environment, leaders are strategic—they vision the direction they want an organization to go, put in place a plan to get there, and articulate results that are measurable. Business leaders manage all resources—financial, human, capital, technological—in ways that support the strategic direction. Sales, marketing, communications are functions that allow both the expression of the unique capacities of the company to meet its customers' needs, and feedback loops for the customers to ask that their needs be met.

After my liberal arts college degree, I faced a choice between the two entry-level business options: sales or finance. I diligently explored both, then chose sales simply because I like people more than numbers. My business career flourished; I eventually earned an MBA in marketing, worked in some technology start-ups, and then entered the family business in computer hardware and client-server development software.

When I left the family business at the age of thirty-one, I set up an internet consulting business helping people determine how to use this new world wide web to support their organization's goals. People were enamored with the technology, all it could do, and wanted to talk about it. I was excited by the collaborative potential of the Internet: bringing like-minded people together for creative and supportive undertakings. And I was utterly uninterested in how the technology works. I started to think more about the people side of the business world.

Pursuing courses in Human Resources Development, I became as "touchy-feely" as a "businessperson" can be. For a final project, I researched The Economic Impact of Spiritual Leadership. For a business audience in the 1990's, spiritual leadership had to be defined without God language. I described spiritual leadership as having the qualities of (1) a win-win outlook, i.e. an ability to be for ourselves and for others at the same time; (2) a commitment to authenticity in all we do, i.e. not being one person at home and another with a boss and another with a supervisee; (3) accountability to a higher good than face-time, politics, or short-term profits. What I found, to my great delight, was that this sort of leadership positively correlates with employee retention, which correlates with customer retention, which correlates with higher profits! And then I started to laugh at myself—trying to sell people on doing the right thing through appealing to profits.

Delving into Torah allowed me to develop and teach a class on how to bring spirituality into everyday work through Jewish texts. It was an extraordinarily gratifying project, and a seminal moment, which helped me connect with my need for a much deeper and substantive religious education. I began to consider rabbinical school at that juncture, but I hadn't lived Jewishly enough to make the commitment.

I was in my early thirties when, for the first time, I felt free to explore the full range of "What do I want to do with my life?" The question became a spiritual one: "God, how am I here to serve You? What is my Purpose?" At first, for a few years, this question of purpose was a completely separate question from, "What is this Jewish identity? And why is it important?"

I learned how to talk to God from the estranged daughter of a Southern Baptist preacher named Gail. Gail taught me to ask for answers and to expect them, and to pray for the highest good for all concerned. During my ninth grade retreats with Temple Israel, Rabbi Zemel had shown us that we could be good Jews without even being sure we believe in God. Our tradition certainly could embrace a wide range of beliefs. So it never crossed my mind until much later, as a rabbinical student, that anything would be strange about a Jew learning to talk with God. I was glad to have a teacher. Learning with Gail was one of many spiritual paths I pursued at the time. I started yoga, went to meditation workshops, and learned the metaphysical properties of minerals.

At the same time, I immersed myself in the Jewish world as volunteer, hoping to answer the questions: Why am I Jewish? What is the significance of Judaism in my life? I began to see how and why "the continuity crisis" was real. The Jewish world was not offering anything compelling for young adults who weren't worried about Israel

or anti-Semitism. I began to see it as my job to answer, first for myself
and then hopefully for the community, why Judaism *is* compelling.
My strength in the business world had always been my ability to help
people and organizations identify the value proposition and articulate
why it's important to the relevant audience or market.

The Reconstructionist Rabbinical College gave me a solid
foundation in Judaism. It took me seven years to learn enough Hebrew,
Jewish history, texts, and practical rabbinics to get through the program
and be ordained. It makes sense to me that it took that long, knowing
one could study all day every day for one's whole life and still not
master Judaism. The vocabulary of Jewish worship, holidays, and life
cycle rituals is vast. But even mastery of all that is only a beginning in
a quest to be a *madrich ruchani*.

Mordechai Kaplan, founder of the Reconstructionist movement,
articulated Judaism as the Evolving Religious Civilization of the
Jewish People. Core to that understanding of Judaism is: (1) that our
tradition—how it is understood, practiced and led—has evolved since
its inception.[1] Accepting this truth is absolutely essential if one is going
to partake in our post-modern pluralistic feminist-theory-influenced
contemporary Jewish life. In other words, today's non-orthodox Jews
must count themselves in the conversation about Jewish life. Jewish life
has always evolved, and contemporary society has always influenced
it. (2) Judaism is a civilization, with its key descriptor being Jewish.
Judaism is not only about the religious parts—it is a way of life. And its
goal, as I understand it, is to provide meaning, connection, grounding,
love, and concrete paths toward partnering with God to repair the
world.

All the Jewish learning from rabbinical school and other places of
formal learning provides the substantive foundation for when I teach
a Jewish class, offer a mourner Jewish wisdom for healing, officiate a
wedding, and lead a service. But to truly be there for people in joyous
and challenging times, to truly even begin to offer Judaism's richness in
a format that is meaningful, I must know myself and be able to receive
the other.

---

1   There is evidence of this even in the Torah itself, and we certainly had a radical shift with spiritual
    continuity after the destruction of the Second Temple.

Martin Buber taught poignantly about the presence of God in the I-Thou encounter[2]—an encounter in which two people genuinely show up to one another's presence, without preconditions, without an agenda or expectations. He contrasts this with an I-It encounter, which is transactional in nature. An example of an I-It encounter might be with a cashier at the market. There is a clear and understood goal for the interaction that the cashier rings up purchases and the customer pays. There is nothing wrong with I-It encounters; they serve an important function. But in an I-Thou encounter, true dialogue can occur, which brings out the best and perhaps even godliness in both people. Buber goes on to describe God as the ultimate Thou. We can only show up; we will know it was real when we feel it; we can not plan or control it.

It is not so easy to just decide to cultivate I-Thou encounters. We all bring a lot of preconceptions and busy minds to the process. So I want to share a couple of practices that have helped me cultivate mindfulness. By mindfulness, I mean both awareness and acceptance of what is really happening, within and without. It is an inner state of being. The Institute of Jewish Spirituality (IJS)[3] offers programs in spiritual practice to rabbis and cantors across the movements. The practice includes meditation, yoga, silence, mindful eating, mindful listening, and mindful Chasidic text study. The idea is not to be meditating all the time, but to be fully awake to all that goes on. This includes treating ourselves with that I-Thou intention.

Jungian therapy helped me get through rabbinical school. I was fortunate enough to work with a therapist and a group of women who appreciate the life of the inner self. The Jungian views I embrace treasure dreams, drawing, dancing, moving, and laughter—anything to give expression to one's creative essence. It's not that I couldn't find it in Judaism—the Torah teaches that we are God's partners in creation—but I could never find the same valence of loving appreciation for the creative act in the Jewish community or school. This Jungian approach also treasures the feminine—the body, the earth, the dark cycles, the unconscious. I couldn't find those loving women role models in the tradition handed down by the rabbis. So I found it elsewhere, and will

---

2   Martin Buber, *I and Thou.* First published in German in 1923 and first translated in 1937.
3   Information about the Institute for Jewish Spirituality can be found at jewishspirituality.org.

hopefully integrate it into my role as a rabbi, so that future generations don't have to look elsewhere.

Business teaches us how to conduct effective transactional encounters. Rabbinic training, as an academic undertaking, teaches us the same thing—with the goal of selling Judaism as the product or service. I could go into a classroom and teach a very information-packed Introduction to Judaism class. I would be transferring the knowledge or information to the students. And a transaction will have happened—they will have the information. Or I could officiate a bat-mitzvah ceremony just like every other Shabbat service, without any particular attention to the bat mitzvah or her family. I will have done my job. She will have performed, and she will have her party. Or I could offer "rent-a-rabbi" wedding packages that teach a couple exactly what they need to know and do for a Jewish wedding, officiating them all the same way.

But that's not the kind of rabbi I am. I am not a transactional rabbi. I don't believe the world needs more transactional Judaism. We, as rabbis of the 21st Century, are called, I believe, to I-Thou encounters with individuals and families. Judaism is the technology—with its language, rituals and customs—that enables people to partner with God, as in Genesis 1, in making the world a better place. *Authority* based on the role of a rabbi has become increasingly less relevant. As the majority of the organized Jewish world grows concerned about the decreasing affiliation, we could be alarmist about future roles for rabbis. But helping people to create meaning, connections, and find support in an increasingly disconnected world, is a job that is truly in demand.

Seven years after ordination, the taproots of my rabbinic education have become a rich root system. As a sales person, my job is to listen well enough to prospective clients to know what matters to them. And then, if something in my product portfolio can help, my job becomes to articulate to the clients how this will be helpful to them. As a rabbi, my portfolio comprises all the Jewish narratives, rituals and conversations that are about creating meaning, hope, inspiration. Finally, my portfolio as a *Madrichah ruchanit* includes all of who I am, and everything I can do to be God's partner in cultivating a loving sustainable world.

During the summer of 2014, **Debra Rappaport** *married the love of her life and moved back to her hometown of Minneapolis. For the previous seven years, she served as Rabbi and Executive Director for B'nai Vail Congregation in Vail, Colorado. She received ordination at the Reconstructionist Rabbinical College in Philadelphia in 2007. After earning her BA at Vassar College, Rabbi Rappaport pursued a business career over the next ten years, in sales, marketing, and management roles, as well as earning an MBA in Marketing from the Wharton School of the University of PA. She currently serves on the Board of Governors for the Reconstructionist Rabbinical College and the Board of Scholars and Advisors for the Vail Leadership Institute.*

Reflecting on the Journey: Officiating at Weddings When One Partner is not Jewish

By Rabbi Jeffrey C. Brown

Introduction and Background

I arrived in Jerusalem as a first year rabbinic student at the Hebrew Union College-Jewish Institute of Religion (HUC-JIR) weeks after completing my undergraduate degree in English at George Washington University. The College-Institute was my academic and spiritual home from 2000-2005. Nine years after receiving the blessing of my teachers to go forth as a *rav u'moreh*, I remain filled with a reverent and humble gratitude for the opportunity to learn from and with them.

In 2005, on the eve of the Placement process that graduating seniors at HUC enter into every January, it occurred to me that in four and a half years, hardly any amount of time in our curriculum had been devoted to the question of marriage between a Jew and a non-Jew[1] and the role of the Reform rabbi in potentially officiating at such a union.

---

[1] My attention turned to interfaith-related issues on the eve of that initial Placement process because my classmates and I were aware and anxious about how the congregations we were interviewing with might inquire about our approach to the issue and factor that into their ultimate hiring decision.

I do not want to suggest that the subject never came up. It was certainly referred to in discussions of contemporary American Jewish history and sociology. In terms of a so-called progressive halachah, it came up in the context of our teachers' desire to convey that the issue of rabbinic officiation at a wedding where one partner was Jewish and the other partner was not was categorically distinct from the equally pressing question of rabbinic officiation at the union of two Jews of the same gender.[2] The vast majority of my teachers[3] were implicitly in favor of us officiating at a gay ceremony (between two Jews) and implicitly opposed[4] to us officiating at a ceremony between a Jew and a non-Jew.

Nonetheless, I was increasingly aware of the fact that we never had the space in any classroom setting to comprehensively study the halachic or sociological issues involved in what I would now call the most significant phenomenon of contemporary American Jewish life: the normalization of exogamy among American non-Orthodox Jews.

The college was not oblivious to the issue. It dutifully publicized to us a weekend retreat opportunity in Denver that was organized by a Reform rabbi. HUC was even prepared to subsidize our travel expenses to attend the optional seminar. Never having the chance to go, though, I entered my Placement process spiritually and intellectually undecided about this most critical question.

The question of officiating at an intermarriage ceremony never came up during that Placement season.[5] I chose to have first round conversations with twelve Reform synagogues, accepted site visit invitations from six of them, and happily matched with Temple

---

2   See *Reform Responsa for the Twenty-First Century* (CCAR, 2010), Vol. 1, No. 5756.8, "On Homosexual Marriage," 213-256.

3   I am specifically referring to those I learned from during my latter four years in Cincinnati.

4   Not all of the College-Institute's faculty and administration were opposed to interfaith officiation. As one example of quasi-institutional support, I would point readers to *T'shuvot* (Responsa) on Jewish Marriage: with special reference to "Reform Rabbis and Mixed Marriage," published in 1985 by the teacher of my teachers, Rabbi Eugene Mihaly z"l (who served as Professor, Dean, and Executive Vice President of HUC-JIR). My reading of Mihaly in Cincinnati planted the seeds for my later journey around this subject.

5   The issue of rabbinic officiation at a same-sex chuppah where both partners were Jewish did come up. At one of my six site visits, the senior rabbi privately informed me that he did not officiate at such ceremonies, and that as a result, I would be prevented in all circumstances from doing so if I came to work there. This was a matter of conscience for him as it was for me. I chose not to rank the position.

Solel of Cardiff, California. There I found a wise, experienced, and patient mentor in Senior Rabbi David Frank. During my seven-year tenure at Solel, I grew as a rabbi and as a person in every conceivable way. It was with Solel's community that I first had the chance to accompany families on the full journey of the Jewish lifecycle. And it was at Solel that I was given the first real opportunity to teach Torah, by exploring with our community the compelling theology and philosophy that could be an avenue toward meaningful engagement with Jewish tradition and modernity.

Rabbi Frank was my guide and teacher throughout this formative period. Whatever merits are a part of my own rabbinate today are due in no small part to the wisdom I was able to glean from him and the nearly 900 other member families of Temple Solel who were my teachers. And yet, dialogue around the question of rabbinic officiation at a wedding in which one partner is Jewish and one partner is not did not happen during those seven years.

Solel was like most other American Reform communities. During my tenure, we presumed that 30-35% of our households included an adult who was not Jewish. And Rabbi Frank, our staff, and our lay leadership enthusiastically created a culture of welcoming, and of outreach to interfaith families, consistent with the programmatic suggestions and norms promoted by the Union for Reform Judaism.[6] But Rabbi Frank respectfully and thoughtfully differentiated between creating a culture of welcoming and offering rabbinic officiation at a ceremony between a non-Jew and a Jew.[7] Solel's Board affirmed that distinction prior to my arrival.

In 2005, I was still neutral on the question, so Solel's position was a non-issue for me. I tried to learn every other aspect of the modern rabbinate. I never had the luxury of time to dwell on my lack of a position on the officiation question, but it was a disconcerting gap in my rabbinic education and identity.

---

6   See the ample resources at http://urj.org/cong/outreach.
7   Rabbi Frank's position is entirely consistent with that of the Central Conference of American Rabbis, which has embraced this differentiation in its responsa literature and resolutions during the last four decades.

Decision-Making: Deliberation Through Study, Reflection, and Communal Dialogue

In 2011, as I began to give serious consideration to my future rabbinate, and as my wife and I gave renewed thought to returning to the East Coast to be closer to our family, I decided once again to enter into Placement—this time for a position as a Solo or Senior Rabbi. I had been well-prepared by the CCAR, mentors and colleagues for the fact that my stance on the officiation issue would be a more significant part of my interview experience this time. The question, in those weeks leading into Placement, was how I would answer those queries.

There were three aspects that I struggled with at that time: To what extent was it realistic for me to reflect on, and decide, this pressing question in the space of four to six weeks while refining my resume and preparing for the job search? How could I reflect in a principled fashion?[8] Given the emotional volatility around this, could I explain to congregations how I made it through rabbinical school and seven years as an assistant rabbi without having a position on this important question?

The advice I received from friends and colleagues ran the full gamut. Friends that were familiar with my general inclination toward more traditional Jewish practice encouraged me to declare myself opposed to officiating. And others who knew I considered myself a theological liberal encouraged me to declare my willingness to officiate. Only one colleague, Rabbi Don Rosoff,[9] affirmed the advisability of not rushing to judgment on the matter. He sensitively discerned that I was not ready to do the hard work of making a decision on the spot. He courageously advised me, instead, to be honest with the congregations that I'd be speaking to during the interview process.

---

8   I was left with the impression that I would be a significantly more marketable candidate if I did officiate at a ceremony between one who was Jewish and one who was not. I wrestled with how I could make a decision during this short pre-interview period in such a way that my decision would not be subconsciously influenced by my desire to get the best job possible.

9   I want to thank Rabbi Alan Henkin of the CCAR for encouraging me to reach out to Rosoff.

Candid honesty, and the sense of rabbinic authenticity implied by it, has always been a touchstone of my rabbinate. Rabbi Rosoff's advice spoke very deeply to me.

I asked the CCAR to send my resume to approximately fifteen congregations at the end of the summer of 2011.[10] I was invited to begin conversations with more than ten of them.

In virtually all of those preliminary conversations, the question of officiation came up. In each of them, I gave a similar answer: "I'm glad you brought up this important subject, which is so directly connected to all of the powerful forces that are shaping American Jewish life today. As it happens, during my five years of rabbinical school, and my six-plus years at Temple Solel, I never had the chance to carefully consider my position on the subject. I'm not certain as to what my position on the question will ultimately be. I do not currently officiate at weddings in which one partner is not Jewish. I am eagerly looking forward to spending the next year of my rabbinate deeply engaging with the question by studying the sources of our tradition, by reflecting personally on the question, and most importantly, by engaging my next congregation in a safe and meaningful dialogue. At the end of that process, I will look forward to making a decision and sharing it appropriately with the congregation that I am privileged to serve."

I have no doubt that several congregations did not want to pursue a further conversation with me because of some *other* aspect of my candidacy, but the search committees' reactions following the officiation exchange were very telling. For several congregations, I could literally see the shift in their body language, giving me instantaneous feedback that my approach to the question was distasteful or problematic for them. Maybe this was on an ideological level, in that they really only wanted a rabbi who would officiate on day one. Or maybe this reflected a judgment about my rabbinic leadership skills in that they wanted a rabbi who was a swift and

---

10 There were two additional congregations that I was interested in applying to that season, but I withheld my resume from them because those job descriptions clearly indicated that their hire would be contingent on the rabbi's willingness to officiate at a ceremony between a Jew and a non-Jew.

decisive decision-maker, as opposed to the slower, more deliberative approach[11] that I intentionally brought to the table.

One of the joys of my preliminary interaction with Scarsdale Synagogue Temples Tremont and Emanu-El (SSTTE) was a sense that we were on the same wavelength around this issue —not in terms of the ideology of officiation per se, but in terms of the process. My process seemed[12] to resonate with them. And that resonance, I think, helped to fuel our interest in each other. I was incredibly honored, and the congregational leadership and I were both excited when I accepted their invitation to lead them beginning on July 1, 2012.

I spent the summer of 2012 getting settled, and successfully navigating that year's High Holy Day services, in which the interfaith issue only came up in passing. But by the time the *chagim* that year were over, my plans had been set. I had already drawn up and begun working through a reading list; I had a group of colleagues and outside experts I wanted to reach out to; and most importantly, I had a vision of how I wanted to engage the congregation around the issue.

The highlights of that congregational engagement[13] consisted of:

- **One-on-one conversations**: As the new rabbi, I had many opportunities to sit with congregants for the first time, get to know them and their families, and hear their history of synagogue and Jewish engagement. Congregants were aware of my lack of a position on the officiation question, and many wanted to talk about it. Some chose to use our time to give me their take on the issue, which often included personal storytelling about their family's interfaith experiences and the Jewish clergy involvement that sometimes went along with

---

11 As some of these first round chats turned into more serious second and third round conversations, I shared that my approach on the officiation question should be seen as representative of how I would navigate other difficult or controversial issues that would inevitably come up later in my rabbinate.

12 Much later on, I came to appreciate that the open-mindedness towards my process on the part of the search team did not necessarily represent the congregation as a whole.

13 See http://bit.ly/1m1TJz7 for my public remarks and correspondence that were a central component of this engagement process.

them.[14] More disconcertingly: others used these meetings to express their anger with me. Why were they angry? Perhaps some were grieving the "loss" (i.e. retirement) of their longtime Senior Rabbi. Others were perhaps genuinely offended by the fact that I had to give thought to an issue that they perceived as being very "black and white."[15] More than a year later, I can now genuinely express my gratitude to all of the congregants who entrusted their sacred stories to me at such an early point in my SSTTE tenure.

- **Small group gatherings:** During my first year, there was also ample opportunity for me to meet members of the congregation in small group settings in congregants' homes. These gatherings were an unofficial extension of the "meet and greets" that the synagogue's transition team organized for me during my initial summer at SSTTE. A typical gathering would begin with some informal schmoozing over coffee, followed by the group sitting together. I'd say a few words about myself, and then invite each person in the circle to share a few words about themselves and their family's journey: how they came to live in Westchester and what had brought them to the temple. If the host alerted me in advance to a particular subject that was on the minds of the invitees, then I would make a point of calling that out at the beginning of the conversation. On many occasions, that subject was interfaith officiation. I strove to listen. When I was asked, I'd do my best to convey how it was that I did not yet have a firm position on the question. I'd invite them to be part of the public

---

14 I learned that my predecessor, Rabbi Stephen A. Klein, did officiate under certain circumstances, and that he had perhaps been one of the first pulpit rabbis in Westchester County to do so. The congregation was very proud of that part of their identity. Congregants presumed that Rabbi Klein officiated at such weddings under all circumstances. The opposite was true: Rabbi Klein had a particular approach that enabled him to marry some, but not all, of the couples that approached him. The search team was privy to Rabbi Klein's approach to the issue, and this, along with a knowledge on their part that not all Reform rabbis officiated helped to create a certain open-mindedness to my process. The rest of the congregation was not as well informed. This, too, created differing sets of expectations of me on this question —from our lay leadership, on the one hand, and from the rest of the congregation on the other.

15 The vast majority of those in this category were strongly, strongly in favor of my officiating. Many reached this position because of personal choices that they, their children, or someone else close to them had decided to enter into a committed relationship with a non-Jew. While I was empathetic throughout this process, I was also occasionally frustrated that my new congregants could not appreciate how complex a question this was for rabbis (or, at least, for me).

dialogue, and I begged their patience as we proceeded forward with the deliberate process that had already been affirmed by the Search Committee that hired me, and our lay leadership. To be sure: the whole range of emotions that were manifest in the one-on-one conversations also came to be a part of these small group gatherings.

- **Public dialogue and study sessions**: From the outset, the centerpiece of the process that I envisioned was a three part series of public lectures with dialogue to follow on three different aspects of the officiation debate. In January of 2013, I addressed, "Can/Should Jewish Law Evolve Over Time?" The following month, I explored "Interfaith Marriage in Jewish History." In April of 2013, I addressed "The Role of the One That Is Not Jewish in Jewish Ritual."

In choosing my study session topics, I was seeking the intersection between subjects that would be relevant or of interest to the members of my community, and subjects that would be key to my own decision-making process. Thus my preparation time for the three lectures was also a big chunk of the study that I felt I needed to do to make an informed decision about this question.

I was committed to dividing each of the lectures in half. One half addressed the topic from the pro-officiation perspective, and the other half addressed the subject from the con side. I was genuinely still on the fence about the question until shortly after the third lecture. Presenting the issue from both sides enabled me to be authentic throughout the lectures. I could easily see the question from both sides, and I wanted the congregation to try to understand that on some level. The approach also mandated that I study the issue from both sides.

Additionally, the Bavli's statement spoke directly to me:

> But now that these and those are both the words of the living God, for what reason did Beit Hillel merit to fix the halachah according to their view? Because they were easy and forbearing, and *because they would study their opinion and the opinion of* Beit Shammai.[16]

---

16 *Eiruvin* 13b, emphasis added.

Our tradition teaches us that there is merit in actively teaching both sides of a difficult question. The Bavli implies that if we follow Beit Hillel's practice, we will be able to move toward a more pluralistic and inclusive communal space. That is not just a central goal of mine in my rabbinate; it was also a specific *need* that I had in navigating the array of strong opinions on both sides that I encountered in my new synagogue.

Almost a year after my engagement with SSTTE on this issue formally concluded,[17] I am able to look back in humble satisfaction. The 2012-2013 year was a significant success for me, my rabbinate, and our congregation.

For some of my congregants, it was a success because I ultimately came to proudly embrace the belief that I was called to officiate at ceremonies where one partner is not Jewish under certain circumstances.[18] Naturally, I also had one group of congregants who wanted me to go further, and another group who were disheartened that I had gone too far.

For me, though, the year was never about ending up at this particular conclusion. It was about creating an authentic and credible process that would enable me to study and reflect on this critical issue in a way that I never had the opportunity or luxury of doing at HUC-JIR or in my mentored assistantship in California.

Some of my New York congregants, after hearing that I had never had the chance to do that learning at HUC or at Temple Solel, openly critiqued my professors and rabbinic mentors for obstructing my learning and professional development by failing to engage me

---

17   I am grateful to Rabbi Adam Stock Spilker for his mentorship as I planned the concluding phase of the process. I am thankful that my SSTTE colleagues Cantor Chanin Becker and Rabbi Wendy Pein encouraged me to reach out to him.

18   At the conclusion of this process, I announced to my congregation that I would be guided by the following factors in deciding whether I would stand with a couple to officiate at their wedding:

- I will stand with a couple under their chuppah if they agree to have a Jewish home, and raise their children as Jews.
- I will stand with a couple under their chuppah if they agree to have a Jewish wedding ceremony, without the participation of a non-Jewish co-officiant.
- I will stand with a couple under their chuppah if they agree to meet with me for seven sessions: one "getting to know you" session, three sessions devoted to studying about Judaism and what it means to have a Jewish home, and three sessions that will encompass both pre-marital counseling and planning for the wedding ceremony.

on this issue. I did my very best to respectfully disagree with their assessment of my teachers and my training.

In fact, I have come to believe that the opposite is true. I am the lucky recipient of a world-class Reform rabbinic education, and I have been blessed with teachers and mentors who continue to school me in the full set of skills, textual and relational, that enabled me to construct and execute the process that ultimately came to successfully define my first year at SSTTE. While many of my teachers will no doubt take issue with my reading of some of the texts I presented in my public lectures, and the ultimate conclusion I chose to draw from those readings, I hope and pray that the decision-making methodology I employed to navigate this vexing question would make them proud. It is to them that this reflection, and indeed all of the good that I modestly seek to do through my rabbinate, are dedicated.

Jeffrey C. Brown *serves as the Rabbi of Scarsdale Synagogue Temples Tremont and Emanu-El in Scarsdale, New York.*

A Shared Model of Leadership

By Rabbis Philip "Flip" & Laurie Rice

We met and courted in Jerusalem during our first year of rabbinical school at Hebrew Union College-Jewish Institute of Religion (HUC-JIR). We married shortly after receiving our respective Master of Hebrew Letters in Los Angeles and were ordained together in New York City in 2001.

While serving separate congregations in Seattle, Washington, the eldest of our three young children asked one Friday afternoon, "Are we going to Abba's Temple tonight or Ima's?"

We looked at each other and both said, "Maybe we should carpool?"

For several years now we have job shared one position, the Senior Rabbi of Congregation Micah in Nashville, Tennessee. We would like to share our perspective on leadership and the model that we use to govern our institution, achieve our mission, and inspire others as we, together, balance work and family life as a rabbinic couple.

We should say at the outset that it was not our initial plan to work together. What became apparent to us was that while serving the needs of two spiritual communities, we were not creating a balanced one for our own family. So we began searching for a congregation where we might both be its rabbis. There were congregations in the Northwest and in Florida that were skeptical and not interested, but Congregation Micah was intrigued by the idea of a rabbinic team. As the interview process proceeded we assuaged any doubters of a co-rabbinate by setting up portfolios where one of us would each take the lead roles: Laurie spearheaded Adult Education, Worship and Life-Cycle Events;[1] and Flip took responsibility for the Religious School, the Bnai Mitzvah process, and supervising the staff. Our portfolios have now blended and the congregants understand that at any given moment they might expect Rabbi Flip, but get Rabbi Laurie.

After nearly a decade, working together still provides its challenges in determining appropriate boundaries. Flip shuts-down when he gets home and would prefer not to discuss work, Laurie likes her inbox clear when she goes to bed so she can start fresh each morning. What we give up is not as important as what we get: we unequivocally trust each other. We are also able to be very present for our children. So we work around the tricky logistics of sharing one job, each with our own contracts and salaries that mirror one another. It is also important to note that you do not have to be married to employ the Shared Model of Leadership. It functions for rabbis who serve solo pulpits, rabbis who job-share, and rabbis who are "co-rabbis" serving one congregation.

The Model

Congregation Micah is mission driven. It is not role driven or ego driven. For us as clergy, for members of the staff, and for lay leadership, it is not about our position, power or personalities. Our finances, our services, programs, and/or events are the results of, not the forces behind what motivates us. Rather, we are united in our shared sacred endeavor of making Micah, "a vibrant and diverse Reform Jewish Congregation where we honor and celebrate our commitment to God, Israel, and our community through worship, lifelong learning and social justice."

Our goal is always about realizing the greatest thing for Micah. Our question is always: "What's best for Micah?" Even as rabbis, we may not always agree upon the correct answer to that question. But as best as we can, we keep it in front of us as we empower our lay leadership. In doing so we ask that all people in leadership positions abide by certain principles in our effort to achieve Micah's mission. We use three principles that guide the decision-making process and relationships between clergy, staff, and executive and board leadership.

---

1   We had Laurie take the lead in all religious matters to make sure that Laurie was seen as senior rabbi, and not as an associate based on gender. In retrospect it would probably have been a non-issue at Micah.

1. Talk first, decide together, and implement with strength

Whether it is something new we are attempting to accomplish or a crisis we are trying to manage, we do the Jewish thing: we talk about it! We do so on a management level and on an executive and board level. We even purposefully engage in dialogue that encourages debate because we believe that, like a page of Talmud, different perspectives produce better decisions and ultimately, better results. Regardless of the idea or issue, we find it best to hash it out, get on the same page, and then endorse our decisions together.

We are sensitive to the fact that the synagogue is sometimes a venue in which people live out those parts of their lives where they could not otherwise do so; they express their passions and can let past traditions and current personal needs cloud their judgment. So in grooming new leadership, we seek individuals who understand the importance of dropping the "get mad or get even approach" when addressing issues of conflict or where we might feel differently than others.

One example of this at Micah was the creation of our pre-school in 2011. After doing the demographic research, creating the business plan and raising the money, there was pushback from a small percentage of the membership. Who would be against the idea of "raising up many disciples" by building a school based on the values of the Jewish people and raise revenue in the process? A very few members of our volunteer religious school staff voiced a frustration that they would be treated as second-class citizens. Once heard, we did our best to assure them that educating all of our children is our priority.

People volunteer for a variety of reasons. While many of their intentions are altruistic, on some level they want to get something out of their experience. Lay leaders want their involvement to be a transformative experience. In order to avoid hurt feelings, our culture is to be tough on the issues, but not each other. We ask all leaders to respect each other's opinions and not take things personally. In doing so we are both many voices and one voice.

2. Authority without authoritarianism

The way a decision or plan is communicated and implemented reveals a great deal about the character of our leadership. Frequent communication between leaders and the congregation helps us avoid surprises on all fronts: from outside the community, from members of the congregation, and from within the leadership team itself. We keep each other informed, and our communication is regular and open. This prevents others from triangulating us, and keeps us from feeling blindsided. We meet as a team frequently, and we stay in touch through phone calls, emails, and texts. We practice and reinforce these principles among the leadership team at Micah through open, honest, civil discourse. Our model may be somewhat unique, but it is not just a show. And it gets tested.

For instance, early in our tenure at Micah, before we developed our current strategy for decision-making, we were frustrated that one member of the team would announce something publicly without thoroughly vetting the idea through others. One Friday night at services, for example, the then President announced, "We are planning to have monthly town hall meetings." We thought to ourselves, "Uh-oh, venting sessions, monthly!" It turned out that the congregation did not want to attend them either.

Now, a good amount of trust exists between the Past President, the President, the Rabbis, the Executive Director, and the Religious School Director. And still, because we feel passionate about any number of subjects (Israel, worship, education), we may become animated in our discussions, but remain professional in our decisions. We also have the extra burden of always being consciously aware that we are the rabbis in the room, and need to act accordingly.

3. Shared responsibility

We relish in each other's successes and help each other through our failures. We take the heat for each other sometimes and are quick to praise each other, too! We attribute most of the success of this model to our ability to trust each other, even and especially when doubt occurs.

There are certain areas of expertise that each of us brings to the table. When there are rabbinic-oriented decisions, we ask that lay and staff leadership support them. At the same time, rabbinic leadership supports lay and staff-oriented decisions. It is important that support is felt both ways and that we back each other up. Here is where our different backgrounds and skill sets are on display. Laurie, for example, is far more musical and so Flip defers to her with regard to music. Flip, on the other hand, is very patient with people, and so he tends to work more closely with children with special needs in preparation of their bar/bat mitzvah.

As rabbinic leaders we model that when we are still in doubt, it is time to trust harder in each other and in God. As our lay leadership team changes from year to year, it is necessary to constantly reinforce the need to trust each other. We cannot underestimate the value of relationships in our work because, as our trust builds, we tend to make better, more conscious, focused decisions together as a team, regardless of our roles. The result is that we remain a healthy, albeit always fragile institution.

When the Model Gets Tested

Jewish leadership has evolved over time. Since the destruction of the Second Temple in Jerusalem some 2,000 years ago, there has been no one single body that has a leadership position over the entire Jewish community. At Micah, the clergy, staff and lay leadership make decisions based on the shared leadership model described above. But what happens when there is a difference of opinion or conflict about what to do?

Name changes in the Bible, like in life, mark significant transitions as well as tell us stories. There is a verse in the Torah in which Moses calls his disciple by a different name. It reads: "And Moses called Hoshea, the son of Nun, Joshua!"[2] Attempting to explain why Moses did this, the great rabbinic commentator Rashi writes: "He called him Joshua because he prayed, 'May God save you from the counsel of the spies!' And the name Joshua means God will save you!"[3]

Why did he need to be saved from the counsel of the spies? The spies had recounted to him a false report. The Rabbi of Ger teaches with regard to this that humble people tend not to stubbornly persist in their own views. Rather, humility invites one to be ready at any time to defer to another opinion. Seeing that the spies were princes of their respective tribes and enjoyed great public esteem, and knowing that Joshua was a humble man, Moses feared that Joshua might be led to

2   Numbers 13:16.
3   Babylonian Talmud, *Sotah* 34b.

defer to their opinion. It is for this reason that he prayed on behalf of him, "May God save you from the counsel of the spies!"[4]

When it comes to leadership, acting humble is not always the best course of action. Persistence is important, too. The Zionist Theodore Herzl once said, "I am not better or cleverer than anyone of you. But I remain undaunted, and that is why the leadership belongs to me."[5] What is important is to know when to persist in one's own opinion and when to defer to the views of others. Like any number of synagogues, we have a wonderful campus: an awe-inspiring sanctuary, a social hall, a pre-school, a religious school, a memorial garden and a cemetery. But what makes Micah tick is its relationships. Relationships are built at Micah in a variety of ways, and people join our community for a variety of reasons. They may want a life-cycle event, access to the rabbis, or a social connection. People may join for their own selfish desires, but they often stay because of the fact that they find a supportive community.

With regard to leadership, we as rabbis spend time building relationships with congregants. The result is that when controversial subjects are approached, whether they are political, religious, social or even conceptual in nature, we already have a rapport with people. It is a different conversation entirely if we already know, respect and trust each other. So we often have coffee or lunch with certain congregants in an effort to make sure that they are heard, and so that when controversy strikes, it can often take the form of banter rather than resulting in someone drawing a line in the sand.

Passion for the Vision

Our rabbinic vision articulates our role in connecting people with God, Torah, and Israel. As leaders of the Jewish people, we are passionate about our work as rabbis; so passionate that we have dedicated our professional and even much of our personal lives to deciding how to go about achieving these three goals. Fulfilling them

4   Alexander Zusia Friedman, *Wellsprings Of Torah: An Anthology of Biblical Commentaries*, Volume Two. Rabbi Nison L. Alpert (Ed), translated from the original Yiddish by Gertrude Hirschler.(Judaica Press, Inc: New York, 1974).

5   Theodore Hertzl, "Quotes: Hertzl Speaks His Mind on Issues, Events, and Men 2," Who is a Zionist, www.wzo.org.il. Obtained July 11, 2014.

regularly requires leadership, vision, and taking risks, all of which we learned as students, interns, and while working with other rabbis and Jewish professionals. As the son of a doctor, Rabbi Flip likes to say that he is saving spiritual lives.

Leaders make things happen that would not otherwise happen. In our tenure at Congregation Micah, we have revolutionized its classical Reform worship, engaged in a capital campaign, built a pre-school, raised the bar on *b'nai mitzvah* students, increased the enrollment of our religious school, and sparked hundreds of members of our community to travel to Israel. All of this required having the vision to see solutions to the problems and obstacles that enable us to set up programs to succeed. All of our successes also required the courage to put those solutions into action, as well as strong partnerships to ensure their realization. Finally, it required challenging individuals and communities to go outside of their comfort zones for the good of the congregation.

Specifics of the Mission

The mission statement of Congregation Micah is our directive. Leaders of Jewish institutions need to know the specific and unique role they serve in the mosaic of the Jewish community. If you cannot clearly articulate why you exist and what makes you unique, then you may try to accomplish everything and so probably accomplish almost nothing. What are you trying to achieve? We unabashedly believe in our mission at Micah. It allows us to be authentic, transparent, and tenacious in pursuing ways to have it come to fruition. Our outgoing phone messages even says, "You have reached the voice mailbox of the rabbi at Congregation Micah, where we seek justice, practice mercy, and walk humbly. I am sorry that I cannot take your call, but I am out fulfilling our mission of..."

People respect passion. Passion helped us learn to fundraise. Why be frightened to ask someone for something that you are certain is good for the Jewish community? People say no to us all of the time, but that is the worst they can say. Our last capital campaign was for a pre-school. We were not asking donors to help us build a nuclear facility. So at Micah, we are not shy about who we are and how we build community. When we take on new projects, we conduct the appropriate research. We create benchmarks. We evaluate setbacks, regroup, and give time for our ideas to mature.

Be a *MENSCH,* Not a *SHMUCK!*

Serving the Jewish community in any fashion can be a daunting task. The overwhelming expectations that lay before us as spiritual leaders of real communities are enormous. In order to succeed at anything, one must differentiate between types of expectations: low, fair, high, and unrealistic. Everyone wants his or her rabbi to be brilliant. The rabbi is expected to be a teacher to the wise, the wicked, the one who does not know to ask, and even the one who does not ask. Everyone wants his or her rabbi to be compassionate. It is a fair expectation to want the rabbi to care. Successful rabbis are authentic. We are the same people on and off of the pulpit. We strive to build on whatever intelligence we have by continuing to learn. And we find enough balance in our own lives to be able to remain present and sensitive when necessary to meet the needs of others.

As spiritual leaders and exemplars of ethics and morality, we try to see the best in everyone and honor the divine spirit that exists in all people, even the ones who annoy us. We try to be as approachable and as available as possible to congregants. As a rule, if someone is coming to see one of us a third time we provide a reference for a professional therapist. We are happy to talk about God, but we know our limitations. We get on the floor with children and bend down so they can dress the Torah easily. We make hospital visits with humility and listen to our elders' stories at every opportunity. We try to connect with singles, marveling at single parents. We embrace the divorced and people of different races and demographics. Anyone who comes through the doors of Micah receives our love.

However, we know that we can be manipulated. We are lied to. And we make mistakes.

Once we wanted to honor the memory of a congregant who passed away many years prior. In writing an article about her, we referred to her as Jenny. Her parents always called her Jennifer. Our attempt to honor her only seemed to remind her parents of their pain and the tradition that had failed them. Rabbi Mordechai Yosef of Ishbitz taught, "A person can only uphold the teachings of the Torah when they have stumbled in them." So we are quick to forgive. Still, we also recognize the difference between being kind and being taken advantage of. The key is to keep the toxicity of any organization to a minimum.

Love and Balance

Rabbinical school prepared us well for leading a congregation. As students at the HUC, we were able to explore the academic side of the rabbinate, while we received training in pastoral care and congregational leadership. By constantly requiring us to be up and in front of others, the college helped us become comfortable with our public speaking. The faculty at HUC taught us how to preach, teach, and create holy moments. In addition, it was while working with other rabbis, receiving valuable feedback and learning from mentors that we learned the true importance of listening to the perspectives of others.

Part of how we keep balance is to remind ourselves, and each other, to find joy and meaning in the sacred tasks of our profession. We are blessed with a job that we love and we understand that it is fragile. So we apply our best practices to keeping communication open, our relationships with staff and lay-leadership strong, and we remind ourselves constantly that while we may officiate at lots of weddings, funerals, *b'nai mitzvah* and baby-namings, each of these life-cycles are flashpoint moments for those participating in them! One time we had tutored a kid for his bar mitzvah, and he was all ready to go. His father was freaking out.

"What's wrong?" we inquired.

He replied, "My bar mitzvah was the worst day of my life!"

To which we said, "Don't make it your kid's worst day."

Finally, we consciously carve out time to spend together and with our children. Yes, it gets interrupted. But when it happens, we believe that we are teaching our children the importance of serving others when we are called away. Most of all, we have the benefit of each other. Even if we were not married, we have appreciated and still consult the moral compasses of the other rabbis we have worked with, all of whom helped us determine what it is we value most. Rabbinical school, our mentors, and our former and current congregants have all made us the rabbinic couple we are today.

Rabbis Philip "Flip" & Laurie Rice *serve as co-senior rabbis of Congregation Micah in Nashville, Tennessee. Raised in Miami, Flip is a graduate of the University of Virginia (1992), and holds a Masters in Western Religious Thought from Florida State University (1996). Laurie hails from Los Angeles, California and completed her Bachelor of Arts at Northwestern University, as a dual major in History and Slavic Languages and Literatures. Together they received their Masters of Hebrew Letters from Hebrew Union College-Jewish Institute of Religion in 1999 and were ordained as rabbis 2001. Flip is passionate about several aspects of his rabbinate, including innovative worship, and teaching how ancient texts can still speak to us today. He also enjoys practicing yoga, sailing, and swimming. Laurie has experience working as a chaplain at the Cedar-Sinai Medical Center of Los Angeles, and as a research assistant to Dr. Eugene Borowitz, the Reform Movement's pre-eminent theologian. She loves running, sipping good wine, and spending time with her husband and three children.*

Growing Rabbis

By Rabbi David A. Teutsch

When I was a rabbinical student over forty years ago, the seminary curriculum consisted primarily of acquiring knowledge and professional skills. Of course both of those are critically important for working as a rabbi in the 21st Century American Jewish community, but given the challenges rabbis face today, that formula has proved inadequate. That is part of the reason that at Reconstructionist Rabbinical College—and increasingly elsewhere—the discussion has shifted from a focus on rabbinic education to one on rabbinic formation. That shift is critical no matter what kind of position—congregation, Hillel, chaplaincy, education, community organizing, programming or freelance—a rabbi serves in.

There was a time when seminaries assumed that their students were knowledgeable, spiritually engaged and ethically grounded Jews. Seminaries today recognize that is not a safe assumption. Many students come to rabbinical programs in search of their place in Jewish tradition. Seminary is a place for them to shape their Jewish lives. Contemporary seminaries therefore have to be concerned with strengthening their students as Jews as a step toward the students growing into rabbis. That adds immeasurably to the complexity and challenge of rabbinic formation.

Of course, the curricular emphases vary seminary to seminary based not only on differences in theology and in assumptions about proper practice, but also on the history and organizational culture of the institution. Nevertheless, the fundamental components of rabbinic formation that the schools need to address remain the same: acquisition of academic knowledge, mastery of sufficient Torah learning and text skills, articulation of personal belief and theology, development of spiritual depth and spiritual practice, cultivation of *menschlichkeit* and the Jewish virtues, understanding of the contemporary Jewish community and its environment, and practical skills relevant to ritual, pastoral work, teaching, administration, group work and leadership.

That's a very long list! But more important than any one entry on that list is the necessity that all of those things be integrated into a seamless whole within the character of the rabbi. The sum is far greater than the parts, as all of us know who have a rabbinic mentor whom we admire. One can acquire more facts or skills later, but if one does not enter the rabbinate with an evident love of Yiddishkeit and of Jews, as well as with integrity and spiritual seriousness, nothing else can make up for that lack. The particulars in any good rabbinic job description spell out expected tasks and relationships, but they cannot be expected to deal with the critical questions about what rabbis need to do to cultivate their personal spiritual resources, to undertake sufficient self-care and to develop the network of familial relationships and friendships that rabbis need to sustain themselves. So the components of rabbinic formation ought not to be developed within departments and programs that are largely separate from each other. Good rabbinic formation depends upon integration of the entire curricular and co-curricular experience. One excellent integrative experience is Clinical Pastoral Education (CPE), which brings together hands-on pastoral work with group support that emphasizes not only the development of skills, but growth in self-insight, help with growing edges and support in integrating the experience with one's personal theology. But full integration can be achieved within a seminary setting only if it is a goal to which the whole faculty and the academic administrators are dedicated.

The emergence of spiritual direction, *Musar*, worship labs, meditation training, attention to personal practice, chanting circles and increased exploration of Hasidic texts are all part of the effort to create greater spiritual self-insight, ongoing and self-sustaining spiritual practice and an improved spiritual toolbox. Awareness of the holy dimension in all of life should shape rabbinic consciousness and guide rabbinic teaching. The consciously spiritual aspect of rabbinic training needs to be integrated with study of codes and of ritual leadership so that spiritual development integrates with the rest of rabbinic study.

Inculcation of virtue and of skills in ethical decision making is an equally critical area that in most schools is still in its infancy. Rabbis need to master professional ethics to guide their personal conduct. They also need to gain substantial insight into bioethics, sexual and family ethics, speech ethics and organizational ethics so that they can teach these critical subjects and provide guidance to Jews and others who come for help with concerns and dilemmas that arise in their daily lives. These together with case studies, *tokhacha*, faculty and mentor role modeling, and explicit exploration should help rabbis deepen their *menschlichkeit*. This Yiddish term has a compound meaning that includes everything that is implied in being fully human. A mensch is someone who reflects the full range of Jewish virtues, including integrity, humility, courage, empathy, kindness, generosity, caring, and sensitivity. Most Jews will forgive a rabbi for almost any mistake for which the rabbi sincerely apologizes, but they will not forgive a rabbi who does not love them, and they will not easily forgive a rabbi who is not a mensch. We cannot assume that rabbinical students come to seminary as fully formed moral creatures, so work on the moral development of rabbinical students needs to be an integral part of the seminary experience.

One of the goals of rabbinic education should be to minimize future burnout. How can seminaries accomplish this goal? Seminaries can attend to the conscious development of rabbis' spiritual lives and increased attention to self-care help. They can ensure that rabbis have good skills in group work and leadership. Shaping realistic expectations about what rabbis can accomplish helps as well. Rabbi Ira Eisenstein once said to me at a particularly hard moment early in my rabbinate that burnout is caused not by hard work, but by heartache. If designed to do so, rabbinic education can help rabbis to develop resilience, to set realistic expectations, to take note of their successes and appreciate their positive impact, and to avoid conflicts that are not *l'shem shamayim* (for the sake of heaven). That will only occur if rabbinic faculty members are trained to undertake this in their role as advisors and teachers. Mentors, too, need training if work in this area is to be part of their mentoring responsibility.

A recent survey showed that rabbis are often resistant to publicly stating controversial views they hold. I deeply believe that rabbis ought to function as moral and spiritual leaders, and that means having the courage to speak out and the wisdom to discern how to do that effectively. One sign that rabbinic training has improved will be the greater willingness of rabbis to articulate difficult stands when morally called for and to take the resulting heat with equanimity. Surely that is one of the tests for *menschlichkeit*.

This is a highly challenging time to be a rabbi. The rate of political, economic, social and techno-scientific change is greater than ever before, and every indicator suggests that it will continue to accelerate. One of the things that people turn to religion for is a sense of continuity, of contact with eternal verities in the face of flux in the rest of their lives. Helping Judaism adapt while at the same time connecting Jews to timeless teaching requires flexibility, excellent listening skills and maintaining perspective. Of course rabbinical schools can teach students what is cutting edge while they are in school, which currently includes such things as use of social media for outreach. But what is new now will be soon be outdated. More important is teaching them the skills of adaptation. When I was a rabbinical student, there was almost no thought given to LGBTQ issues or to how to serve the intermarried family. I wrote my senior thesis on a typewriter. No one was yet talking about the way that settlements on the West Bank would impact any future peace negotiations. There was no thought of the Internet or cell phones. Successful rabbis must adapt to ever shifting social and technological realities. Developing character and openness to change is critical to the success of the next generation of rabbis because we cannot possibly anticipate the changes they will see in their lifetimes.

One of the problems of the American rabbinate—and I believe the rabbinate across the world—is that rabbis are often put on a pedestal, or treated like parental figures, or alternately fawned over and belittled—and sometimes all of these within the same community. This adds to the way that rabbis are wounded, so their situation is that of wounded healers. The flattery and special treatment that go with the role explain the ego inflation and concomitant insecurity that seems to accompany some rabbinic roles. One of the tasks of rabbinic school is to inoculate rabbis, making it less likely that they will be infected by rabbinic ego inflation. Refusing to stand on a pedestal, sharing questions and doubts, and remaining aware that much of the feedback reflects the rabbinic role rather than the rabbi's essential self are practices that can be acquired in rabbinical school—and they should be.

The rabbinate can be a lonely profession. Often there is only one rabbi working in a particular setting. Rabbis need to seek out *chevrutas*, clergy support groups, mentors, supervisors and ongoing professional education if they are to continue to grow and maintain perspective as they move through their careers. They will do so only if they are trained to recognize the importance of these activities while they are students. Learning experiences that help students see the value in devoting time and money to these activities can help to sustain careers that will span most of a century.

I did not devote much of this essay to the key questions of language acquisition, decoding Jewish texts, the study of history and a host of practical curricular questions. It is around these kinds of questions that there will necessarily be the greatest differences among seminaries. And seminary faculties are used to focusing on these questions and continually tinkering to improve their curricula. This is a process that goes back hundreds of years. I trust that each faculty does the best it can. But we are still in the early stages of thinking about rabbinic formation more broadly. Our largest challenge as we look ahead is the creation of rabbinic leaders whose vision, inner lives, and caring for others can continue the advancement of Jewish civilization.

Rabbi David A. Teutsch serves as Director of the Center for Jewish Ethics and the Louis & Myra Wiener Professor of Contemporary Jewish Civilization at the Reconstructionist Rabbinical College. He was Editor-in-Chief for the groundbreaking six-volume Kol Haneshamah Reconstructionist prayerbook series, and he is currently working on A Guide to Jewish Practice that takes a values-based approach to both ethical and ritual matters; the first volume of the Guide won a National Jewish Book Award. He has previously served as Executive Director of the Federation of Reconstructionist Congregations and Havurot and as a congregational rabbi. As an honors graduate of Harvard University ordained by Hebrew Union College-Jewish Institute of Religion, he earned his Ph.D. at the Wharton School, where his dissertation dealt with organizational ethics. Rabbi Teutsch is a widely published writer and a well known organizational consultant and trainer.

The Chisma Curriculum

By Michael Marmur

Creating a curriculum for the education of rabbis is a complex and fascinating task. Ideological, theological, sociological, political, and institutional dimensions are included in the equation. Every generation is convinced that it is living in remarkable and unprecedented times. At the risk of falling prey to this kind of historical hubris, educating rabbis has never been as uncertain or as intangible as it has become in non-Chareidi Judaism in the 21st Century.

Factors contributing to this complexity include the challenge posed to the denominational model, which has held sway for decades; economic pressures on graduate level professional education in general; and palpable shifts in the cultural landscape. Opening programs that offer rabbinical ordination is easier than ever, while recruiting students to justify this proliferation is hard work.

Thinking creatively about rabbinical education requires discourse with a variety of audiences. There must be a constant conversation with students about their experience of and hopes for the program in which they are enrolled. Sessions with alumni have also proven to be particularly helpful— encouraging graduates to reflect on their education from the perspective of what they currently do in the field helps those responsible for seminaries to think about many aspects of the work of pre-service rabbinic education and the need for in-service continuity. Faculty colleagues are constantly engaged in the trial and error of course preparation, mentoring, and other forms of guidance. Administrators, scholars, mentors and teachers in sister institutions have much to teach each other, and opportunities for open dialogue are usually of great worth. The wider world of seminary education and other kinds of professional training also offer inspiration and perplexity in roughly equal quantities.

I am charged with the task of working with the faculty of my institution to devise a course of study and overall experience rich enough to send a generation of Reform rabbis out into the world. Such a task can only be undertaken with curiosity and humility. Curiosity because the work at hand should involve anthropology, sociology, psychology, hermeneutics, history, education theory, and pastoral care. Humility because one can only ever hope to be an amateur in most of these fields, and also because there is no evidence that expertise is a key to efficacy or excellence. After all the articles have been read and written, all the studies commissioned and undertaken, after the soothsayers have sifted through the entrails of our contemporary situation, there remains an intimacy and a mystery to rabbinical education. This is an area characterized by a plethora of deeply-held opinions and a dearth of real expertise.

The sources of rabbinic literature have much to teach us about rabbinical education. My colleague Larry Hoffman, one of the great modern masters of this field, has emphasized the gulf separating our situation from that of our forebears: "Whatever our ancestors of the Talmud may have been, "sages" (as we like to think) or "holy men" akin to Zoroastrian magi, rabbis are hardly that."[1] While it is hard to fault Hoffman's statement, there are at least three reasons why looking to ancient rabbinic sources as we contemplate current rabbinical dilemmas can be seen as a worthwhile exercise. Firstly, the term "rabbi" spans the generations and the social contexts. The fact that Jews across the denominational spectrum afford significance to the title and imbue it with different kinds of significance should encourage us to explore the use of this term in earlier times. The title "Rabbi" continues to display remarkable resilience at a time of great

---

1   Lawrence A. Hoffman, "The Professionalization of the American Rabbinate," *Rabbi-Pastor Priest: Their Roles and Profiles Through the Ages*, Walter Homolka and Heinz-Günther Schöttler (ed.s) (De Gruyter: Berlin, 2013) 129. There is a burgeoning literature on the institution of the rabbinate in the period in ancient Palestine and elsewhere. For a fine example of the state of historical research in this area, see David Levine, "Rabbis, Preachers, and Aggadists: An Aspect of Jewish Culture in Third- and Fourth-Century Palestine", *'Follow the Wise'—Festschrift for Lee I. Levine*, Zeev Weiss, Oded Irshai, Jodi Magness & Seth Schwartz (ed.s) (Eisenbrauns: Winona Lake IN, 2010) 272-294.

fluidity and change, and that term carries with it layers of meaning, which deserve examination and understanding.

Secondly, perusal of these sources often reveals that the chasm we believe separates the rabbis of today from those who preceded them centuries ago is not always as deep or as wide as we might imagine.

Thirdly, this is what rabbis should do—turn to the literature of our people in search of direction and meaning. And if we bring our own prism of interpretation to the sources we choose to read, we are enacting the finest and most enduring aspect of a rabbinical imperative spanning millennia. Looking to rabbinical literature (and indeed other periods and genres of our tradition) as part of our deliberations about rabbinical education is justified in intrinsic terms and is also an enactment of the best of what the rabbinate can be: a bridge spanning Judaism and the Jews, history and contemporaneity, timeless resonance and timely relevance.

According to the relatively meager sources available to us,[2] Rabbi Elazar Chisma was a significant tanna of the second and third generation, perhaps both a contemporary and a disciple of Rabbi Akiva. It may be that Chisma is a locative name, suggesting that he came from the place known today as Hizmeh. In some sources he is ben Chisma, which would imply a familial link. Within a tradition within the literature of the Midrash itself, however, Rabbi Elazar came by his name as the result of a great moment of post-ordination in-service rabbinical education. This source is to be found in Leviticus Rabbah 23.4 and in Songs Rabbah 2.7.

We are introduced to the teaching about Rabbi Eliezer in the context of a discussion of the biblical phrase "like a rose among the thorns." It is taught that a person who knows how to behave in a liturgical or ritual situation when nobody else is sure what to do—to recite the blessing for a bridegroom or a mourner, for example— such a person is to be likened to a rose among thorns. Against this backdrop the tale of how Rabbi Elazar came to be called Chisma is

---

2   See Aaron Hyman, *Toldoth Tannaim Ve'Amoraim* (Pri Haaretz: Jerusalem, 1987, volume 1) 217-218. On the traditions in the name of Rabbi Elazar, see Levine, Diane. "Elazar Hisma", *Persons and Institutions in Early Rabbinic Institutions*, William Scott Green (ed.) (Scholars Press: Missoula, 1977) 149-205.

recounted. The translation offered here, like all translations, is no more than one version of how the story might be understood.

Rabbi Elazar went to a certain place where he was asked to read the blessings before the Shema. He said to them: I do not know them. They said: lead us in the Amidah prayer. He said: I can't.

The man who comes to this anonymous congregation is not himself anonymous. He has attained the title Rabbi, and as we shall presently see, he has already earned something of a reputation as a learned sage. He is asked to perform a standard task and declines because he does not know how. The host congregation may have thought this aberration was connected to a particular section of the liturgy, or perhaps they suspected that he was refusing them because the offer was beneath his dignity. But when they invite him to take on a yet more central part of the liturgy, he declines again. This noted rabbi seems unable to perform the tasks expected of him by the field.

They said to him: this is the man of whom people make such a fuss? What is he called Rabbi for?

The response of the host congregation is swift and merciless. After these two strikes, he is out. They do not simply impugn his skills as a service leader, but rather they seek to undermine his rabbinical status and reputation. This is the same Rabbi Elazar everyone has been talking about? He can't even fulfill rudimentary performance expectations. And if he can't do that, why is he called Rabbi at all?

The people who educated and ordained Rabbi Elazar had not seen it necessary to teach him these particular skills. In a parallel tale of a newly-minted rabbi failing to make the grade in his first congregation, it is explained that he forgets everything he knew and is therefore incapable of answering the legal and philosophical questions posed to him by the lay people.[3] Here, however, as the continuation of the story makes clear, these are skills which Rabbi Elazar had not been taught. As a teacher of rabbinical students, I am acutely aware of everything we don't teach and they don't learn which one would want a rabbi to know. If there were a contemporary rabbi incapable of or uncomfortable when leading a prayer service, we would bemoan the fact that he or she did not come from a thick

---

3   See PT *Y'vamot* xii. 13a and parallel sources.

Jewish environment. But in the case of Rabbi Elazar we might speculate that his inability to act as prayer leader reflects not only his own skills and predilections, but also the attitudes and priorities of his teachers. When the graduate comes into contact with the clear expectations of the Jews in the pews, his ivory tower education seems to have served him poorly.

He was deeply mortified and went to Rabbi Akiva. He said to him: why does your face look so sickly? He told him what had happened. He then said to him: Sir, would you be willing to teach me to learn?

Wounded, Rabbi Elazar makes his way to Rabbi Akiva. At times these two men are presented as contemporaries and colleagues, while elsewhere Rabbi Akiva appears to be Elazar's teacher. In any case, it is to Rabbi Akiva that the demoralized rabbi turns. Akiva sees that his colleague or student is not himself. The fact that Rabbi Akiva notices is noteworthy. The finest teachers are often those who combine good pedagogy with great humanity. The learning moment which is about to take place would not have happened had not the great Rabbi Akiva looked into the face of his erstwhile student and realized that something was awry.

Next is the lynchpin of this tale. "Will you help me learn what I need to know to pass the congregational test?" Some translations of the Aramaic text read this question as being addressed to Rabbi Akiva by Rabbi Elazar. Others suggest that the question is posed by Rabbi Akiva as, "Are you interested in learning from me?" In either case, the key motivation for learning comes from the encounter of the graduate with the realities of the field. There is a triangle at play here, and each angle is acute—the seminary (represented here by Rabbi Akiva), the student, and the demands, needs and expectations of the world. This triangulation leads to a moment in which the newly-minted rabbi comes back to his teacher and is now ready to learn a skill he needs in order to be the kind of rabbi he needs to be.

In some versions of this tale the questioner calls his interlocutor Rabbi. This is easy to understand if Rabbi Elazar is addressing Rabbi Akiva, but at first glance this seems implausible the other way around. After all, why would the great Rabbi Akiva call the rattled Rabbi Elazar by this term, one which denotes not only a certain status but also an acknowledgement of seniority? There is, however, another understanding of the scene. Rabbi Elazar has internalized the criticism he received from the unforgiving congregants. He doubts the validity of his own rabbinical status. In that moment Rabbi Akiva shows immense tenderness. Just as he asks Rabbi Elazar if he would like to learn, he calls him Rabbi. "You are my student for the purpose of this particular skill. You are also a rabbi—my rabbi." This is how we should teach our students. There is an echo here of the blessing given some years earlier by Rabban Gamliel to Rabbi Joshua: come in peace, my rabbi and my student![4]

He consented and taught him. After some time he returned to the same place. They invited him to say the blessings before the Shema. He did so. They asked him to lead the Amidah prayer. He did. They thereupon said: Rabbi Elazar itchasam and they called him Rabbi Elazar Chisma.

After Rabbi Akiva and Rabbi Elazar speak and agree upon the learning contract between them, the actual learning of the particular skill is not described in any detail. The assumption here appears to be that a bright student motivated by a bracing encounter with the professional environment, tutored by a great teacher, will have little trouble learning the requisite capacities. We know in our own work that motivation and talent are not always enough for great student learning outcomes to ensue. There may be learning challenges, or the teaching may be ill-conceived, or the expectations of the field unrealistic. The essential point, however, is as true today as ever it was. When the teacher, the learner and the milieu are aligned, the chances of imparting the subject matter effectively are enhanced immeasurably.

How should we understand the title given to Rabbi Elazar by the congregation after his successful return to the site of his former embarrassment? The root ĥ-s-m covers a broad semantic range, so the conclusion drawn by the congregation once it has seen that Rabbi Elazar can now pass this practical rabbinics test is open to broad interpretation. It may mean that he has now become stronger, more resilient in the face of criticism. The checkpoints in contemporary Israel are *machsomim*, barriers capable of exclusion. In this sense the title given Rabbi Elazar by his congregation is not an unalloyed compliment. Now he is strong and capable and perhaps

---

4   Mishnah *Rosh HaShanah* 2.9.

also less approachable. There is now no barrier on his mouth—he is a fluent exponent of the dictates of tradition. But perhaps another kind of barrier has been erected? In the Mishna we find our verb used to describe a utensil which has been completed.[5] It is as if the congregants are saying, "When that rabbi first came to us, he was still in a molten state. He had not yet found his full rabbinical form. Now he is the real deal, the finished item." It is not clear that to be finished, to be completed, is the most essential rabbinic virtue. I would argue that in the rabbinate one expects a level of competence likely to inspire confidence in those being served, but also a certain aspect of incompleteness, the same cocktail of curiosity and humility described above.

It is hard for a rabbi to appear unfinished. There are the expectations of one's congregation, often there are denominational politics at play, and of course each rabbi has expectations of herself as well. However, we might observe that the best rabbis are like implements fit for purpose but not yet in their final state.

The root from which Elazar's nickname is taken bears many meanings: impermeability, strength, completeness, fixity, hardness, silence, and hesitation. It may be that the indeterminate nature of the term they apply to the rabbi also carries with it an important teaching. Our congregations and institutions give us all kinds of reputations and imbue us with any number of talents and shortcomings. We carry around with us the names given to us by the people we serve. For this reason, it is particularly important to know our own name, the identity we have independent of the interaction with the field. Many of the saddest tales of rabbinical meltdown seem to take place when a rabbi forgets his first name and is only identified through the expectations and projections of his community. It is good to have both names.

I recently had an opportunity to study the Chisma text with my predecessor as Provost of Hebrew Union College-Jewish Institute of Religion, Norman Cohen. With his eagle eye for nuance in rabbinic literature, he noted that in a number of manuscript versions of our

5   Mishnah *Keilim* 20.2.

story the name given to Elazar is not Chisma. Rather, the impressed congregants say of the returning rabbi—now he is capable and knowledgeable, using a word from the root meaning wise. Learning, emotional intelligence and intellectual curiosity play a key role at the heart of this process. It is only a coincidence that the Hebrew Union College was established by Isaac Mayer Wise, and that the Jewish Institute of Religion was founded by Steven S. Wise. You don't have to be Wise to establish a rabbinical seminary, but you do have to be wise to make your name as a rabbi.

The midrash has an epilogue. Immediately following the tale of Rabbi Elazar's experience of just-in-time professional coaching, we find a teaching concerning Rabbi Jonah, an *Amora* of the fourth generation who was the head of the yeshiva in Tiberias. Here, then, is the testimony of a seminary president:

Rabbi Jonah used to teach his disciples the bridegrooms' blessing and the mourners' blessing, so that they might be ready for any to call upon them.

This teaching relates to the earlier context of the midrash. A person who knows what to do in peak life cycle moments when everyone else is too overcome or uncertain or uneducated, such a person is to be compared to a rose among the thorns. Rabbi Jonah's practice is included in the text here as if to say, "We are aware of all these examples, including the tale of how Elazar Chisma got his name, and we have altered our curriculum in order to include these skills as a regular part of in-service instruction." The curriculum of rabbinical schools has always been in dialogue with the needs and preferences of the fields in which our graduates will toil. The curriculum, then, is not impermeable or completed. It should strive to demonstrate the curiosity and humility we expect of our graduates.

It may be a stretch to imagine Rabbi Jonah meeting with representatives of the Central Conference of Galilean Rabbis, the Board of the Union for Amoraic Judaism, or for that matter experts and master practitioners from the Kinneret Institute, and demographers pouring over early findings from the fourth century Pew study, along with focus groups of students and alumni. All this is fanciful, but it is less improbable to believe that Rabbi Jonah and his faculty considered the needs of the environment for which they were training their rabbis, and factored in the body of teaching they were committed to impart whether or not the field articulated a clear need for it. To design the curriculum solely to teach how to perform a smooth wedding is to sacrifice depth on the altar of ratings. To ignore the skills and sensitivities called for out in the world— interpersonal and pastoral skills, marketing and budgeting, new trends in communication, liturgy and music, and all the rest—is to ignore the sacred responsibility of the seminary.

Often in discussions with members of my faculty, I am struck by the tension they feel between the formal curriculum they are striving to impart to our students and what might be described as the shadow curriculum. The shadow curriculum includes any number of co-curricular additions, many of them experiential in nature, which form a major and perhaps increasing proportion of our students' time. I don't know how to solve the tension, which is real. Our students are overwhelmed with the need to balance existential, spiritual, economic, intellectual, academic, personal and spiritual demands. Perhaps we can take comfort in the fact that the tension is, in fact, very ancient.

I am open to the discussion of how much should be crammed into the pre-service part of rabbinical training and what should be fed into the sixty-year curriculum—the life of learning and growth to which all rabbis should aspire. There is a professional basis one has a right to expect from a doctor on her first day after being qualified, and the same could be said for her rabbinical counterpart. I am convinced that the deep knowledge and passion for learning which our rabbis exhibit will be as significant for the future of Judaism as their ability to interpret a spreadsheet. We are constantly striving to work out what should get taught how and when in the arc of an education. Much— perhaps most—will indeed be taught after ordination. Twenty centuries after the curricular discussion began, its next iteration promises to be bracing, unsettling and exciting.

Welcome to the Chisma curriculum. Better to rely on it than on charisma. In this curriculum, the seminary gives you your title. The encounter between you as a person and the persons you serve is what gives you your name.

Michael Marmur is the Jack, Joseph and Morton Mandel Provost of Hebrew Union College - Jewish Institute of Religion (HUC-JIR). He lives in Jerusalem.

Rabbinical School Curriculum

By Rabbi Kassel Abelson

I recently discussed with a medical school student her medical school's approach to curriculum. The medical school had recently introduced a new approach to the courses offered in the first year. The first year's program was a mixture of traditional courses in the various sciences combined with interviews with patients, shadowing doctors in clinics and hospitals, and joint meetings with nurses and technicians in training. Medical schools in past decades concentrated their science courses in the first two years and then students applied their new knowledge to realistic challenges in the concluding years of the medical school. The new approach reflected the conviction that even abstract science courses needed to show that the knowledge acquired was relevant to dealing with real medical issues and real medical personnel.

A Rabbi Looks Back

This impressive, innovative and pragmatic medical school curriculum approach for training physicians is very different than the approach to training rabbis I got when I was a rabbinical student at the Jewish Theological Seminary in the 1940's. The Seminary offered a curriculum in Biblical and Rabbinic texts taught by outstanding scholars. The approach was a scholarly one, blending classical texts with a modern historical approach. I had the feeling that the professors' approach was to train scholars with little thought given to the realistic challenges involved in being Conservative rabbis in modern synagogues. I liked my professors and enjoyed the material that I studied, but they did not help me to understand and deal with the challenges that lay ahead.

The only courses that dealt with the real challenges that rabbis would face when they graduated was the course taught by Dr. Mordecai Kaplan on Jewish philosophy and the course by Dr. Simon Greenberg on Homiletics. From Dr. Kaplan I began to understand that Judaism was a religious civilization that involved all aspects of contemporary Jewish life, and from Dr. Greenberg I learned how to write and deliver a sermon. I also learned that being a rabbi would mean that I would have to deal with theological questions and find answers to questions asked by congregants about God and the meaning of life.

When I graduated the Seminary, I decided to take a job as an assistant rabbi to Rabbi David Aronson at Beth El in Minneapolis, Minnesota. This proved to be a very good choice. I learned from Rabbi Aronson what a modern synagogue should be and how to help it become the institution for Torah study, for worship, and for human interactions.

In 1951, I became a chaplain for a two-year term in the Air Force. This was a very good experience in developing rabbinic skills. First and foremost I learned how to relate to non-Jewish clergy, which proved very useful in my many years as a rabbi in the general community. In chaplains' school I also took a course on counseling and had to deal with a wide variety of problems that our airmen faced. This helped prepare me for my role as a personal counselor in my many years as a congregational rabbi. I never stopped learning new things and applying them to new issues as they arose.

Rabbinical Schools for the Future

Present day schools for training rabbis and other Jewish clergy have changed since I graduated. A multitude of new courses have been introduced which have helped graduates through the years prepare for rabbinic careers in congregations, as Jewish educators, and as administrators in Jewish communal institutions. However, I would like to apply the new approach that is now used in some medical schools of mixing the practical with the scholarly from the very beginning of the years spent studying to become a rabbi. I do this with the prayer that this will help develop even more effective rabbis, and relieve the stress involved in the early years serving as a rabbi.

Though I thoroughly enjoyed my rabbinic studies, I soon learned that they were not easily translated into education courses for congregants. I had to review every text that I wanted to teach and develop my own study materials that would be of interest to laypeople. Hence, I would strongly recommend that the rabbinical school also teach courses that would introduce rabbinical students to the materials developed for adult use, and how to best utilize them. This should include utilizing the Internet to obtain relevant material.

The Role of the Synagogue

We are told that the Synagogue plays three major roles in the Jewish community. It functions as a *beit midrash*, a *beit t'filah*, and as a *beit k'neset*. This, in a way, is a practical application of the rabbinic saying that "the Jewish world stands on three things: Study of Torah, worship, and the performance of deeds of loving kindness."

Let us look at the rabbinical school curriculum in the light of these three basic values. We begin with the synagogue as a house of learning. The study of Torah at a seminary should not be seen as an academic pursuit, but rather preparing a rabbi to teach Torah to his or her congregants. My hope in this recommendation is to marry serious text study of the classics with real world, practical applications to congregations and other rabbinical settings. Relevancy should be a priority of lens used in the study of classics. Additionally, using contemporary texts coming out of the tradition in class will encourage rabbis to use this scholarship in their vocations. Teaching future rabbis to be at home in Jewish texts should include more relevant yet scholarly work from the movement.

Beit Midrash, Torah Study

The Torah: During my years at the Seminary, we never studied the *Humash*, the Five Books of Moses, probably, because the Bible Professors did not want to teach the *Humash* from a historical and critical point of view. However, the Torah is the most important book of Judaism, and it is central in the life and thought of the synagogue.

In addition to a course on studying traditional commentaries, there should also be a course that is studied in the rabbinical school utilizing contemporary materials developed for adult study. The *Etz Hayim* is a widely used Torah translation and commentary. Congregants look at it every Sabbath during the reading of the Torah. To familiarize the student with its contents, the *Etz Hayim* should be used as the basic text in the study of *Humash* for rabbinical students. Classroom discussions should involve the commentaries in the *Etz Hayim* and the essays in the back of the Humash. This will help the rabbi to prepare for teaching an adult education class on the Torah and to comment from the pulpit. The *Etz Hayim* also has material for the haftarah, which should also be studied in such a class.

The Bible: Courses on the other books of the Bible should include the historical books of the Bible as well as the Prophets and the Writings. The courses should include discussions on the available Jewish English commentaries and how to develop courses for adult education. There should be discussions on the Christian and Muslim approaches to the Bible and the differences in approaches of the three major faiths.

The Mishnah: An introductory course on the Mishnah should include references to available materials for study and for teaching. I believe it important to make an assignment for a private daily study of a Mishna with an appropriate commentary. There should be regular meetings with the instructor to review what has been privately studied. It's also important that *Pirkei Avot,* the Ethics of the Sages, be a separate assignment. It is a book that will be studied in every synagogue sooner or later. *Pirkei Avot* should be assigned with a modern commentary, and be discussed from the historical and ethical points of view.

The Talmud: The courses in Talmud should be, at least partially, based on selecting Talmudic sections that would be of interest to the lay members of Conservative synagogues. These sections can later serve as the basis for adult study courses in synagogues. The professors of Talmud should be asked to teach, with an eye to contemporary relevance and reference to available supplementary sources. Talmud study *chavurot* can be set up utilizing sources such as Koren Talmud Bavli, which are available with English translations and contemporary commentaries. This will help rabbinic students to become aware of available resources for future adult courses. It also makes the students knowledgeable about the value of *chavurot*.

Medieval and Modern Writings: Whatever the courses cover, an overall English language text which covers the field should be assigned, such as *Jewish People, Jewish Thought*. This will help the student to refer to a context when discussing a Jewish philosopher or historian in a future congregation.

Conservative Judaism: A course in the History of Conservative Judaism should be a requirement for every student. It should be based on a book like *Conservative Judaism, The New Century* by Neil Gillman. The course should include a detailed study of *Emet V'Emunah*. Part of graduation requirements should be an essay by each student outlining his or her understanding of Conservative Judaism.

Halachah: It is essential that our rabbis be acquainted with the traditional codes and responsa. However, it is not less important that they become acquainted with the contemporary responsa as well. They should be introduced to the CJLS by attending at least one meeting. A course in the responsa of the CJLS and the Masorti Movement should be required, and each student should have to write a responsum on an assigned *sh'eilah*.

Beit T'filah, Synagogue Services

The main responsibility of the rabbinical student who chooses a congregation when he or she graduates will be to conduct services in the synagogue. It is essential that the student be well prepared for this responsibility. I remember one incident from my days serving as a chaplain in the United States Air Force that illustrates this need. I was serving in Morocco and the High Holidays were approaching. A young Moroccan Jew had been recommended to be our cantor for the High Holidays. I was reviewing the services with him, and I mentioned the *Kol Nidre*. He asked, "What's the *Kol Nidre*?" shocking me beyond measure. I began to point it out to him in the *machzor* and he said, "Oh, yes, I remember now, Al Jolson in the Jazz Singer." Al Jolson had played the role of a cantor's son in the movie. He did not want to be a cantor like his father. He wanted to be an entertainer, a jazz singer. He was tremendously successful, but his father was heart broken. In the concluding scene of the movie, Jolson goes to the synagogue on Yom Kippur night, and the movie ends with him singing the *Kol Nidre*.

The Sepharadim do not have *Kol Nidre* in their Yom Kippur Service. The Sephardic have a special Minchah ceremony on Yom Kippur where they release vows. The Sefardic Liturgy has undergone a totally different development from the Ashkenazic Liturgy. I took this experience to dramatize to me that what is important to one branch of world Jewry in liturgy may not have the same importance to another. This incident influenced me through the years, helping me to be flexible in adding or dropping prayers from our prayer books, knowing that Jews the world over had been doing this through the centuries. The presence of Aramaic prayers such as *Kol Nidre*, *Kaddish*, and *Y'kum Purkan* in the services should be used to explain the introduction of English prayers into the services and the choice of which prayers should be explored. Today, with so many different styles of prayer available on the Internet, it is very easy to make prayer a more enriching experience by keep a fixed body of prayer for services, but regularly introducing multiple styles of prayer from Jewish communities around the world.

Liturgy Program: I believe it to be essential that our rabbinical students have a basic course in liturgy and utilize the Mahzor Lev Shalem, both the High Holiday and the Sabbath prayer books. They should be taught how the liturgy developed, and the many changes that took place, so that they know what is essential when they plan services with the ritual committee. Though I am not musically proficient, I believe it essential that rabbinical students become familiar with the melodies of the different services and participate in conducting services during their years at the seminary.

The instructors in the courses on liturgy should arrange for students to attend services at the various area synagogues, and follow up with discussions on what they observed. It is important that students also go to synagogues in other parts of the country and report back in writing on what they saw. Since they are at the seminary where there are cantorial and education students, it would be helpful to have regular meetings with them to explore the varied approaches of these future professionals. Congregational rabbis should be invited to meet with the classes and discuss how they plan services with their staff and how they meet with Ritual committees to discuss the nature of the service and how they introduce innovations and changes.

Beit K'neset, Interpersonal Relationships: The Synagogue plays a key role in bringing Jews together as a community, not only to do *g'milut chasadim,* deeds of loving kindness, but for all kinds of meaningful activities. Rabbinical students should be introduced to these activities in a course devoted to interpersonal relationships in which they will have to a play a part. The course should include role playing by the students, by the teachers and by invited guests.

Rabbis and Congregants: Rabbis should be invited to speak to the students about their experiences dealing with congregants and with the synagogue board. Presidents and congregational officers can be invited to speak to the rabbinical students about their thoughts and reactions to being active in their congregations and their thoughts about their conceptions of a rabbi's role and responsibilities in the congregation. Arrangements should be made for students to shadow rabbis as they go about their duties from day to day in their congregations. These can be combined with the student giving a sermon to the congregation.

Funerals: The most common lifetime ritual involves dealing with families that have lost a beloved. After a presentation by the teacher on the funeral ritual and writing a eulogy, a meeting with the bereaved family can be role played by the teacher, by guests, but also involving some of the students. The "rabbi" should lead the meeting with the family, asking about the circumstances of the death, helping the family members deal with their loss, extending condolences, explaining the ritual of the funeral and gathering the necessary information about the deceased for writing a eulogy. The students should be asked to compose a eulogy, based on what they heard and learned at the family meeting. The eulogies should be discussed at a class meeting. The teacher should also discuss the funeral ritual, the graveside ceremony, and the shivah that will follow and the role that the rabbi will play in the follow up.

Weddings: The teacher needs to discuss, at length, the ritual of the wedding. The role that the rabbi plays in the preliminary meeting with the couple should be discussed in detail, for this is an opportunity to enroll future members in the Synagogue. In this pre-marital meeting the marital relationship should be explored in detail, as should the wedding ceremony. The discussion should be followed by an enacted wedding, role played by the students. Each student should be asked to write a wedding talk which should be discussed in the classroom. These are merely some ways that the rabbi can develop a relationship with a couple that can last a lifetime, by helping them realize the relevance of Judaism and the value of a relationship with a rabbi.

In Conclusion

Students who will enter the rabbinate and serve congregations have many responsibilities. They should be defined and become the subjects of classroom discussions using the recommended techniques. If the students expect to go into other aspects of Jewish professional life, there should be parallel programs that will help them learn and experience at an early stage the challenges they will confront in their chosen areas of Jewish communal life. This should be done with the goal of having the rabbinical students understand the challenges that they will face when they become rabbis and have some practical experiences to deal with them. This will be of help both to the new rabbis and the congregations that they will serve.

Rabbi Kassel Abelson graduated from New York University in 1943, was ordained from the Jewish Theological Seminary of America in 1948, and became Assistant Rabbi at Beth El Synagogue in Minneapolis, MN, immediately upon ordination. After a hiatus of seven years, when he served as a chaplain in the U.S. Air Corps, and then as a solo pulpit rabbi in Columbus, GA, he returned to Beth El in 1957. Rabbi Abelson has been a pioneer in the fields of Jewish education, youth work and camping, inter-religious relations, biomedical ethics and Conservative Judaism. He is a past president of the International Rabbinical Assembly and a past chair of its National Committee on Jewish Law and Standards (CJLS). He has put his stamp upon an approach to Conservative Jewish law as editor of the CJLS proceedings and author of numerous responsa. He still serves as Rabbi Emeritus of Beth El and is one of America's longest serving congregational rabbis.

Red Rover Red Rover Let Torah Come Over

By Rabbi Jessy Gross

I take a moment from playing hostess and planner of the Hanukkah Brew Ha Ha to look out over the crowd of nearly two hundred people gathered. Standing beside me is a friend whose childhood rabbi would likely name as "least likely to attend a Jewish event as an adult." I see friends from my personal community, friends of the host site Union Craft Brewing, regular participants of Charm City Tribe, young Baltimore Jews and non-Jews feeling the Hanukkah spirit, a few hipsters, enthusiasts and skeptics, *kippah* wearers and tattoo sleeves and, of course, complete strangers. It's quite a turnout.

On top of a beer-brewing platform, my friend holds the menorah while two others each hold up a poster of blessings in Hebrew, English and transliteration so that everyone can participate in the ritual. We light the menorah this seventh night of Hanukkah. I welcome the group, expressing gratitude for their presence and for the community partners who helped to make the night possible. At the Brew Ha Ha, young adults can socialize and come together to celebrate and mark Jewish time. I invite them to explore Jewish tradition and culture through creative and meaningful ways, to become a community that celebrates diversity and is open to others interested in exploring the same. I invite them further to the playground[1] of identity formation and Jewish exploration, to come together around the Jewish holiday

---

1   I'm grateful to my teacher, Rabbi Tali Zelkowicz, who introduced me to the idea of creating playgrounds, not museums, for people to create community in.

cycles and shared values relevant to this chapter of life in 21ˢᵗ Century American society.

The Brew Ha Ha is a success for many reasons. We expected fifty people and two hundred show up. People are so happy and engaged that the evening goes long. The opportunity to see the professional and lay leadership of the JCC, my employer, enter a space packed with young adults "missing from our Jewish communities" is both personally and professionally rewarding. Most importantly, I test my hypothesis: one need not pick between socially engaging events and meaningful Jewish content. People can engage with one another and the themes and ideas relevant to the holiday simultaneously, resulting in an experience that might transcend just another night out on the town.

The platform to the beer kettle may not be the typical bimah. But I look out onto this crowd of unaffiliated, missing, opted out young adult Jews and see people open-eyed and in no rush to leave. As the Director of Charm City Tribe and Baltimore's "Rogue Rabbi," I have the opportunity to see a generation of people marking Jewish time, eating latkes from a local food truck, and sipping on etrog-infused beer that seeped eight days and eight nights, saved from Sukkot. Community partners are engaging participants in activities that bring the themes of Hanukkah to the surface. Young people are introduced to organizations doing great work that relate to these timely themes year round.

I told my parents I might want to become a rabbi at thirteen, but I also spent extensive energy trying to talk myself out of it. The terrorist attack on September 11, 2001 came as I began my final year of undergraduate studies. I feared there would be no place for a rabbi seeking to serve those in the moderate middle. Would my generation seek extremism and fundamentalism and avoid religious tradition that marked time, engaged with the holiday cycle, and built community based on moderate interpretations of Jewish themes and values? My generation, in fact, would create "the Nones"—a silent majority of people opting out of civically engaged communities believing they will not be able to find an ideological home.[2] My own rabbi suggested how important it would be for people like me to

---

2   Robert D. Putnam and David E. Cambell, *American Grace*, (Simon & Schuster: New York, 2010).

occupy space in the future of Jewish leadership. She suggested that for some of us who loved Judaism and the Jewish people, who offered alternative styles and interpretations to the mainstream norm, taking on a leadership role would be the only way in which the masses of my generation would have the opportunity to see their connection to Judaism as valid and acceptable. She suggested that the rabbinate would likely provide a good entry point to do that work.

Always a bit of a boundary pusher, I approached my mid-20s and decided that going to rabbinical school was actually more radical than going on a Phish tour. However, my experiences on that Phish tour and exploring alternative communities complemented my love for Torah. Not to mention, there are minyans upon minyans of Jews at those shows! Could they be integrated? I entered into the rabbinate because of a deep love and passion for Jewish learning, ritual and community coupled with a frustration with stalely packaged Judaism. I didn't understand why youth group and summer camp experiences felt like a lively laboratory while Hebrew school programs geared towards the bar mitzvah often felt like another period of school with a standard often comfortably set around regurgitation. I knew more people who grew up being told that their bar mitzvah was the end of Hebrew school rather than the beginning of a lifelong journey to figure out what it means to be a Jew on a personal, communal and societal level. I was interested in why twenty Jewish college students who would never step foot into Hillel would regularly come together for Shabbat dinner in my college apartment, just doors down from Hillel. Together we would make *Kiddush*, share a meal together and then play music and sing songs long into the evening. More intriguing was the high percentage of graduates of Jewish summer camp and youth groups who the organized community identified as lost or unaffiliated but who were active participants in their own micro-communities. They shared common interests such as sports teams and music that become the foundation of people's relationships in their young adulthood years. We didn't only get together to do Jewish, but often it was notable how many Jews were a part of our community. Over a decade later, this same community of folks has come together to mark time in the life cycle. We have danced at one another's weddings, welcomed babies into the Jewish people and have grieved together, too. I imagine and pray that we will continue to do so for many decades still to come.

During my time at the Hebrew Union College (HUC), I often struggled with the curricular balance of traditional Jewish textual learning and the myriad of classes meant to prepare future rabbis to succeed in the vocation of rabbi in 21st Century America. I would return from summers spent farming in the morning and *beit midrash* learning on Jewish agricultural law in the afternoons and beg for more time to dive into the copious amount of literature of our people and tradition. Despite the fact that our program director was a Talmud teacher herself, she reiterated how developing skills related to the practitioner side of the rabbinate would strengthen us as rabbis in the field and ultimately allow us to dive deeper into our own Jewish learning. My time in the seminary was to develop a toolbox and skills, not to learn every piece of Torah and tradition available in the Jewish canon. A primary goal during the six years spent at HUC was to learn how to use the tools and materials of Jewish tradition to create and lead, to help strengthen the foundation upon which others might create their own toolboxes to use as they construct a meaningful Jewish identity.

The nature of a rabbinic program rooted in both the American educational system and the values of traditional Jewish learning allowed for a dynamic experience as a rabbinic student. When I wondered why we could not specialize more in our own areas of interest, I was told to trust the process. A control freak by nature, it was difficult for me to trust my teachers. However, that resistance was quickly met with a feeling of safety and security created by the incredible wisdom and leadership of the teachers and mentors making curricular decisions. I completed Masters degrees in both Hebrew Letters and Jewish Education, and the opportunity to self-select topics in the tradition that I wanted to explore further became readily available.

My time at HUC was a time of experimentation of practices, ideas and hypotheses. I brought all of my criticisms and questions into a seminary that sees critical analysis as important and values asking good questions and debating possible answers. While not a legally bound movement, my teachers taught me how to develop consistent criteria and operating values that would give form to my Jewish journey and not simply create an experience of solely picking and choosing.

I struggled in areas of Hebrew language and technical writing, but also had tremendous support to grow through the support and the alternative experiences offered. The opportunity for cohort learning accompanied with the various one-to-one student/teacher attention served as a model for how to engage groups of people in Jewish content and the intimate parts of one's Jewish journey. The most critical moments of my own learning were often the moments when I recognized my teachers modeling methods and approaches that I would ultimately practice on those pursuing Jewish knowledge and seeking a spiritual home. I often felt enclosed in an ivory tower learning theory and practical application. Yet I quickly realized how that experience shaped my understanding of what my role would be as a teacher of Jewish tradition and facilitator of Jewish community in my rabbinical work in Baltimore. I often felt like I was faking it as an academic in order that one day I could hit the streets and apply my learning outside the realm of footnoted papers. We all built a foundation to enter the world as rabbis with Jewish knowledge, tools, and skills to apply those tools to succeed as a professional. It amazes me the diverse work that my colleagues are doing today around the country.

With the help of my loving teacher, Steven Windmueller, I developed hypotheses about my generation built on the scholarship of those asking similar questions—how we function in community, what is similar to previous generations and also what is unique given the circumstances of this time and place in history vis-a-vis technology, mobility, and privilege. My time at HUC did not necessarily allow me to test these hypotheses, but rather provided time and distance to nuance and mature them so that I could prepare to test them upon entering into the field. HUC helped me think outside the box with an authentic Jewish foundation. The ongoing mentorship and support was perhaps even more valuable than the support I received during my time as a student.

My seminary understood the role that individual preference and choice plays in Jewish decision-making. That helped me understand how to meet people where they are at and withhold assumptions about where they ought to be. Many non-Orthodox Jews in their 20s and 30s feel unclear about how to step into Jewish life as an adult. For those more inclined to partner, buy a house and have children, the likelihood that they will join a synagogue when it comes time to educate their children is still a probable scenario. However, with an increasing number of folks not walking that traditional path or coming to it later, how will we engage this generation of Jewish adults?

I was blessed to find a job in a community that I already had some rooting in, thus allowing me to dive right in relationally. Perhaps one of the most rewarding aspects of my work as a community rabbi is the focus on the adult. I am interested in learning to pass along to the next generation, but I am more interested in learning for the sake of lifelong spiritual and communal growth. We become better teachers when we are first the students, and adults require something more compelling than memorizing a Torah portion and a morning prayer to prepare for a bar mitzvah. My generation is one that constantly asks, "What's in it for me?" Shouldn't we be able to answer that question as it relates to Jewish tradition beyond simply that we have to pass it along to the next? There must be value and meaning for ourselves if we are to connect deeply enough to desire to pass it on. We must know something about who we are if we are to teach others to know the same.

I knew that becoming a rabbi would require me to be a good translator. Sitting in *kitah alef* in Jerusalem, I worried that I might not be able to succeed at translating in the ways my classmates who were in more advanced Hebrew classes would. I could not figure out my grammar tables, and I would need to acquire some level of proficiency in Aramaic along the course of my studies. I supplemented my lessons with time spent with Israeli friends who refused to speak English me. They offered me priceless support so that I would actually become quite strong in street Hebrew even if I will likely always struggle with the written language. I offered them their first insight into a world where there is serious engagement with Judaism not grounded in law alone and in which women can become rabbis and also enjoy a good beer. Often the ability to translate meaning is not in making sense of the biblical Hebrew or Aramaic alone, but in translating the particularities that Judaism offers when people are already quite fluent and connected to a similar idea in their universal form. My goal as a teacher and translator is often less about translating the ancient text into modern. More so, I make connections to Torah where people might otherwise think the universal meaning is good enough. I like to argue that the particularities that give way to stories, ritual and practices that have nurtured many generations of our ancestors may actually enhance our experiences as both human beings and as Jews still today.

The Baltimore Jewish community created a position to hire a rabbi to find Jews who have left the fabric of Jewish life and create opportunities for meaningful re-entry into Jewish community. It was born out of the findings from a 2010 community study which identified that 55% of non-Orthodox Jews between the ages of eighteen and thirty-four living in Baltimore felt positive feelings of connection to being Jewish while only 11% of that same demographic believed that belonging to a Jewish organization was important. While in the beginning I identified that 44% differential as the sweet spot in which I was hired to work, I now think about it as a silent majority waiting to find an entry. Our synagogues and Jewish organizations are relevant; however, I worry that the perception that they are irrelevant is one reason why folks don't show up.

While a Reform Jew in rabbinic ordination and ideology, I am a pluralist who believes that diversity and different approaches to tradition is good for the Jewish people. I speak openly about looking to Chabad as a model for meaningful engagement and often joke that part of my success with the demographic I serve is simply because I don't have a beard and do have a colorful wardrobe. So we deck our mobile sukkah with Baltimore Ravens swag and empty beer cans from the local brewery, include a disco ball. We take the sukkah to the streets so people can fulfill the mitzvah of shaking the *lulav* and *etrog* and sitting in the sukkah. I love to take the best of what the Jewish people have and find ways to lift them up to invite the moderate, progressive, highly secularized Jew to feel connection to Jewish time and ideas.

I start from a place of assumed shared interest. For example, I am a music lover. Music has often fueled my spiritual identity and informed my Jewish journey. I also know that it is easy to spark a conversation with other people who appreciate music. Thus, when I make the case for why celebrate Shabbat, I start in a place that may seem somehow distant from the end point. I out myself as a diehard music fan and acknowledge that any lover of music understands that songs have different rhythms and sounds as a result of different tempos and methods of keeping time. Madonna's "Material Girl" is a very different sounding song than the Grateful Dead's "They Love Each Other." Only then do I make the suggestion that the rhythm of the week could also feel different when we move from a 5:2 rhythm and that of a 6:1. Most of us operate according to the weekly song that five days you work and two days are the weekend, but the intended rhythm of our Jewish song is one in which time actually beats to a different tempo. The potential gain of that difference is a fruitful discussion to hopefully follow, but on a simple level, just the understanding that something can feel different when the framework is adjusted is a great starting place to spark someone's interest. Just as there is a different song that comes out when the tempo is different, so too the possibility of a different experience when we orient ourselves to the rhythm of our tradition in contrast to that of the American work week.

When we internalize music that we love we can bring songs with us and sing them wherever we go. Within the big tent of music, there is something for everyone be it jazz, funk, hip hop or opera. When we find something we like, and we dive deeper into it, we stand to internalize those songs—for them to become a part of us and for the words and the vibrations of rhythm to impact our spiritual pursuits. People come to better understand the Psalms when presented with the idea that they are similar to song lyrics, often accompanied by instrumentation and written to be sung. People who say they don't pray may very likely be able to name a song that they listen to at least three times a day—often because of the message the words send and how it leads them to think about the bigger themes they touch upon. In that respect, I sometimes wonder if we are a generation that doesn't pray or has just learned to tap into that prayerful place using the liturgy of our secular society rather than the words of our tradition. In starting with music, something accessible and seemingly universal, I am able to make a case for the particularities that might apply to Jewish practice and learning. I stood on that beer bimah that evening and two images came to mind: the first of Jacob after he wrestles with the angel. He discovers something he hadn't previously been able to see that will ultimately change his course. The other image was that crowded space where folks convene before going into a concert. The buzz shifts from anticipation to arrival. I softly sang, "Once in a while you get shown the light in the strangest of places if you look at it right," and then offered a *Shehecheyanu*.[3] It was a moment when the song of our tradition and the Torah I understand today were in perfect accord, strengthening my hunch that Torah might be timeless after all.

It is at this intersection that I find myself as both student and teacher of how to be a committed and engaged, non-halachically observant Jew in the 21st Century. It is incumbent upon our generation to be able to learn the song of our tradition and to find ways to create a link strong enough to take the Judaism and communities we inherit from our parents to the generation that will follow us. I was brought up in and trained to become a rabbi in a movement that celebrates the changing nature of society and embraces the gifts of modernity and the world at large as fertile ground in which Torah and Judaism remain relevant. And yet, I know that my time at seminary was only a launching point to confront the role that I am to play as someone who opted in amongst a generation that many fear will ultimately opt out. Every day I offer thanks to the Holy One that I am on a journey that engages both the things I love and the things I struggle with about what it means to be a Jew. I am grateful to have had the mentorship of rabbis and teachers who challenged and guided me during my time there to teach me the timeless questions of our tradition and to contextualize them in the landscape of what it means to be a rabbi at this particular moment in history. The teachers gave me a toolbox that I feel honored to carry along with me to use daily in pursuit of the contribution I hope to make to the Jewish people and among my generation.

Looking forward to yet another mobile sukkah and Hanukkah Brew Ha Ha, I am still reeling from a successful community seder held at a

---

3   Lyrics from "Scarlet Begonias" by the Grateful Dead.

local art gallery on the second night of Pesach. The Holy Hallel Band presented the traditional music that comes after the meal and we read from a Haggadah placemat that was concise, colorful and structurally *yotzei*. I am grateful to the teachers who reminded me that Judaism flourishes in places analogous to playgrounds more so than museums. They give me the courage to test the creative limits of how to do Jewish in a meaningful way, inviting others to do the same. The training in the seminary, the knowledge I acquired and the incredible support from the Baltimore Jewish community to pursue this unchartered territory for Jewish engagement are, without question, the platform upon which I feel much of our success has happened to date and hopefully will continue for many more years to come.

Rabbi Jessy Gross lives in Baltimore and works as a community rabbi and the Director of Charm City Tribe—a community project of the JCC that creates creative and meaningful ways for young adults looking to tap into Jewish tradition and culture. She received a B.A. from the University of Maryland, College Park and Masters in both Hebrew Letters and Jewish Education, as well as rabbinic ordination from the Hebrew Union College - Jewish Institute of Religion in Los Angeles, CA.

The Roar of the Cat Rabbi:
The Vital Role of Introverts in the
Congregational Rabbinate

By Rabbi Edward C. Bernstein

I still cringe when I think about that day. I finished a lesson on the weekly Torah portion with the third grade of a local Jewish day school. I then rushed through the hallways to get to my next appointment. While heading for my car, I saw two women from my congregation engaged in deep discussion near the main entrance. Without breaking my stride, I tried to make eye contact with them to acknowledge their presence verbally or non-verbally. I knew that was a good rabbinic thing to do. Neither of them looked my way, so I kept going.

I might not have given that day another thought except a few weeks later I faced an annual review. There were a number of positive comments concerning central areas of rabbinic practice: my sermons were thoughtful and addressed timely topics; my teaching was engaging and learned; my pastoral care during times of crisis was warm and caring; my eulogies consistently captured the essence of the deceased. I sat tall in my chair happy that I was doing the things a good rabbi was supposed to do. Then, the other shoe dropped. My reviewers noted that I often appeared quiet, even aloof, not interested in engaging with congregants on a personal level. When I asked for an example, a member of the review panel cited the two women I saw that day at the Jewish day school. The women were offended that I did not stop to say hello to them. They felt that I was ignoring them.

"Seriously?" I thought to myself. I responded, "I did not want to be rude to those women. What if I had stopped their conversation? They would have been offended had I interrupted." My lay leaders weren't convinced. They made clear that the congregation wanted a social butterfly to burst out of my tight cocoon. At least that is how I heard the feedback.

I am an introvert. There is no doubt about it. I have taken the Meyers Briggs Type Indicator assessment on multiple occasions. Without fail, I score squarely as an "I" for "Introverted," as opposed to "E" for "Extroverted." There is no value judgment associated with "I" or "E" or other MBTI personality indicators. The test measures personality preferences with the understanding that while these traits are hard-wired into each individual, awareness of one's preferences maximizes productivity in interacting with the outside world.

I understand intellectually the value of MBTI as an assessment tool; however, for much of my career, longer than I care to admit, I have been self-conscious of my introversion. I have taken to blaming myself for not being more outgoing. American society's premium on extroversion as an ideal personality preference stokes my anxiety. "If only I were a backslapping schmoozer, I'd get the respect I deserve in the rabbinate," I have occasionally muttered to myself.

I have always been drawn to the multi-faceted vocation of the pulpit. I find fulfillment in synagogue life through serving as a Jewish guide for people of all ages. Still, I have had my share of challenges, often related to my introverted inclination and how it is perceived by others. When I receive feedback about my introversion, such as in my annual review, I take it hard, because I know it's important. As Ron Wolfson writes, "It's all about relationships."[1] That is, if Jewish institutions such as synagogues are to remain vibrant in this century, their constituents need to feel like they matter and that others in the community, especially the rabbi, care about them. If my introversion hinders me in this regard, it's a problem.

Nevertheless, the introverted rabbi need not fear. Gregarious, extroverted rabbis do not have a monopoly on "relational Judaism"

1   Wolfson, Dr. Ron. *Relational Judaism* (Woodstock, VT: Jewish Lights, 2013) 3.

or the pulpit rabbinate. The synagogue membership model is under assault. The Jewish community needs to reach people with different personality profiles and cultivate leaders of different types who can connect with them. Research shows that between one third and one half of people in our society are introverts.[2] In this moment of truth for the Jewish world, it's all hands on deck. Our multi-faceted community will benefit most from the leadership of both introverts and extroverts. Introverted rabbis bring significant qualities to bear and can draw upon various tools in order to maximize success. We must ensure that such leaders are not left out in the cold.

Conventional Wisdom and Its Limits

Conventional wisdom would divide rabbis into two categories, extroverted and introverted, and assign specific professional positions based on these traits. Extroverts would serve the pulpit and campus Hillels, while introverts would enter chaplaincy and academia. Such conventional wisdom was expressed most explicitly in Rabbi Dan Cohn-Sherbok's 1995 essay, "Dog Rabbis and Cat Rabbis."[3]

Cohn-Sherbok struggled in several pulpit positions early in his career then shifted to academia where he has flourished for several decades. In assessing his pulpit woes, he writes: "I tried and tried and tried—yet over and over again I failed to satisfy the demands of my congregation. I fell into every trap. I just couldn't be the friendly, enthusiastic, sympathetic, and attentive pastor that my congregation wanted. But I am not a quitter."[4]

He describes his journey to congregations on multiple continents. "I shriveled up inside when I had to act as master of ceremonies. I dreaded bar mitzvahs. I loathed weddings. I detested kissing each lady 'good Shabbos.'"[5]

Cohn-Sherbok contrasts his style with that of a friend serving a congregation:

---

2   Cain, Susan. *Quiet: The Power of Introverts in a World That Can't Stop Talking* (New York: Crown, 2012) 3.

3   Rabbi Dan Cohn-Sherbok, "Dog Rabbis and Cat Rabbis," *CCAR Journal*, 42:1 (Winter-Spring, 1995) 21-23.

4   *Ibid.*, 21.

5   *Ibid.*

> Unlike me, [Rabbi] Brian [Fox] loves to be with his congregants: he greets them as long-lost friends, not because it is politic to do so but because he genuinely likes them. He kisses all the ladies—from the oldest to the youngest—with gusto. He wishes everyone 'good Shabbos' with relish. He is perfectly at ease with the members of the Temple and they in turn love and value him.[6]

Cohn-Sherbok never uses the terms "introvert" and "extrovert," though he clearly implies them. Rather, he invokes the metaphor of dogs and cats, dogs as extroverts, cats as introverts. Applying this metaphor to the rabbinate, he asserts:

> The congregational rabbinate is designed for dog rabbis. A good rabbi must behave like a dog, loving everyone, greeting each person with enthusiasm, rounding everyone up and metaphorically wagging his tail. Right or wrong, this is ultimately what congregants want: a rabbi must be friendly and public-spirited, he cannot be a solitary recluse.[7]

I empathize with Cohn-Sherbok's agony in the pulpit. I endure my own struggles with the public persona that the congregational rabbinate demands. Yet Cohn-Sherbok makes assumptions and generalizations that are neither realistic nor helpful in providing guidance to current and aspiring rabbis in the 21st Century.

Cat rabbis are just as capable as dog rabbis in serving congregations. Also, cat rabbis do not have safe havens in the rabbinate away from the pressures of the pulpit. In a rapidly changing world, every field of the rabbinate requires a wide toolkit of skills. Academia, for example, requires professors to interact with students, navigate internal faculty politics, pitch their scholarship to publishers, supervise departments and speak to donors. This is hardly a hermit's existence. As author Daniel Pink writes, "Like it or not, we're all in sales now."[8] No industry can afford cat-like people who curl up, hide and avoid all interaction. Cohn-Sherbok is correct that it would be inadvisable for a pulpit rabbi to be a "solitary recluse." No one denies that the highly

6   *Ibid.*, 21-22.
7   *Ibid.*, 22.
8   Daniel. Pink, *To Sell Is Human* (New York: Riverhead, 2012) 2.

public nature of the rabbinate would not be a good fit for someone at such an extreme end of the spectrum.

Cohn-Sherbok's artificial dichotomy of dog rabbis and cat rabbis became more engrained in public discourse as a result of Rabbi Bradley Shavit Artson's 1998 article "My Life As a Dog Rabbi."[9] He accepts Cohn-Sherbok's basic premise and describes himself as a dog rabbi who enjoys great success and fulfillment from the pulpit:[10]

> To be a good rabbi, you must love and identify with your congregants. No gift of eloquence, administrative skills or bedside manner can compensate people when they sense a rabbi's disdain, distance, disinterest. When you love your congregants unconditionally you feel their pain. When you go to someone's home who suffered a loss, and you have to be there for them and to help make a Shiva minyan, you cry when you see them crying. When you stand by their hospital bed, it can be wrenching. When you hear their family troubles, your heart can break.[11]

I agree with Artson completely. The rabbi must be both authentic and present for the congregation. However, both extroverted and introverted rabbis must relate to congregants in the way that Artson describes. Authentic relationships are not the exclusive domain of extroverted dog rabbis. These qualities are equally achievable by extroverts and introverts. They may even come more naturally to many introverts.

In the two decades since Cohn-Sherbok's article appeared, psychological and social science literature has exploded with groundbreaking research on personality traits. Susan Cain's best seller *Quiet: The Power of Introverts in a World That Can't Stop Talking* synthesizes the scientific literature and argues for a fresh look at the significant role that introverts played in history and can continue to play with greater awareness and sensitivity throughout society. The

---

9   Rabbi Bradley. Shavit Artson, "My Life As a Dog Rabbi," *Jewish Spectator*, Spring, 1998, p 13.

10   Rabbi Artson published this article while serving as spiritual leader of Congregation Eilat in Mission Viejo, CA. Since 1999, he has served as Dean of the Ziegler School of Rabbinic Studies at American Jewish University in Los Angeles.

11   *Ibid.*, 13.

Jewish community will benefit from looking anew at the strengths of introverted rabbis.

Shy and Introverted Are Not the Same

In the 1990's Cohn-Sherbok and Artson seem to have conflated introversion and shyness when they described the angst of cat rabbis. In light of Cain's research, we must distinguish between the two terms; they are very different. As Cain explains, introverts are neither hermits nor misanthropes, and are not necessarily shy. She writes, "Shyness is the fear of social disapproval or humiliation, while introversion is a preference for environments that are not overstimulating. Shyness is inherently painful; introversion is not."[12]

People often confuse introversion and shyness because they sometimes overlap. Some psychologists map the two tendencies on vertical and horizontal axes, with the introvert-extrovert spectrum on the horizontal axis, and the anxious-stable spectrum on the vertical. With this model, you end up with four quadrants of personality types: calm extroverts, anxious extroverts, calm introverts, and anxious introverts.[13]

Shyness, like any form of anxiety, is an acquired trait that one develops as a result of experience. Anxiety can be overcome by systematic exposure to the source of anxiety in modest doses. For instance, fear of public speaking can be overcome by finding small, friendly venues in which to practice public speaking, like a Toastmasters club. Regular exposure to the anxiety-causing stimulus reduces the fear of personal danger associated with that stimulus.[14]

The introversion-extroversion spectrum is different. These traits are hard-wired at birth. Researchers have found that one's place on this spectrum is a function of reaction to stimulation

One can be a shy extrovert who is energized by heavy metal rock concerts but cowers from stage fright when called upon to perform. On the flip side, non-shy introverts may keep to themselves, but

---

12 Cain, 12.
13 Ibid.
14 Ibid., 126-129.

are unfazed by the opinions of others.[15] An introverted rabbi can work the room and schmooze as well as anyone without any shyness; however, that rabbi may tire more quickly than the extrovert.

I straddle the introvert-calm and introvert-anxious quadrants. On one hand, there have been times when I've taken principled stands, spoken out on various subjects and carried out many initiatives of which I am proud. On the other hand, I can think of times when I listened intently to what others said during meetings and took copious notes but refrained from offering comments of my own out of fear that what I had to say would not be considered important or that I would not be able to articulate my case adequately. Awareness that this anxiety is not innate is a huge step forward in managing it. Having uncoupled shyness and introversion as separate phenomena, the question remains how an introverted rabbi can manage the highly stimulating environment of the pulpit and enjoy a successful and fulfilling rabbinate.

On a Mission from God

I am able to function as an introverted pulpit rabbi and do so with great fulfillment because of my deep sense of mission in serving the Jewish people. I am inspired by many examples of introverts—even shy introverts—who demonstrate leadership and make vital contributions to humanity because they tap into their deepest values that propel them into action. Twentieth Century examples of this include Gandhi,[16] Rosa Parks[17] and Eleanor Roosevelt.[18]

Within Jewish tradition, starting with the Torah, introverted characteristics are singled out for praise. Jacob was a studious tent dweller, while his swashbuckling twin brother Esau was an active hunter.[19] Jacob pays a heavy price throughout his life for his acts of deception, and the narrative emphasizes "what goes around comes around." Nevertheless, Jacob is the hero of the story. He experiences profound personal growth. His new name *Yisrael* (wrestling with

---

15   *Ibid.,* 12.
16   *Ibid.,* 197-200.
17   *Ibid.,* 1-3, 58-60.
18   *Ibid.,* 130-133.
19   Genesis 25: 27.

God)[20] reflects that he has struggled with his youthful missteps. Jacob's introversion, ultimately, is the wellspring of his growth and renewal.

The quintessential introvert in the Torah is Moses. He protested to God that he was "heavy of speech and heavy of tongue"[21] and not able to carry out God's charge that he appear before Pharaoh and demand that he lead the Israelites out of Egypt. Moses stuttered and expressed fear to God at the burning bush. God does not let him off the hook, and allows Aaron, Moses's brother, to be the spokesman. Moses calls the shots for Aaron, the face of the operation. Before too long, though, Moses grows into his public role. Propelled by righteous indignation over the plight of the Israelites, Moses finds his voice. Moses begins his career as an inarticulate stutterer, yet by the end of the Pentateuch, the entire book of Deuteronomy is, in essence, one long speech! While Moses grows as a leader, his fundamental character never changes. Moses is described later in the Torah as the most humble of men on the face of the earth.[22]

Within Talmudic literature, much praise is bestowed on humility and quiet. *Pirkei Avot*, a treasury of rabbinic wisdom, quotes Rabban Simeon son of Gamliel, "Throughout my life, I was raised among the scholars, and I found that there is nothing more becoming of a person than silence; study is not the essence, but action, and excessive speech leads to sin."[23] Rabban Simeon's father, Rabban Gamliel, was a larger than life figure and domineering personality.[24] I imagine his studious son struggling to assert his place in the shadow of his father, offering a generational corrective in leadership style.

One more image of introversion in rabbinic literature is attributed to none other than God in a discussion of the festival Sh'mini Atzeret. After a week of festivity during Sukkot, the rabbis understood the Torah's word *atzeret* to convey stopping or delaying. "'I have stopped (*atzarti*) you, from leaving,' [says God]." The Talmud then contrasts the sacrifices between Sukkot and Sh'mini Atzeret. The seventy bullocks sacrificed in Temple times during the seven

---

20 Genesis 32:29.
21 Exodus 4:10.
22 Numbers 12: 3; see also Cain, 60-61.
23 *Pirkei Avot*, 1:17.
24 Mishnah *Rosh HaShanah* 2: 8-9 and Babylonian Talmud, *B'rachot*, 27b-28a.

days of Sukkot are in honor of the seventy nations of the world. On Sh'mini Atzeret, just one bullock is sacrificed, symbolizing the relationship of God and Israel.[25] It is as if throughout Sukkot, God is working the room of a big party where all the nations of the world are guests. At the end, though, God craves a quiet, intimate conversation with Israel. God has an introverted side, and Shemini Atzeret is its celebration.

The American ideal of extroversion that took hold in the early 1900s[26] stands in contrast to Judaism's more introverted ideals. When attempting to translate Jewish ideals into an American idiom an American rabbi, irrespective of individual personality preferences, will face an almost irreconcilable tension. For a rabbi with a greater tendency towards introversion, however, the tension is more profound.

Nevertheless, the cat rabbi need not fear. Introverted leaders such as Jacob and Moses in the Torah and Gandhi, Rosa Parks and Eleanor Roosevelt in the 20th Century all draw from a common reservoir: mission. When a mission rooted in one's deepest values is at stake, the introverted rabbi not only faces the challenges, he or she often excels.

Rabbi Jack Bloom defines the rabbi's mission as a "Symbolic Exemplar" who stands for something other than one's self, specifically the totality of Jewish tradition.[27] According to Bloom, "It is this symbolic exemplarhood that enables the rabbi to be taken seriously in the first place and the myth that surrounds this symbolic exemplarhood provides much of the rabbinic power to touch individual lives and direct the future of the Jewish community."[28]

I was inspired by positive Jewish experiences as a teenager to dedicate my life to serving the Jewish people. I understood intuitively in high school and college that I longed for the symbolic exemplarhood of the rabbinic mantle rather than another form of communal service. Now that I have served in the field for fifteen

---

25 Babylonian Talmud, *Sukkah*, 55b.
26 See Cain, 19-33 for a history of the shift in American consciousness from an ideal of character to an ideal of personality.
27 Rabbi Jack. Bloom, *The Rabbi As Symbolic Exemplar: By the Power Vested in Me* (Binghamton, NY: Hayworth Press, 2002) 136.
28 *Ibid.*

years, I believe that symbolic exemplarhood provides me with the enormous satisfaction I derive from my service. I wake up every morning committed to serve the Jewish people.

Bloom notes that symbolic exemplarhood is a double-edged sword. Just as Moses frequently expresses frustration with the burdens of shepherding a stiff-necked people through the wilderness, the rabbi as symbolic exemplar also confronts professional hazards. The pulpit rabbi encounters isolation and alienation that are endemic to the field. Criticism comes from all sides. The rabbi's family, not to mention the rabbi, lives behind a glass wall.[29] These are serious challenges for anyone entering the field. Introverts and extroverts alike are equally vulnerable to burnout. Therefore, in order for the challenges of the rabbinate to seem worth it, the benefits must outweigh the costs. The rabbi as symbolic exemplar is on a mission from God.

A sense of personal mission is a powerful force and propels the most unlikely players to make significant and lasting contributions for the causes about which they are passionate. Dr. Adam Grant refutes conventional wisdom in his thorough analysis of givers and takers, particularly in the work place.[30] Takers care more about personal benefit from their jobs, while givers care more deeply about serving other people. Through exhaustive research, Grant shows that givers often achieve more measurable success than takers. In other words, he disproves the infamous adage attributed to Leo Durocher, "Nice guys finish last."

An important factor in predicting a giver's success in relation to a taker is the giver's sense of mission. Grant performed an experiment with students working in a university call center whose job was to cold call alumni to solicit donations to the school. Like most telemarketing jobs, university solicitations are often thankless; prospective donors repeatedly hang up on callers. Initially, takers outperformed givers, closing gifts by a three to one margin. The result surprised Grant; he figured since the givers knew that the funds they raised were going to student scholarships they would be more highly motivated. Grant's hypothesis was not wrong, though. He made one change, and

---

29 *Ibid.*
30 Adam Grant, *Give and Take: A Revolutionary Approach to Success,* (New York: Viking, 2013) 162-165.

suddenly the givers outperformed the takers. The key was reading to the callers letters from students who wrote about the significant impact that the scholarships had in enabling them to attend college. When the callers were introduced to a student beneficiary in person, revenue soared even more. All callers improved, but the givers improved most dramatically. For givers, monetary compensation for their time was insufficient. Positive feedback that they made a difference for other people is their greatest reward.[31]

Society imposes biases and stereotypes on the giver-taker spectrum and the introvert-extrovert spectrum. Takers and extroverts are both generally perceived as stronger and more likely to succeed, while givers and introverts are generally perceived as weaker and less likely to succeed. Thankfully, research shows that such assumptions are false. The common thread between these two pairings is that a strong sense of mission propels the stereotypical weaker party onto equal and often stronger footing with the stereotypical stronger party.

When I remind myself of the larger mission to which I am committed, I am more likely to step out of my introverted comfort zone. In order to achieve the goals and objectives of the rabbinate, I willingly subject myself to higher levels of stimulation than I might otherwise. In the three pulpits in which I have served, my mission-driven perspective has borne fruit in various ways including: spearheading a family retreat weekend, organizing and leading congregants on a trip to Israel and soliciting gifts and bequests to support congregational programs. All of these are vital to sustaining a vibrant congregational atmosphere.

Based on my experience and the burgeoning literature on introversion, deep commitment to mission is a greater predictor of success in the rabbinate than personality traits. Mission is a significant motivating force, but is only part of the story.

Focus

An introverted rabbi often draws upon another key leadership quality—focus. In the first decade of the 21st Century, there was a competition among Wall Street investment banks for a prestigious

---

31   *Ibid.,* 164-165.

piece of business. Members of the winning team celebrated and bedecked themselves in matching baseball caps and T-shirts emblazoned with the letters FUD for Fear, Uncertainty, and Doubt. The letters FUD had been crossed out with a red X. The statement was clear: to win business was to vanquish FUD.[32] For Susan Cain, these Wall Street bankers were the ultimate extroverts. The behavior advocated by their regalia was a major factor in the global financial meltdown of 2008. According to Cain, the financial services industry is dominated by extroverts who took inappropriate risks that brought about the Great Recession. Evidence shows that introverts on Wall Street offered warnings, but they were ignored. Jack Welch, former chairman of General Electric, has a slightly different perspective. He told Cain that "the extroverts would argue that they never heard from the introverts."[33]

There is no difference between introverts and extroverts in terms of intelligence: both score equally well on IQ exams. Differences, however, are found in an area of brain research called reward sensitivity. Dopamine is the neurotransmitter—more commonly known as the reward chemical —released in response to anticipated pleasures. "The more responsive your brain is to dopamine, or the higher the level of dopamine you have available to release, some scientists believe, the more likely you are to go after rewards like sex, chocolate, money, and status."[34] Research finds that extroverts' dopamine pathways appear to be more active than those of introverts.[35]

Extroverts are not only more likely to take risks than introverts, they are more likely to speed up and take more risks after initial failure. Extroverts, therefore, are said to have a high degree of reward sensitivity. Introverts, in contrast, tend to downplay reward and scan for problems. In sum, introverts are geared to inspect; extroverts are geared to respond.[36]

Cain's analysis of the Great Recession reminds me of a challenging incident in which I confronted reward sensitivity. I was

32   Cain, 164.
33   Ibid., 173.
34   Ibid., 160.
35   Ibid.
36   Ibid., 166.

working with a synagogue search committee to fill a professional staff position. One candidate made a particularly strong impression. Before offering the job, we checked references. I contacted rabbis with whom the candidate had worked in the past. Some raised serious concerns about the candidate's qualifications and advised not to make this hire.

I informed the committee what I learned. They heard my concerns, but they liked the candidate and were eager to conclude the lengthy search process. We made the hire. Within weeks, it was clear that the new staff member was not a good fit. After about six months, the employee was relieved of all duties, and the synagogue bought out the contract. Needless to say, it was a highly embarrassing situation for all involved and for the congregation.

In retrospect, it seems that the allure of an attractive new face stoked the reward sensitivity of influential extroverts on the committee. I focused on important concerns when I reported the candidate's unsatisfactory references, yet I was not heard. It weighs heavily on me that we could have spared the candidate and the synagogue much heartache by not making the hire in the first place had I asserted more strongly my reservations.

Focus, along with mission, is an important leadership quality that introverts who are geared to inspect often bring to the table. It is vital for the multi-faceted role of congregational service. A focused rabbi is a "canary in a coal mine" who guides others from danger. At the same time, such focus is of little use if the rabbi is not heard. The rabbi must trust his or her gut in order to be heard and maximize influence. Therefore, an introverted rabbi must draw upon a set of tools in order to reap the benefits of mission and focus.

Toolkit

In this age of social media clutter, with people and organizations vying for our attention, it's easy to assume the best way to be heard is to outshout everyone else. I take a different view. Now more than ever, our society and the Jewish community will benefit from more consciousness of the gifts that introverts possess. Introverts need to be heard. Furthermore, as Daniel Pink notes, "We're all in sales now." The pulpit is the retail end of the business of selling Judaism to our flock. Introverted rabbis can be heard by adopting various tools to articulate our values-driven perspective without burning out from attempts to copy extroverts.

In finding our voices, it is helpful for introverts to realize that we all fall on a spectrum. The world isn't as neatly divided into two groups of extroverts and introverts as one might think. Most people fall somewhere in between. Daniel Pink and Adam Grant have provided us with the convenient term ambivert, a person with both introvert and extrovert characteristics.[37] In a study of software sales representatives, extroverts slightly outperformed introverts, but they were both beaten soundly by ambiverts. As Pink writes, "[Ambiverts] know when to push and when to hold back, when to speak up and when to shut up."[38]

We need more calm introverted pulpit rabbis with tools who can stretch toward ambiversion. An effective pulpit rabbi needs to navigate the delicate balance between inspecting and responding. An overly extroverted rabbi might talk too much and listen too little. Such traits could drive people away. In contrast, an overly introverted rabbi (perhaps one who lands in the introvert-anxious quadrant described above) would be too timid to initiate contact with congregants and engage them in Jewish life.

There should be neither shame nor stigma attached to introverted preferences. At the same time, knowing that I fall somewhere in between polar opposites of introversion and extroversion is liberating. I am not chained to a particular set of behaviors by virtue of innate personality preferences, and most people are not either. Related to this point, Cain notes two important truths: 1) Our inborn temperaments influence us regardless of the lives we lead; and 2) We have free will and can use it to stretch and shape our personalities. She calls this pairing the rubber band theory of personality.[39]

In my congregational service, I stretch and contract my inner rubber band to suit the needs of the moment. I accept that I don't have to be the loudest, most forceful speaker in the room in order to influence others. I might have a different style than extroverts, but I

37   Pink, 81-84.
38   *Ibid.*, 84.
39   Cain, 117-118.

can still be heard. I communicate my thoughts in writing. I reach out to allies to help advance my ideas. Of course, when I have to, I speak up, driven by the call of my tradition to serve the Jewish people. I find that when I recognize and utilize various tools at my disposal to stretch my internal rubber band, I am more successful in executing my larger mission.

Dr. Ron Wolfson is among the most inspiring spokespersons for reimagining and transforming the 21st Century synagogue into a center of welcome and warm relationships. Wolfson has appeared in synagogues across the country and inspired thousands of lay members, clergy and professionals. He is a highly engaging, energetic speaker who models a culture of welcome. Wherever he speaks, he personally greets every person in the congregation. He starts with a simple, "Hi, I'm Ron!" When speaking at a meal, he opts not to eat; rather, he works the room. Wolfson tirelessly engages one person after another, and each connection energizes him more. In other words, Wolfson is the quintessential extrovert.

For a rabbi on the more introverted end of the spectrum like me, Wolfson's personal style could be intimidating. After all, if congregants are smitten by his style, as they usually are, won't they expect their rabbi to be like Ron? Perhaps, but Wolfson himself comes to the rescue.

Wolfson has been able to reflect on his own personal social gifts, break them into digestible parts, and make the art of relationship building accessible to all people. For example, he offers seven tips for great greeting. These include specific pointers on personal presence, body language and appropriate things to say. His prescription to say specific words such as "Welcome" and "Shabbat shalom" are empowering to those who might not mingle naturally. Wolfson also includes introducing new people to others and thanking them for coming.[40] Wolfson lovingly guides the introvert towards Daniel Pink's ambiversion. Simultaneously, his tools remind the extroverts that they have to listen, care and be authentic. Wolfson steers extroverts towards ambiversion as well.

One Wolfson-esque practice I adopted recently has worked wonders. Our ritual committee recommended that at the end of

---

40   Dr. Ron Wolfson, *The Spirituality of Welcoming: How to Transform Your Congregation Into a Sacred Community.* (Woodstock, VT: Jewish Lights, 2006) 69-70.

Shabbat morning services (our most attended service of the week), the rabbi and cantor walk down the center aisle and greet congregants at the rear of the sanctuary as they exit to *Kiddush*. It was suggested that the receiving line of the rabbi and cantor would enhance our culture of welcome and create a friendlier adjournment to *Kiddush*.

Within short order, I realized the additional advantage of this practice for me as an introvert. It is a tool in my toolkit for meeting people in a structured setting. I greet everyone who passes by. If a congregant begins a conversation that I can tell will take some time, I ask this person to wait until everyone else passes then focus on him or her. Though I still circulate among tables while people are eating during *Kiddush*, I feel less pressure to hit every table and greet every person. For many congregants, if not most, the initial contact with clergy after services conclude is sufficient. For those who need more time with me, the receiving line gives me a basic sense of who needs more attention at *Kiddush*. After the last person has passed, I'm able to enjoy a few quiet moments for myself and regroup. Cain refers to such a break as a "restorative niche," a quiet pause from stimulation.[41] Those precious moments give me the energy boost I need to return to *Kiddush* and mingle with my congregants.

Another favorite tool of mine is my Torah tie collection. Over the years, I have accumulated themed neckties that I connect to the weekly Torah portion, Jewish holidays and other special occasions. They act as great props for conversation starters. When meeting people, we often discuss the tie-Torah connection, which often leads to a more extensive conversation. I had been doing this tie shtick for several years before I discovered that according to psychologists a prop job is a common trick among introverts for engaging in conversation and building relationships.[42] More recently, I have taken to blogging about my ties each week and enjoy a global audience.[43]

The Internet is another useful tool to level the playing field between introverts and extroverts. Granted, the Internet has cluttered our universe with information overload in a way that has raised the collective noise level. It has become more challenging to be noticed.

41 Cain, 219-220.
42 Marti Olsen Laney, *The Introvert Advantage*, (New York: Workman Publishing Company, 2002) 184-185 (iBook edition).
43 For examples, see www.rabbiedbernstein.com or on Twitter, #TieBlog.

Advantage extroverts. On the other hand, social media provide outlets of expression to introverts that did not previously exist. For introverts, the Internet is a vehicle for thoughtful curating of ideas and an outlet for building connections.[44]

In the Jewish world where community building and in-person relationships lie at the heart of our existence, social media platforms are not a substitute for relationships, but a tool for building and strengthening them. In my congregation, my professional colleagues and I participated in the Darim Social Media Bootcamp. Our focus was using social media outlets, such as Facebook, to enhance the culture of welcome in our congregation.[45] For me, as a rabbi who tends towards introversion, social media allows me to connect with others and share my creativity in ways I could not have previously imagined.

The Roar of the Cat Rabbi

The dog rabbi/cat rabbi dichotomy proposed in the mid-1990s was a false dichotomy then and remains so. The Jewish community needs maximal inclusion and openness towards different models of leadership. Introverts should not be stigmatized or excluded from leadership opportunities to serve the Jewish people.

Seminaries should teach aspiring rabbis about different personality traits and guide them towards applying their personal gifts in any leadership situation. At the same time, they can coach students on how to stretch their inner rubber bands in order to master the art of relationship building.

Congregations must recognize that many introverted rabbis have made significant contributions to the congregational rabbinate over the years and have inspired many thousands of Jews to engage more deeply in Jewish life.[46] Lay leaders should recognize that rabbis on the more introverted end of the spectrum often are motivated into service

---

44   Aryeh Bernstein, "Virtual Strength: How the Internet Fosters Community," *Sh'ma: A Journal of Jewish Ideas*, June, 2014, 5.

45   Edward Bernstein, "Using Social Media to Strengthen Culture of Welcome," *JewPoint0: The Official Darim Online Blog*, May 29, 2013, www.darimonline.org.

46   Susan Cain dedicates her book to the memory of her grandfather, Rabbi Israel Schorr (not named in book), who led an Orthodox congregation in Brooklyn for more than six decades and whose funeral brought throngs of people into the streets. She describes his introversion as the source of his success. See Cain, 267-268.

by a deep sense of mission and are adept at intense focus on vital issues. To the extent such rabbis may still need to develop tools to cultivate relationships more effectively, congregations should nurture and support their rabbis in this effort. They must recognize that most rabbis fall somewhere on the spectrum in the large area of ambiverts. Therefore, rabbis have flexibility to stretch their relational skills while still remaining authentic to themselves. Congregations may consider investing in an executive coach for their rabbis in order to hone their relational tools.

Finally, introverted rabbis should not sell themselves short. The stigma associated with introversion is false. Rabbis on the introverted end of the spectrum possess special gifts that are vital to the rabbinate including caring, compassion, keen listening skills and deliberate decision making. It may be time to retire the cat rabbi label. Perhaps it is apt to remain in the feline family, though. A lion has always been a symbol of courage and quiet dignity. When necessary, the lion springs into action to land its prey. Otherwise, they quietly observe the animal kingdom. If cats are introverts, lions are ambiverts. It's time for the cat rabbi to roar.

Rabbi Edward C. Bernstein is the Spiritual Leader of Temple Torat Emet in Boynton Beach, Florida. He was ordained by the Jewish Theological Seminary in New York in 1999. He has held various leadership positions in rabbinic and Jewish communal organizations on the local, regional and national levels. Rabbi Bernstein has also been a fellow in several continuing education programs including Greenfaith and STAR-PEER. He blogs on Judaism for the Huffington Post *and at www.rabbiedbernstein.com.*

Living the Tension and Balance Between Form and Content

By Rabbi Norman M. Cohen

The first time I saw it, I did not understand. There were two different grades at the top of my paper. Was this an indication that the teacher could not decide which one I deserved? Did he read it twice and assign a different one for each of the readings? That was my English teacher's way of introducing us to the reality that there was more than one thing to think about as we offered our presentations for his evaluation. Once he explained that there were two grades for every assignment: one for form and the other for content, it became an indispensible guideline. I have never stopped thinking about that distinction and weighing these two separate but equally significant elements in writing and presenting.

Our work in the rabbinate can be like that as well. We strive to attract the interest of the people who come to us for a variety of reasons. We work at form and style. We keep up with technology and the latest means of communication and marketing. Long ago we read the Fein Report, *Reform is a Verb*, years later the demographic surveys of the Federations at the turn of the 21st Century, and the more recent Pew Report to help us figure out who our community is and what they are seeking. We want to create a "delivery system" that will attract a significant audience. Many lay leaders, who come from the world of business, operate by the numbers. And if we are honest, we also like to see those numbers. Rabbis are known to count the house and exaggerate the actual turnout. Yet we also console ourselves with Jeremiah's message in the name of his son:

Sh'ar Yashuv, a "remnant" will return. Aim high but take comfort in the quality of those who partake.

How often have we worked on a project for days and weeks only to be disappointed by a poor turnout? We cannot argue with those who use technology to reach a greater audience and creative advertising techniques to make things inviting. This is the form of the rabbinate. Yet, we rabbis also seek to keep the content rich and enriching, helping people to understand that there is a cumulative result in learning more of our sources, the texts that are the core of our tradition. We want them to want more, interesting them in the things that our tradition can provide. We want to believe that the content should be the message. If people truly got it, there would be no need to entice them. The daily work of the rabbi is to find a creative tension and balance between content and form.

Accessing the Conversation Between The Ages

I like the story about the rabbi who was interviewed by a reporter writing a story on Judaism. The scholar invited the man to accompany him for a week while he went about his rabbinic duties. Time and again, during counseling sessions, answering phone calls, and talking with people, the rabbi went to his bookshelves and pulled down a *Tanach*, a tractate from the Talmud and a volume of commentaries, and moved from one to the other, seeking a quote, a text, an anecdote that he shared with the person sitting opposite him at his desk, or on a couch in the corner, or with the faceless voice on the other end of the line. Sometimes it was a line from the Torah, at others it was a First Century sage's words. Still others brought the practical advice of Rashi or the multilayered wisdom of the Rambam into the conversation. After a week of observing and learning some historical contexts of the various sources, the reporter said, "It seems to me that Judaism is a conversation between the ages."

My grandparents had a "party line" telephone, a primitive phone option in which several homes shared one telephone line, each home with its own private number, but a trunk line that could only be used by one at a time. Often when you picked up the phone to make a call, there was someone already using it. The polite thing was to hang up immediately and wait until the line was free to make your own call. Sometimes I imagine people stayed on the line listening. I would guess that one had to stay on the line for some time before it made any sense. The same is true for that ongoing conversation we call Judaism.

The Jewish conversation makes more sense when we know what the discussion has been about, what words were used and how those words have been understood in subsequent historical and cultural contexts.

Our faith is rich with content. The rewards of Torah and text speak for themselves. How often do we smile from ear to ear when an adult learner at Torah study makes a connection of this text and that from another session months or years ago? How many times do we want to applaud when in the midst of Torah study, a social action activist exclaims that this is why she organizes the food shelf, serves at the homeless shelter, or volunteers at the hospital?

Al achat kammah v'kammah, how much more important is this for Jewish leaders, rabbis, cantors, and educators. We must drink at the font of Jewish sustenance frequently, maintaining our study and replenishing the sources that we have accumulated throughout our rabbinates, beginning in rabbinical school. We must maintain our connection to the seminary and offer our input into what curriculum should include, so that we continue to strengthen our own resources and offer our experience to help shape the learning process for future professional Jewish leaders as well.

The False Dichotomy

When I was in rabbinic school there appeared to be a dichotomy in the division of studies and a tension between form and content. There were our text courses and then the practical rabbinate courses. It seemed that our professors and administration placed a certain higher value on the courses related to Bible, Talmud, and commentaries. Indeed that is the core, the content, and the essence. To be honest, I always took more pride when the higher grade of the two on my high school English papers was for content rather than style. That dichotomy should not have been, not intended however strongly we perceived it to be. We need to combine them and integrate them. Form and Content—two grades in English classes in high school have their parallel partners in this rabbinic school separation.

At HUC, the courses in speech, homiletics, counseling, and education seemed to be add-ons. Afterthoughts. That must have been fine with my classmates and me. Our *chevruta* certainly spent an inordinate amount of time in preparation for the exams of the text courses. I cannot remember anybody getting together to study for education, speech, or human relations courses.

Some teachers' curriculum seemed at first to be a waste of time. One began his classes with "goodies," cartoons from the New Yorker, projected onto the blackboard by an overhead projector. Actually, in looking back it seems an appropriate and helpful metaphor: humor, contemporary vehicles for stimulating thinking, and using the technology of the day. Yet, it was up to us to make the bridge, the synapse, and the connection between what our tradition says about the content of that cartoon. That same professor used to revel in asking us his mind-breaking riddles: What color is a giraffe's tongue? And why does a man have the obligation to teach his son to swim? Today Google would provide the answer in seconds. Then we had not only to research the answer, but also try to understand why such seemingly absurd questions are important at all.

Form and substance are not a Kierkegardian either/or. We need to embrace both. We recall the rabbinic anecdote about the learned man who respected the wealthy man because he saw what things he could do with those resources. Yet, the wealthy man failed to respect the knowledge of the scholar. That may be one of the myths of the rabbinate. People do come to the synagogue because they have respect for the power of our tradition. They want access to it so that their lives can be enriched. Years in the rabbinate have informed me that we are in need of both areas of expertise.

Our tradition and history is filled with examples of how we must adjust in form while not giving an inch in content. The *m'turgeman* of old made the tradition accessible to the general population, most of whom had lost touch with their Hebrew skills. Prayer books are still written today after countless hours of debate and compromise about the form and content, the use of literal and interpretive translation and transliteration. What can we convey and how to do so most effectively? The Talmud and other sources of our tradition suggest that we limit the length of our services and sermons so as not to tire our congregations.

Our job is both to create interest in our tradition and to deliver the goods. As my friend and colleague Rabbi Steven Bob likes to say about the rabbinate, "We bring Torah to the people and the people to the Torah."

I often use the image of standing with one foot on Mount Sinai and the other in the modern world to convey the tension a Jew feels today. Standing at Sinai is the core image of being a Jew and serves to describe what rabbis must feel as we try to lead, balanced between our ancient tradition and modernity.

Delivering Torah Via Life

There can never be less emphasis on texts. Yet the fact remains: substance and content will always remain the same. Delivery systems will change. The seminaries cannot possibly keep up with every new technology nor predict what will be in the future. Growing up in my home in the 50s we had rabbit ears on a TV that took fifteen minutes to warm up. One of us would sometimes have to stand next to the TV and hold the aluminum foil that we wrapped around the metal to get better reception. Today's shortcuts on our computers will be outmoded way too soon for our seminaries and training institutions to stay current. But they can continue to cultivate an attitude of openness toward new technology and the means to connect it to the tradition and vice versa. A page of Talmud seems to me to be like the first website, connecting us to a myriad of related thoughts and ideas from a variety of sources and ages.

Perhaps we need even more emphasis on modern responsa literature than was taught decades ago. This is a kind of literature that appeals to congregants and provides opportunities to bring in texts from every era and stage of rabbinic development to answer contemporary questions.

I recall an ordination address by Helen Glueck, the wife of the famous Nelson Glueck, our seminary's one time *Rosh Yeshivah* who also spent much of his time riding camels between archaeological sites. She told us that people do not come to the synagogue to hear the headlines from *Newsweek* and *Time*. They come to hear what Judaism says about life. She was not referring to *Life* magazine.

We had a professor in human relations who challenged us with socio-drama exercises that dealt with the personal problems we would face in the lives of our congregants. He raised the issues of sexual boundaries, intimate counseling, transference and counter-transference. We may have rather been studying *M'chilta*. Yet, these tools must be part of our toolbox if we have hopes of effectively engaging our people.

While the classes at HUC provided a range of material for learning, the visits to professors in their studies were most valuable. There we could pick their brains. But there we also engaged with them as human beings. We built relationships. That is what we do with our congregants in our congregations. Soon after my ordination in 1977, there was still an emphasis on sermons and frontal teaching. Somewhere along the way, the arenas for communication changed. In our congregation, we offer a sermon at most once a month. Instead, we interact with more people through briefer *divrei Torah* online and from the bimah, teaching in the sanctuary during so-called life cycle ceremonies, through our charges to *b'nai mitzvah* students, confirmands, at weddings and funerals, and in more informal settings such as adult Torah study sessions, retreats, and family education programs.

At HUC, we were sometimes invited to our teachers' homes. Sheldon and Amy Blank always invited half a dozen students at Shabbat morning services to come later in the day to their home for tea, cookies, and wonderful conversation. I often spent Shabbat lunch at the table of Chanan and Millie Brichto, hearing stories and anecdotes, participating in lively discussions and debates on some current topic laced with humor and a multitude of references to our sacred texts. Most of all, I experienced Shabbat as it was meant to be. This is where we learned the most about how to be effective in the rabbinate—one on one relationships and personal interaction. Ron Wolfson's book title *Relational Judaism* accurately captures what should be the core of Jewish life.

Role of the Rabbi

Feeling authentic as a rabbi is something all of us contemplate. I remember one of my first Shabbat services at Rockdale Temple in July 1977, when I was fresh out of HUC. I was on the bimah with Harold Hahn, my beloved senior rabbi. He began the service, and at a certain point I was supposed to take over, my first formal appearance at the reading desk. I looked around in the congregation that morning and saw Jakob Petuchowski, Fred Gottschalk, Jacob Marcus, a few of my professors from HUC. I was nervous, like at my bar mitzvah. I said to Harold, "How can I get up there and lead services with all of them sitting there?"

He leaned over and whispered in my ear, "They are just professors—you are the real rabbi!" Their signatures were all on my *s'michah*. That proves it! That was form at its best. Harold had a knack for that. I look at those signatures sometimes. Most of them have gone to the *Beit Midrash Shel Maalah*. But seeing their names on the *s'michah* reminds me of what is the real proof of my authenticity. It's the content, the *M'Korot* I have learned and continue to study; it is every opportunity to read the *parashah* and all those commentaries through the new technology of websites and YouTube. I often remember that story, usually as we gather outside the sanctuary before ascending the bimah to lead the community in prayer and study.

At the same time we need to feel our authenticity without being filled with ourselves, arrogant, haughty, leading to the narcissism that infects too many of us. It is an easy seduction. All those people coming to you, telling you how much you mean to them, what you have done for them, and how you have affected their lives. It is a nice perk to the position, but too many rabbis believe their press clippings. We need our reality checks, our feet brought back to the ground. Sometimes our spouses, close friends and colleagues help us with that. In the end, it is something we must do for ourselves.

To exude that excessive self-assuredness is to fail in form and style, to make it more difficult for our congregants to accept the content: the teachings and gifts we want to share with them. The Pew Report, like other sociological tools, tells us something is not working. While our authority comes from our knowledge of Judaism, and our capital is found in the texts that are at the heart of what we do, we cannot bury our heads in the sand when it comes to being aware of our effectiveness. The future of the Jewish people depends on our willingness to examine our shortcomings. The seminaries can help us with this. As one of our professors told us, "The best advice I can give you to be a successful rabbi is: Be yourself. However, if you are a schmuck, then be someone else." But then it must become part of our core. When I first was ordained, I used to call my former professors for advice and support. Most of them are no longer available. The witch of *Ein Dor* is nowhere to be found.

The seminaries are designed to help prepare us for as much as possible. Today's mentoring programs are a valuable extension of seminary training. If we are fortunate we will have older colleagues in our community to whom we can turn for mentoring, advice, and the benefit of their experience. My senior rabbi, Harold Hahn, was a marvelous role model, teacher and mentor who became ill with cancer months after I came to work as his assistant. He was the main attraction for me at Rockdale Temple. He helped me to understand how to put into practice the things I had learned at HUC. He showed me that we may learn the texts in school, but we begin learning the many ways to apply them in real life only after the ink on our *s'michah* has dried.

After Harold died, I had the unique opportunity to become close with Rabbi Victor Reichert, Rockdale's emeritus, author of the Soncino Bible's volume on Job. Besides helping me, a twenty-nine year old temporarily leading a 1000 family congregation, Victor invited me to his home every Thursday for lunch and Talmud study. There we enjoyed *Mo-eid Katan,* discovering a great text with a multitude of insights into many facets of life. But the gem of it all, according to Victor, was the teaching that the house of *Baitus,* though possessing a special resource for imprinting matzos, was entitled to no more privilege than any other ordinary Jew. Being a rabbi was a privilege with responsibility, not just perks.

Our seminaries and older colleagues cannot prepare us for everything. After all is said and done, the most powerful source of rabbinic learning, training, and support came then and continues to derive from my closest classmates. The words of *Pirkei Avot* were never truer. Get yourself a teacher and make yourself a friend. From our first days in Jerusalem when we met as twenty-two-year olds, we formed a bond that became richer and deeper through our seminary days. Throughout our rabbinates, not a week goes by without conversations, phone calls, emails, vacations, even sometimes planning and spending our overlapping study leaves together. They are reality checks and sources of great wisdom and advice.

Our *chevruta* culminated at a celebration of Rabbi Mark Dov Shapiro who was being feted by his congregation for twenty-five years of his leadership as their senior rabbi. Instead of the usual testimonials and tributes to him, he invited the five of us to come to the bimah during Erev Shabbat services and sit in a round table discussion of the things that were most important to us on our journeys, especially the part of them that overlapped with one another. The time flew by with stories and recollections, smiles and even a few tears. The next morning, we each presented ten minutes (a rabbinic ten minutes!) on a topic that we had studied in depth over the years. It was an inspiring meaningful hour of *chomer* for life. This is a unique way of life. Not just being Jewish, but being a rabbi. It is not just a job, not just a career, not only a role. Not just what we do when we go to the temple. It is who we are. It is not something you leave at the Temple when you go home.

The biggest personal challenge for most rabbis is how to nurture our own spirituality and continue to study while maintaining the hectic schedule of a pulpit rabbi. Time management needs to be an essential part of the seminary curriculum. Some are fortunate to arrange study leave and sabbatical to take advantage of opportunities like the Hartman Institute, CLAL's rabbinic study program, STAR, Hebrew College's Oraita retreat and online and in phone conference forums with various movements' tremendous offerings of seminars and lectures by some of the leading teachers of today. Our *chevruta* also met in New York and continued studying with Rabbi Larry Hoffman for several years after ordination. We must remain Jacob wrestling with the angels that are our texts.

There are so many such opportunities through modern technology. It reminds us when we are frustrated with the computer how much benefit there is as well. These are the "goodies" of today. And like fire, the original technology in the Midrash, modern technology can be used for good or bad. Imagine Hillel vs. Shammai. Hillel would have an iPhone and would be on Twitter. Shammai would throw technology to the ground.

The Sine Qua Non of the Future

An essential for rabbis, especially in the American Jewish non-Orthodox world is interfaith relations. Not only do we interact with non-Jews in a traditional way—dialogues, church visits, celebrating Thanksgiving and other national occasions together, but we must also face, and even embrace, the fact that many of our congregants have Christian relatives. In fact, a significant number of people sitting in our pews are non-Jews who are related to Jews, some of whom are members and involved in many activities of our communities.

Rabbis in training and in the field must continue to seek opportunities to interact, teach and learn, preparing ourselves in every possible way. Perhaps my four years at Holy Cross College as an undergraduate was my determining factor, my wake up call. It was there as the only Jewish student for much of the time that my Jewish identity became reinforced and much more significant to me. There I first became interested in Christian literature and interfaith activities. At HUC, I was blessed to have as my teacher Michael Cook and I also got to know Sam Sandmel who was no longer teaching but still on campus and came, on occasion, with his family to Rockdale, the Temple I served after ordination.

I enrolled in every course that Michael Cook offered, and eventually I did my thesis work in New Testament and its relationship to the personages of the Hebrew Bible. My thesis was not only a rigorous exercise in learning and scholarship. It has also been a calling card and key to the door that has opened up the world of significant collegial relationships with ministers and priests and invitations to speak at churches, where many refer to me as their rabbi!

Annual visits to my alma mater in Massachusetts to work with today's Jewish students and faculty there have reinforced that and in June 2014, I was privileged to co-lead a trip to Israel with Fr. Jim Hayes, Holy Cross classmate and good friend along with forty of our classmates and their families.

I also co-led an interfaith trip with my good friend, Rev Steve Thom, a UCC minister with whom I have had a dialogue and deep friendship since we met as neighborhood colleagues nearly two decades ago when he first moved to the Twin Cities. As our discussions unfolded I was pleasantly surprised to find a UCC minister who was so pro-Israel, with a deep commitment to defending the Jewish state against so many of the insidious and not so subtle attacks by some church leaders in the UCC and other liberal Christian denominations. He reached out to me at some of those critical times and taught me about an organization called Christians for Fair Witness in the Middle East. This is one of the benefits of our investment in interfaith relations.

Thursday evenings became an important evening of conversation. Over scotch or martinis, we discussed our particular challenges in congregational life, life cycle functions, and congregants' issues. We discovered that we shared, in so many ways, the same calling, with different faces, different rituals, but the same human needs and the same sweep of concerns. The words of *Pirkei Avot* were never truer. Get yourself a teacher and make yourself a friend. My interest in interfaith activity included a sincere interest in learning about the other, not just teaching the other about us. This I believe is a key that many of our colleagues miss.

My thesis and prior studies at Holy Cross were the passport and visa. They were the form that has given me entry into that world. The content came through my studies with Michael Cook. It was through the substance of that learning that I was able to carry on those discussions and create those relationships.

Interfaith work also includes the issues of intermarriage and the role of the non–Jew in the synagogue. Our congregation helped to set some standards. Rabbi Alexander Schindler pointed to our congregation during his outreach campaign and the CCAR Responsum on the challenge of how to be inclusive in *b'nai mitzvah* ceremonies, making specific reference to what we do at Bet Shalom. Finding a way to publicly show the community that a non-Jew can have a role, different and distinct from a Jewish parent, respecting the boundaries of Judaism but acknowledging the significance of their contribution to the future of the Jewish people is something we all need to contemplate. As rabbis we can show the way.

Our approach to mixed marriage officiation may change during our rabbinic careers. It certainly is a topic from which we cannot flee. It is never a simple yes or no if we want to engage our congregants and create a respect even when we differ. I was adamantly opposed to officiation in my younger days, but experience and interaction with many of my colleagues has helped me to evolve in my approach.

Our seminaries need to help us focus on the flexibility we must have in developing so many of the programs that are a part of the everyday rabbinate. Conversion cannot be a set prescribed path. Our experience teaches us that people come to this threshold from a variety of backgrounds and with differing needs. As gatekeepers we have to learn the variety of entry points and the journey for each person must be individually planned along with them.

All of these issues are what led me to a deep and intensive study of the book of Ruth. The study of Ruth has my interest because of its attention to conversion, intermarriage, welcoming the stranger, and relational Judaism. It is my hobby and passion. To discover an attraction to biblical and textual sources can enhance our study time and enrich our personal resources. Once again, we are led back to Torah.

Becoming Torah

Torah and text are the source of our authority. Without it, what are we? Those in congregational life know the answer. There are many people in congregations, some leaders, who want social workers, program directors, and camp counselors. Congregations can provide these but not by transforming their rabbis into them.

Form is an ever-changing adaptive vehicle for delivering the goods. The world's culture is evolving. The way we understand our tradition is different. But the tradition at its core is the same.

The Pew Report suggests we concentrate more on the form— the way we present our resources to the Jewish community. People are interested in different things from their synagogue. Many of the preferences seem to suggest that congregations become more like community centers offering what social workers would offer.

JCC's are responding with that kind of programming. Federations are looking to redefine themselves and find a new purpose.

I think synagogues need to repackage what we offer as well. However, the content needs to remain the same. It is Torah and text study that has sustained our people from time immemorial. Our responsibility is to find ways to present the sacred content in a way that people can appreciate all the wisdom and life meaning that lies at the core of the Messages from Sinai. Rabbi Jeff Salkin's title of his book for teenagers, *Text Messages* is ingenious in its ambiguous use of a modern reference to the oldest of all texts.

When we study Torah in an appropriate setting with our congregants, it is not the same as studying academically in a university or on a college campus. There is something about *chevruta*, reciting a blessing, and making it a sacred activity. It becomes such an activity by its context. We experience *ahavah*—we fall in love with Jewish sources.

What you do is sometimes Torah—in a mystical and rational way—Abraham coming out to greet the strangers. That is Torah—embodied in *hachnasat orchim*. We must be as welcoming as our Biblical and rabbinic models. We teach Torah and in many ways for our congregants, what we do becomes Torah. In that sense the form and content are the same.

One of the most influential pieces I was assigned to read in seminary was Haim Nachman Bialak's article "*Halakha* and *Aggadah*." Although it is considered secondary literature, there is nothing more primary than the metaphor it has imprinted on my heart and in my brain. The tension between "harsh" halachah and "warm" aggadah is symbolized by ice and water flowing through a river. While many imagine those two to be separate entities, they are of the same essence. This is how I envision content and form, substance and style. Rabbis are the stewards of the content of Judaism, the sacred texts and their interpretations and applications in every generation. We are also the creators of the forms in which this precious content is to be offered and served. May we be granted the wisdom and creativity to combine them in the most successful manner to help ensure the future of the Jewish people as Jews who appreciate our tradition.

Norman M. Cohen is the founding rabbi of Bet Shalom Congregation in Minnetonka, Minnesota. He is an annual visiting consultant to the chaplain's office at his alma mater, Holy Cross College in Worcester, Massachusetts, where in 1972 he received his bachelor's degree cum laude. He earned a Master's degree, ordination, and a Doctorate of Divinity from HUC in Cincinnati. He has taught at both of his alma maters, as well as Xavier University, St. Olaf College, United Theological Seminary, the College of St. Catherine, and Macalester College. Rabbi Cohen is the author of the book Jewish Bible Personages in the New Testament as well as numerous published articles and sermons. His most recent publications are a chapter in the book Text Messages, and an essay he co-authored in Society and Business Review: Leviticus on how to make and distribute profit. Rabbi Cohen is past president of the Midwest Association of Reform Rabbis, the Minnesota Rabbinical Association and has served, on behalf of the CCAR as a developer and member of the Joint Mentoring Institute, the National Commission on Rabbinic Congregation Relations and as the vice chair of the Joint Commission on Synagogue Management and a member of the Rabbinic Placement Commission. He currently serves on the President's Council of HUC-JIR. He spends part of his summer each year at OSRUI, the oldest of the Reform movement's camps.

Shaping the Evolving Congregational Rabbinate

By Rabbi David Lerner

Sometimes, my mind would wander during Talmud class in rabbinical school. Instead of exploring the intricacies of a Tosafot (12th Century commentators on the Talmud), I would start making an ambitious chart about my future life as a congregational rabbi. On the top, I would list the seven days of the week, each hour of the day, on the left. In the middle, I would list what I would do: daven, learn Torah, answer phone calls, study with a *chevruta*, meet with people, go out for lunch, research a sermon topic, attend a meeting and teach a class. I would leave plenty of time for exercise, family, and relaxation.

Fast-forward a couple of decades: things are not exactly the way I imagined they would be. Thankfully, I daven every morning, but rarely do I have time to learn Torah, other than the Torah I am planning to teach. The rabbinate has changed dramatically in the fifteen years since I was ordained at The Jewish Theological Seminary.

When my rabbinate commenced, the pulpit rabbinate was a stable and sound career. Having turned away from other options (law, restaurant-owner and politics) and having a father who was a rabbi, I thought I knew what I was getting into. But things change.

When I began as the second rabbi in North Suburban Synagogue Beth El in Highland Park, Illinois, I daily received from congregation members: three personal letters, five emails and ten calls. Now, I receive barely a letter a week and still ten phone calls, though they are more likely to come through my cell phone. But emails have multiplied ten-fold and now, I must respond to dozens of text-messages and direct messages through Facebook and Twitter. A good part of my day is spent in front of a computer or my smartphone, not with our people's greatest texts, or even spending time with my congregants face-to-face as much as I would like.

This technological revolution has allowed incredible advances— my classes are recorded and put up on my shul's website, I post my sermons as graphic blogs on the *Times of Israel* website and my assistant rabbi and I have a YouTube channel where we post our videos. The most popular Jewish article I have composed is not in prose, but a music video based on a Calvin Harris song "I Feel So Close to Shul." Some weeks, we reach thousands of people through our use of technology. But at the same time, these connections lack depth. If they spur someone to come to shul, great, but if not, they only scratch the surface. Real relationships take time and occur face-to-face. The meetings I have to help someone during a personal crisis, the visits to the hospital, the pre-funeral conversations, the time with *b'nai mitzvah* families, preparing with a couple before their wedding, exploring the possibility of a new family joining our community—these are the moments that truly make a difference because they enable me to enrich people's lives by connecting them with our traditions and texts. They are always the most meaningful part of my day.

Beyond technology, the Jewish world continues to change—at times, at an alarming rate. The recently published Pew Study of American Jewish Life demonstrated the extent of assimilation and the figures are not good. In addition, the number of Conservative Jews is declining precipitously. Further, more and more young Jews choose not to affiliate with a synagogue. While the default used to be that a Jewish couple would join a shul when they moved into town, that is no longer the case. These developments mean that shuls are on the decline, especially Conservative synagogues, and we must work twice as hard to convince Jews to try out our shul and join.

Synagogue dues have emerged as a new challenge. Younger Jews look at synagogues the way they look at other expenses in their lives—more as an à la carte experience. Shuls were not built for that and thus, new models are being explored, including not charging dues which, of course, puts synagogue communities with their dues structure into competition with groups that do not charge. In general, finances are becoming a greater and greater challenge.

In the last fifteen years, rabbinic job security has also changed. It used to be that a beloved rabbi could count on spending many years in a shul, but today, rabbis in their 50s and 60s—sometimes just a few years before retirement—have been let go, often replaced by someone younger who can be paid less and, it is hoped, bring in more young families. In general, rabbis face a more challenging environment, as there are more and more rabbis for fewer and fewer jobs.

Rabbis are pulled in many directions. In addition to working long hours and developing skills they never knew they needed, rabbis are asked to play many roles. As the joke goes: the ideal rabbi is thirty-five years old with twenty-five years of experience. Over the last few decades, rabbis have become much less formal. Rabbis can hang out with their congregants in many more situations. While I would argue that is a good thing, it can also be complicated as it is sometimes unclear if the rabbi should be one of the crew or the rabbi in a given situation. Being a regular person has brought down boundaries and helped rabbis connect with their congregants, but it has also brought with it a fair amount of role confusion.

All of these changes have created a more stressful environment for the congregational rabbi. Not only is she or he in a fishbowl, but the rabbi's family is often placed in difficult situations. This can lead to undue pressure on the family, to marital instability and other major stressors. Rabbis are burning out at a higher rate than before. Sadly, some suffer from depression that is exacerbated by this work and that can lead rabbis to make bad choices. It would behoove communities to encourage their rabbis to have a serious program of self-care in place.

Given all these changes in the world and in synagogue life, I have learned a few critical lessons:

1) Be Open to Learning

After five years as an assistant and associate rabbi in a large synagogue, ten years ago, I became the sole rabbi of my current synagogue at the age of thirty-two. While I thought I knew a lot, the reality is that I had much to learn, and I am still learning.

One of the areas where I learned a tremendous amount from my community was around the issue of intermarriage. While I had never thought one should be particularly open to intermarried families (the only option I knew was that non-Jewish partners should convert before marriage), my shul presented a newer model. They not only allowed intermarried families to feel welcome on a superficial level, but they also actively pushed themselves to create a more inclusive and welcoming environment for them.

Our Keruv (welcoming) Committee helped me be open to welcoming non-Jewish members of our community and today we celebrate their involvement in our synagogue life with the honor of leading the prayer for the community on *Rosh HaShanah*.

2) The Need for a Partner and Mentors

Being a rabbi can be lonely. It can also be hard. One needs a great partner (and not just the kind that you marry, though I am blessed to have that as well!) in a shul.

I worked as a second rabbi and have had two assistant rabbis in my current shul. The partnership I have with my assistant rabbi, Michael Fel, is such a gift to me and my shul. He and I work closely on almost every area of synagogue life and have a real meeting of the minds. The two of us work hard together, but also have a great time doing so. If a rabbi does not have another rabbi with whom to share the pulpit, he or she should look for another staff member or even a rabbi outside her or his shul, with whom she or he can meet regularly. The stress of this work and the loneliness require this.

In addition, the need for good advice is ever-present. I have been blessed to have a number of mentors whom I have called upon over the years. They have consulted with me in matters such as halachah (Jewish law), my contract negotiations, staff issues, and encouraged me every step of the way. I cannot thank them enough and encourage all rabbis to find a person—or more than one—who can serve in this role and that rabbinical organizations should create programs to match rabbis with rabbinic mentors.

Beyond mentors, a supportive family is invaluable. I have been blessed with an incredibly supportive wife, parents, children and extended family. There is simply no way I would be the rabbi I am today without their love and support.

3) The Importance of Process

As much as the ends matter (and they do), the process of getting there is just as crucial.

The best example of this done well in our synagogue occurred around the issue of gays and lesbians. While for many years, we have welcomed gay and lesbian Jews into our shul with open arms; we did not perform same-sex weddings.

In 2006, as the Rabbinical Assembly was deciding this issue, I realized that we needed a process to help move the community forward. Perhaps it was because I myself had not decided what I felt was right that I needed a thoughtful process. I opened the issue with a sermon on *Kol Nidre* where I framed the topic.

After the holidays, I convened a group of people from the shul––a couple who were opposed to change in this area and others who wanted us to be more accepting of gays and lesbians. These people were from a wide variety of backgrounds and perspectives. We met with a member of the shul, Dan Rothstein, who co-founded the Right Question Project. Dan helped us refine our questions around this issue and in the process, helped us determine how we should proceed.

We developed a year program, which included speakers on both sides of this issue: Rabbi Joel Roth of JTS (opposed) and Rabbi Avram Reisner (in favor) and a *Shabbaton* with Rabbi Steve Greenberg, the first openly gay Orthodox rabbi. I also taught a session about the Rabbinical Assembly's Committee on Jewish Law and Standards in general and another session specifically about the *t'shuvot* (religious responsa) on this topic. We had more formal and informal sessions where members of the community could share their perspectives. The process concluded with another sermon on the topic the following Yom Kippur where I announced the change we were making: we would perform same-sex ceremonies. While not everyone was overjoyed at the decision, no one resigned from the shul over it, and everyone felt heard due to our rigorous process.

Ignoring process, I have learned, results in bad feelings and sometimes the derailing or loss of significant initiatives.

4) Don't be Afraid to Experiment and Change

Some of my best ideas have been risky. Could we really have a BBQ on a Friday night before Shabbat? Yes and hundreds of people come! Would people really come to Tishah B'Av Minhah services held in the middle of a weekday? Yes. Would people come to shul to meditate? Yes. Would they want to in the main service? Not yet! Can a *Yom* Ha'atzmaut (Israel Independence Day) celebration work on the actual day of Yom Ha'Atzmaut, even when it falls on a weekday and not on Sunday? It's more challenging, but yes. Could we create a successful Shabbat morning experience that allowed people to choose from many options? Yes—thank you Synaplex! How would people come to yoga in shul on a Shabbat morning? In yoga clothes and then they change for shul. Can a woman who has never put on a tallit learn how to recite the *Birkat Kohanim* (Priestly Benediction) and lead that wondrous blessing of the congregation? Yes—in her magnificent tallit!

5) Stick to Your Values

It's important for rabbis to honor what they believe. When I first came to my shul, they told me that they played music on Shabbat in an alternative minyan, which met once a month. While I was uncomfortable with this, I realized that because this alternative minyan had standing long before my arrival; I would not interfere with their practices.

However, just a few weeks before Simhat Torah the shul told me that they also utilized musical instruments in the evening service of that most communal of celebrations. I had to make a decision— would I compromise my values and leave things as they were or should we make a change?

With little time for any process, I considered my options: not attending—that would not have looked good for a new rabbi, attending with the music—I would have compromised my values and felt forced to be in an uncomfortable role—hardly the first impression I was hoping for as well, or I could simply make a change. While normally, I believe in having change rooted in process; here, I had to make a quick decision which was to eliminate the instruments and utilize singers, microphones and "banging on the *amud* (the reading table)" in such a manner that it mimicked much of the previous musical experience. For me, it was essential that I stick with my core values.

6) Don't Get Too Discouraged

The congregational rabbinate is often filled with moments of disappointment. There are times when you connect with people and those connections are incredibly meaningful and times when you simply do not.

My wonderful teacher at The Jewish Theological Seminary, Rabbi William Lebeau, taught that there are "two percenters" in every shul. Two percent of the congregation, no matter what you do or say, will not be happy with you. He stressed to my senior class that we should not get too worried about this group. That is not to say that we should not care about them; we should. But we should also realize that we couldn't please everyone all of the time and that is okay.

Just a few months into my tenure in Lexington, Massachusetts, I was having problems with a couple of people in the shul. I felt badly that we were not connecting; our interactions seemed always to put us at loggerheads. I called Rabbi Bernard Eisenman, the rabbi emeritus of the congregation, for his sage input. When I told him what was going on he asked who the difficult people were. I gingerly asked him if he ever had any difficulty with them.

He said, "Oh, yeah, every week." He told me that often people act or speak in a way that is more reflective of who they are and what they are grappling with.

That said, when people resign from my synagogue to join another local community, it is still incredibly painful. Sometimes they leave because they have found a better match or they want a religious school experience with fewer demands; sometimes they leave because they are upset with me and that is the hardest.

Perhaps my most difficult personal moment in the rabbinate occurred around this. A family with whom I was friendly left the shul over an incredibly personal and painful issue of halachah (Jewish law). When I explained the law they asked me to ignore it; I could not. Sadly, not only did they leave the shul, they terminated our friendship and never responded to the phone call, email or letter that I wrote them. That was one of the most disappointing experiences I have had in my rabbinate.

7) Open All the Doors

There are numerous barriers to joining a shul: the cost, the lack of interest, the feeling of inadequacy, of not knowing much about the tradition, the difficulty of meeting people and forming friendships, and just not feeling a need to join. Given all that, we need to open every door into our buildings and our communities. At Temple Emunah, we do that on numerous levels: we have two softball teams, mah-jongg, movies and book clubs. We make our services more accessible with learning minyanim, transliterated siddurim (prayer books), themed minyanim, Skyping the minyan or call-in phone numbers for those who cannot make it to shul, and spiritual services and meditative minyanim and meditation sessions. Our lay-led *Ivrit lakol* (Hebrew for Everyone) program helps adults conquer the difficult task of feeling comfortable in a Hebrew liturgy.

Beyond opening the doors, we meet people all over. Every Monday morning, a group of cyclists meets me at my house for an early morning ride. This fall, nine of us plan to travel to Israel as part of the "Lexington Minutemenschen" raising money for the Arava Institute as part of Hazon Israel Bike Ride where we will ride 350 miles from Jerusalem to Eilat. In the last seven years, I have led four multi-generational congregational Israel trips taking some 300 people to Israel. Not only have these experiences been incredibly fun and powerful in and of themselves, but they have also helped strengthen the bonds among members of the community.

Rabbi Fel and I try to connect with people wherever they are. We hold Coffee with the Rabbis at local coffee shops, special holiday events at the local Barnes and Noble and our local Stop and Shop supermarket. We provide kashrut supervision for some products at a local fruit and vegetable market and at a supermarket. In shul, we hold special Synaplex Shabbat services, which present participants with multiple options from yoga to learning to singing *niggunim* (Jewish wordless melodies). We reach out to young families with a host of special programs from stroller walks to baby massage classes.

8) Reaching Beyond Your Immediate Community

Being a rabbi is a fairly busy existence and the instinct is to remain within one's *dalet amot* (literally, four cubits; figuratively, immediate domain). However, that is a mistake. Rabbis must engage with the larger Jewish and non-Jewish community to be most effective in fulfilling the mission of spreading Torah in the world.

Working with interfaith clergy associations in Chicago and Boston is among the most powerful experiences I have had. I took fourteen Christian ministers to Israel with the JCRC of Greater Boston—this was important since it provided not only a rich, textured portrait of Israel, but also of some of the deeper nuances of both faiths. In the Rabbinical Assembly, I have worked hard to try to bring colleagues together in our New England region and help us think thoughtfully about the complexities of keiruv toward intermarried couples. Recently, a wonderful and engaged group of lay leaders and I started the Community *chevra* Kadisha Burial Society of Greater Boston to bring the mitzvot of *taharah* (ritually preparing the body for burial) and *sh'mirah* (being present with a dead body) to a wider, non-Orthodox community. As of now, thirty different synagogues and minyanim and Jewish institutions affiliated with a variety of Jewish religious streams have partnered to create a pluralistic *chevra* that has allowed a new generation of volunteers to participate in this *chesed shel emet* (ultimate act of loving kindness).

While it is not easy to find the time to start new organizations or give our time to additional projects, these types of initiatives and efforts are such an integral part of what the rabbinate can be.

9) Speak From the Tradition

Torah informs what I do. It is not ancillary to my rabbinic practice, but at its core. When I speak, teach, lead, counsel—in groups and one-to-one—I am always conscious that Torah, in its broadest and richest definition, is part and parcel of my message, just as it is part and parcel of my persona.

While I try not to be preachy, I see my role at its core as representing Jewish traditions and texts. Whether I am teaching my seventh grade students or teaching at 2am at our all night *Tikkun Leil Shavuot*, I present traditional texts in Hebrew. This is not a tradition that I serve in a watered down format. I ask participants to read in Hebrew so that the words with their original ancient echoes of the past come to life in our ears.

We sometimes forget that we have been given a 4,000-year-old treasure chest to draw upon. It has insights that guide me in moments as diverse as singing the *Shema* with a group of preschoolers or kicking off a basketball tournament. We ignore it at our own peril.

10) Speak From the Heart

Finally, and most importantly, while the world and the rabbinate are changing, the core idea of being a rabbi remains the same. We must be ourselves, our authentic selves to truly connect with others and our community.

We must be totally present with people so we can be a supportive presence for people when they are in need. And, we must speak from our own experience. The most powerful sermons and teachings I have offered have never been the talks I thought were the most brilliant ideas woven together with poetic language. They were stories I told about being a parent, about being me. Those stories, sometimes even the ones that have made me somewhat more exposed and vulnerable than a rabbi already is, have resonated with people most strongly. And, of course, they reflect and underscore the Jewish teachings to which they are linked.

We must speak from the heart and when we do, we have the ability to touch people's hearts in a manner that can truly move them. And thus, they and we are transformed.

While my days are not exactly as I would have imagined (YouTube, Facebook, Gmail, and texting were not on my radar in rabbinical school); thankfully, they are filled with learning and teaching, engaging people and experiencing meaningful moments. The rabbinate of the future will require even more creative flexibility and the ability of rabbis to reinvent themselves and their communities to keep up with the times. That said, we are blessed to have a reservoir of ancient wisdom and the richest set of rituals and ethical insights to call upon. If we can be authentic to that and to ourselves, we will be ready to face the challenges that lie ahead.

Perhaps my dreaming in Talmud class was not so far off after all.

Spiritual leader of Temple Emunah, Lexington, MA since 2004, **Rabbi David Lerner** *also serves as chair of the Rabbinical Assembly's Commission on Keruv, Conversion and Jewish Peoplehood, a member of the Rabbinical Assembly's Social Justice Commission, vice-president of the Massachusetts Board of Rabbis and founder of Clergy Against Bullets and the Community Hevra Kadisha of Greater Boston. After his ordination at The Jewish Theological Seminary, where he was a Wexner Graduate Fellow, Rabbi Lerner served at North Suburban Synagogue Beth El in Highland Park, Ill.*

Rabbinic Pioneer or Pariah?

By Rabbi Geela Rayzel Raphael

After thirty-five years of working at specific jobs in the Jewish community, I am now a freelance rabbi. This means I mostly serve interfaith and intercultural families by officiating at weddings—mostly interfaith—baby-namings, and funerals. My whole career at this juncture provokes controversy. I had no plans to be a freelance rabbi, nor had anything I had learned in rabbinical school prepared me for it either emotionally or technically. I have had to learn entrepreneurial skills, marketing and social networking, and to manage the anxiety that comes with running a private practice. I have had to grow my *emunah* (faith) that "God will provide" as long as I am on the right path of service. This essay will explain how I got to this place, what have I learned along the way, what did and did not prepare me for this journey, and what skills I had to acquire to serve in this capacity.

Introduction to my Personal Journey

Growing up in Tennessee in the 1950s and 1960s, there were not that many Jews near me in Knoxville. The few of us learned to treasure each other and stick together to ward off the efforts of our neighbors to convert us. The Young Lifers of the evangelical churches were forever trying to save our souls. We also grew to appreciate any newcomers to town; they increased our numbers and made the discussion around our Shabbat table more interesting. They brought new tunes and traditions, and my parents modeled the Southern hospitality of "Let all who are hungry come in and eat."

I internalized that message and took it with me to Indiana University, where I worked at Hillel cooking and doing outreach. It took me to graduate school at Brandeis in Jewish communal work where I professionalized my outreach skills. When I became Executive Director of the Hillel and worked on campus at York University from 1977-88, I used that message to welcome students. At every pulpit I have served, the message has been to welcome the stranger, make them comfortable, and help them feel at home.

While I was studying for the rabbinate at Reconstructionist Rabbinical College, an assignment in Talmudic codes introduced me to the concept of *ger toshav*—the resident alien. Reb Zalman Schacter-Shalomi had pointed me in this direction, and I was intrigued by this obsolete Biblical category to address a contentious issue in my congregation. We had a man who wanted to convert, but some felt he was not really able to understand the Jewish concepts. It split the congregation. By looking at the category of *ger toshav*–"the stranger who dwelt among us"—perhaps I could find a compromise position.

The whole matter took on a sense of urgency when a rabbinical friend of mine was horrified that her husband had been asked to be a witness for a *ketubah* of a couple about to intermarry. In her opinion, although the groom had done *mikvah*, he was not prepared to call himself a Jew. The rabbi had considered him a *ger toshav*, someone who had allied with the Jewish people and was willing to perform the marriage.

I called the rabbi who was doing the wedding and asked her to explain her rationale. She said that she was trying out this new formula as a way to deal with intermarriage. "Conversion is a scary word, and most people are not ready to give up their past identity. However, many non-Jews have agreed to raise their children Jewish and affiliate with the Jewish people."

I thought back to my experiences with synagogues and community. Yes, inevitably in just about every situation there had been a non-Jew who had never fully converted, but was accepted as part of the community. I was intrigued enough to investigate the traditional ramifications of the status of *ger toshav* and see if I could find rabbinically valid grounds for creating a new category of people who affiliate and live with us. Perhaps this catogory would support the goals of outreach to intermarrieds.

Background on *Ger Toshav*

There are five places where *ger toshav* is mentioned in the Torah.[1] This term *ger toshav* is translated as "temporary resident," "landed immigrant," or "resident alien"— someone who has a "green card" and is accepted into the society except for a few key privileges. God discusses the rules of the

---

1   Exodus 12:45, Leviticus 25:6, 25:40, 25:47 and 25:55.

Sabbatical year, and with it a promise of abundance. We are obliged to share food produced during the Jubilee year with our slaves, hired laborers, guests and all who live with us. The community of Israel accepts and welcomes the stranger and resident. Foreigners are an integral part of our communities. However, Leviticus 25:47 indicates that Israelites are not to be at the mercy of any strangers. The Torah assumes that there are a number of different types of foreign people who live in our communities. They are accepted fully in some respects, but not others.

In Numbers, God is describing to Moses what the Israelites should do when they finally enter the land. They are to bring sacrifices for payment of vows and/or voluntary gifts to one of the feasts.[2] The strangers are bound by our laws and are accepted in as part of our communities. Further, Zechariah, the prophet, also makes a statement regarding the nations that will come together worship God.[3]

Historically, Chaim Clorfene and Yaakov Rogalsky explain how Israelites taught the gentiles the seven commandments. "During the 410 years that the first Temple stood and the 420 years that the Second Temple stood, Gentiles who wanted to dwell in the land of Israel had to agree to fulfil the Noachide laws and had the right to enter the Holy Temple and offer sacrifices to God."[4]

Rambam's defines a *ger toshav* as a former heathen who has since forsaken the worship of idols and agreed to observe the seven Noachite commandments.[5] *Gerim toshavim* are not circumcised or immersed. Jews are under their own sovereignty and have the power to issue visas and make the rules, so to speak. Rambam clarifies that the people living by the seven universal Noachite commandments agree not to worship idols, not to curse God, not to kill, not to steal, not to engage in sexual immorality, not to eat the limb of a living animal, and to establish courts of law to enforce these laws.[6] They become one of the *chasidei umot haolam*, the Pious Ones of the Nations, and receive a share of the eternal world.

This is just a small sampling from my extensive study on *ger toshav*, which I did on my own outside of my formal rabbinical training.

Applying the Concept of *Ger Toshav* to Interfaith Outreach

After working through issues around the *ger toshav* in my first pulpit, I began to work for Jewish Family and Children Service of Greater Philadelphia.

---

2   Numbers 15:14-16.
3   Zechariah 14:16-18.
4   Chaim Clorfene and Yaakov Rogalsky, *The Path of the Righteous Gentile* (Targum Press, Jerusalem 1987) 16.
5   *Mishneh Torah, K'doshim*, Laws of Forbidden Relationships.
6   *Mishneh Torah*, Laws of Kings 8:11.

There, my docket was specifically to develop a program to welcome interfaith families and to make the Jewish community more welcoming. That project, funded by a Jewish Federation continuity grant, was called the Jericho Project and later Interfaithways. Our mission was to reach out to interfaith families and make our synagogues and temples friendly to interfaith families. During my time at Interfaithways, I began to officiate at intermarriages in order to be in line with the values of the program. I simply could not make a couple feel welcome if I turned them away when they asked me to officiate at the wedding.

In the beginning I only did weddings where the couple had decided to raise the children Jewish. To ease my own internal guilt about doing a particular wedding, I invited a couple to Shabbat dinner at my house as part of the preparation for their big day. I had to work through my own internal voices to be able to do this work. As a Jew, I felt *hachnasat orchim* was the value to hold central. Hadn't Abraham run to greet the strangers in the heat of the day while he was recovering from his circumcision? As a rabbi, I was conflicted about whether this was the proper way to serve, but I was certainly being called to it! As a mother, I would want my own children to feel nurtured and welcomed; how could I turn someone else's children away? As a universal being, I realized that love was at the foundation of this work. If I could foster love and connection, it was indeed a holy task. I had to suppress the voices I had absorbed from sources all across Jewish culture that said, "Intermarriage could be the end of the Jewish people."

At the time the Jewish Outreach Institute was holding professional development conferences to further the cause of reaching the unaffiliated. At those conferences I realized that I had been actually doing outreach my whole career. I began to offer more Shabbat dinners for interfaith couples that were either thinking of getting married or already engaged. Again the Shabbat dinner table was where the magic happened. We had time for some education about the rituals, time for conversation, and of course the experience of a relaxed Shabbat meal.

The conversations around my table were profound. Here were young couples, wrestling with their parents, their identities and each other. In one of the early dinners, I had a young couple that had been dating for four years. The boyfriend was son of Holocaust survivors, one parent Israeli, who belonged to one of the prestigious congregations in town. He felt he just must raise his children Jewish! The girlfriend was a devout Catholic, and she had to raise her children Catholic! They were both in university and had taken religion courses to understand each other better. Here they were at my Shabbat table wondering how to get through the impasse. At the end of the evening, I asked how they felt about the experience. The young woman replied, "We have been arguing about Shabbat for four years, but I had never been to a Shabbat dinner. Now at least I know what I'm getting into!"

I said, "You mean to tell me his parents have never had you to dinner in all four years?"

She replied, "No, and maybe if they had, I would have been more willing to raise the children Jewish." I was stunned. Here was the recipe and it was that simple: make Shabbos, invite the interfaith families, let the Spirit work its magic, and save the Jews.

Since then I have done dozens of weddings and hosted many couples around my table: Quaker-Jewish, Catholic-Jewish, Methodist-Jewish, Hindu-Jewish, African American-Jewish and many more. It has been a fascinating adventure. The conversations have been wonderful, intense, educational and joyous. I have also heard such stories of pain, being rejected by one rabbi after another—or in some cases, by grandparents and parents.

I have come to understand that most of these families will enrich the Jewish experience if both sides are committed to understanding each other and the journey they have chosen. The Jew is sometimes more interested in his or her heritage than ever before. My work is to guide them through the losses so that something new can emerge.

In time I believe the practice of welcoming the non-Jewish partner in marriage will increase the strength of the Jewish community "gene pool." Inevitably, it will change what we call Jewish practice. The Jewish home will be more ethnically diverse and celebrate numerous holidays. We will create allies for the Jewish people. The great North American Jewish experience is still in its infancy and only time will tell the outcome. In the meantime, I vote on the side of supporting love as the unfolding of God's plan.

As of this writing, I have been performing weddings for over twenty years, and interfaith weddings for about fifteen years. After a number of years, I decided to try co-officiation for one year and then would evaluate. My one-year experiment with co-officiation took me to many places, both figuratively and spiritually. I met interesting priests and ministers that I would never have come in contact with. I learned and experienced many traditions I had only read about. My contact with couples grew deeper and richer as I helped them untangle the beliefs and assumptions they had inherited or absorbed from their families of origin. Wrestling with my own prejudices, I grew to appreciate a diversity of customs cross-culturally. I was doing interfaith outreach as well as interfaith dialogue. I have met wonderful priests and ministers who are curious about Jewish customs. Most of the non-Jewish families love our rituals. One Catholic priest in particular says he counsels his couples to raise the children Jewish as we need the numbers. I have sensitized many a minister and the couples about leaving Jesus out of the ceremony as not to alienate the Jews present.

Over the years, I have used the category of *ger toshav* for those partners of Jews who have no other major religious practice, or have agreed to raise their children Jewish. I usually raise the question when they are filling out their *ketubah*. Does the non-Jewish spouse want his or her name transliterated or are they ready for a Hebrew name to signify the beginning of their journey with the Jewish people? We then have a conversation to find them a name. And if, according to *midrash*—the Hebrew letters can create the universe—then certainly they can create a spiritual path for one person![7]

My Calling: Welcome the *Ger Toshav* with Open Arms

When my job ended at InterFaithways, I felt pain, not only from the lack of work, but also from the loss of the opportunity to welcome these families. It had been such a meaningful part of my career, not just for me, but also for my whole family. Since then I have written many grants to organizations that may be interested in this kind of work, asking them for support to continue. No one has yet seen the value and responded favorably as it is a labor-intensive process. I have also written numerous grants to work with the rabbis who do the work of freelance weddings. They are the gatekeepers to these couples—also to no avail. There is a gold mine out there and the community only seems to want these families when they are ready to commit to the education of their children. I have decided to strike out on my own and create a community of my wedding families—built around Shabbat gatherings. And yes, I am passionate about this work, it's our future and our chance to increase our numbers, our gene pool, and our diversity.

Implications of the Call to Welcome

Yes, my work means we will have a different looking Jewish community. But just as adoption in Jewish families changed the face of what Jews look like, these interfaith families will as well. Some will do two sets of holidays and will put up a Christmas tree or eat Christmas dinner at Grandma's. Some will raise their kids Catholic, but instill a love for Israel—therefore creating allies for the Jewish state.

I have had to work through the self-esteem issues around this—from being an employed professional in the community to unemployed or self-

---

7   For a longer discussion of this see my post, "Naming the Stranger: A Defining Interfaith Moment," on interfaithfamily.com from January 30, 2013.

employed and performing the job of the community that most rabbis don't want. Sometimes, I do the dirty work of co-officiated weddings before sundown on Saturday. Given that I've interpreted this holy work as *pikuach nefesh* (saving a life)—which is allowed on the Sabbath, I've made peace with this path. Yet I've heard freelance rabbis referred to in derogatory terms such as "Rabbis who will do anything for a buck," or the work as "marrying anything that asks." The assumption is that these couples will never build congregations or create communities, and we free-lancers are undermining the community by serving them. I'm willing to be the pioneer and bear the stigma of pariah and prove some of this is wrong. These couples do care; they want a rabbi at their wedding—it means something! We must let the future generations speak for themselves.

My Recommendations for Rabbinical Schools

As for rabbinical school, I may have had one class on interfaith weddings—certainly not enough to craft a personalized meaningful ceremony for the variety of couples I have encountered. A best practice course on interfaith weddings would have been invaluable. The concept of *ger toshav* needs to be taught with applications for interfaith families. Perhaps new rituals, prayers and certificates of authenticity can be developed as part of the course.

As more and more private foundations enter the Jewish communal landscape, grant writing is an excellent skill to have, and one that rabbinical schools already possess. I was not taught any of the grant writing skills needed to find support for my visions. The entrepreneurial skills of marketing, social media, Google Analytics, and promotion were also not part of any curriculum, and I have had to learn them on my own to create a niche.

Finally, "How to Create Community" would have been a fabulous class to take. How to gather random people and create a functioning, sustainable group would be invaluable to me now. Managing group dynamics, developing infrastructure, and growing a diverse community is crucial to know for those of us who are striking out on our own. I have the couples, I have the families, and they are calling me back for their baby-namings. How do I harvest this for the Jewish community? I want to give them the skills and tools for building community and a rich Jewish life. Do I have to do this alone?

Intermarriage in the American Jewish community is here to stay. Our tradition already has a Biblical category to which we can ascribe membership for the non-Jewish partner. The category of *ger toshav* provides a vehicle for the non-Jewish member of a new couple to enter our community, rather than inviting the Jewish spouse to leave it.

In order to make it possible for the rabbinic community to serve these mixed Jewish families, rabbinical schools must train students to think of service to these families as kosher and not illegitimate. The entrepreneurial skills needed to support work that takes place outside of already-sanctioned Jewish institutions must be available to rabbis-in-training, with no stigma or opprobrium associated with seeking these skills. Finally, the greater Jewish community needs to study the impact of differential approaches to welcoming the non-Jewish partner or spouse into Jewish life. I am passionate about this cause of outreach—even willing to take the road less traveled—and believe it is the right approach for our families, our communities and our rabbinical schools.

*Rabbi G. **Rayzel Raphael** is an "unorthodox" rabbi. For the past 15 years her career has been devoted to welcoming interfaith families to the Jewish community. She has a private practice in the Philadelphia area counseling interfaith couples, performing lifecycle rituals, and welcoming couples to her Shabbat table. Rabbi Rayzel has also been the spiritual leader of three congregations, served as chaplain and worked for Hillel doing outreach to students. Currently she serves Temple Israel of Lehighton, PA. Geela Rayzel was ordained at the Reconstructionist Rabbinical College and studied Religion at Indiana and Brandeis Universities. She also studied in Israel at Pardes and at the Hebrew University of Jerusalem. Rabbi Rayzel is also a visionary artist and award winning songwriter/liturgist with five recordings to her credit. She teaches about "the Jewish Mysteries" - angels, dreams, Kabbalah, through music and art. Her most recent creation is a deck of Shechinah Oracle cards researched from Jewish text and tradition. For more information visit www.shechinah.com.*

The Praxis of I-Thou in the 21st Century Rabbinate

By Maury Hoberman, M.D.

In the 1968 American Jewish Year Book, the esteemed sociologist Charles Liebman, ז״ל, argued that the rabbi is the most important figure in American Jewish life:

> While individual scholars, educators, administrators, philan-
> thropists, or even politicians may assume leadership posi-
> tions and preeminence in Jewish life, none is as important as
> the rabbi. None has the direct and immediate contact with
> American Jews as the rabbi. And all leaders, to a greater or
> lesser extent, depend upon the rabbi to mobilize the Jewish
> community in support of the goals or programs they seek to
> achieve.[1]

More recent literature continues to support Liebman's assertion. In Rabbi Sidney Schwarz's now classic book, *Finding a Spiritual Home*, individuals sought synagogues in which they were comfortable. In every case, these were synagogues in which the rabbi led his congregation to a place in which each individual interviewed felt at home.[2] In *Sacred Strategies: Transforming Synagogues from Functional to Visionary*, Isa Aron, Steven M. Cohen, Lawrence A. Hoffman,

---

1   Charles Liebman, "The Training of American Rabbis," *American Jewish Year Book* Fine, Morris, Milton Himmelfarb, ed., 1968, vol. 69 (Jewish Pub Society, 1968) 5.
2   Sidney Schwarz, *Finding a Spiritual Home* (Jewish Lights Pub, 2000). Sidney Schwarz, ed., *Jewish Megatrends: Charting the Course of the American Future* (Jewish Lights, Pub, 2013).

and Ari Y. Kelman find that for any initiative to be successful in a congregation, that program must have the rabbi's full support.[3]

In my discipline, medicine and surgery, there are two aspects of developing a competent and effective physician. The first is a deep sense of responsibility to each encounter with every patient with whom that physician comes into contact. The second is the pursuit of excellence in whatever field and whatever endeavor that physician undertakes for the sake of his or her patients, as well as his or her sense of completeness. By completeness, I mean that the physician is accomplishing the goals that he or she set for himself when that physician entered the medical profession. At the end of the day, if the physician keeps these two goals always before him, he will have achieved and know that he has had a successful career.

Does this formula apply to the rabbi? I think it does. I have witnessed what might seem like a lack of realization of the impact that each rabbi has on each member of his or her congregation. We know that every word that a person says impacts the person who is hearing it. There is no place for a casual or non-considered word. This is especially true of our rabbis. Most involved Jews take the word of their rabbis very seriously. It is important, then, for the rabbi to consider every encounter with someone, congregant or non-congregant, with maximum care. In today's world, many consider the rabbi as the most knowledgeable figure they know. This may not always be the case, but that is the perception and that is what they want to believe. In that belief, the impact of every encounter is of utmost importance and the rabbi must be aware of this power in his or her execution of his or her rabbinate.

As a physician, my charge was to save lives. A rabbi's job is to save Jewish lives. My physician colleagues took our charge very seriously. I cannot say with certainty that very many rabbis see themselves in such a critically important role. Perhaps, what I see as a distortion of the rabbinate is not a 21ˢᵗ Century phenomenon. Yaakov Yosef of Polony, a disciple of the Besht (1710-84), describes the failure of the rabbinate of his time as due to:

---

3   Isa Aron, et. al, *Sacred Strategies: Transforming Synagogues from Functional to Visionary* (Alban Institute, 2010).

1. *The breakdown of the place of Torah*, which became, for the scholar, a means of achieving glory and fame.

2. *The drive for personal security*, which resulted in corruption and subservience to the rich.

3. *The concern for spiritual security*, the salvation of the leader's own soul, which led to the neglect of the people's salvation.[4]

How do these precepts apply to today's world? We learn so we can teach. One of the most important duties of the rabbi is to teach Torah to his people in such a manner that they can absorb the teaching, so that it stimulates curiosity, questioning, and a desire to learn even more. A subject must be taught according to the needs of each individual. In some cases, perhaps because of a lack of command of the subject matter, the teacher leads the student in a narrow path limiting the exposure to the larger subject matter, which would stimulate thinking and further investigation by the student.

The drive for personal security is evident when the rabbi lacks confidence in his or her vision and the sense that he or she has the capacity to fulfill that vision. Too often the leadership or board of a congregation pulls the rabbi away from his or her strengths to participate in meetings and projects that lay leadership is well qualified to carry out without rabbinic participation. Soon the rabbi feels comfortable in his or her role as the chief executive officer rather than the "chief rabbinic officer." The congregation and board of a congregation can pull the rabbi in so many ways until he or she neglects the original vision for entering the rabbinate. The rabbis fall into a trap and, then rather than being the people they dreamed of becoming, they become the people that Jonathan Rosen describes as "clerical administrators."[5] Could they also be called ecclesiastical functionaries?

In prayer life, some rabbis tend to lead their congregation's approach to prayer in rote performance of communal services. In those congregations, after many years, the conduct of services without passion becomes the standard to which the congregation becomes familiar, not knowing that there can be deeper experiences in personal and communal prayer. I believe that Dresner's book is worth a read

---

4   Samuel Dresner, *The Zaddik. The Doctrine of the Zaddik According to the Writings of Rabbi Yaakov Yosef of Polnoy* (Jason, Aronson, Inc., 1960) 86.

5   Jonathan Rosen, *Joy Comes in the Morning* (Frarrar, Straus, Giroux, 2004) 308.

and a re-read by every rabbinical student and every rabbi to help him or her keep grounded in their objectives without distortions and lapses into these pitfalls.

The requirements for educating a rabbi, perhaps more than any other profession, need to be multifaceted. He or she must have a firm foundation in Jewish texts, history and liturgy. Rabbi David Gordis points out that rabbinical schools have failed to differentiate between their roles as graduate schools of Jewish studies and professional schools. The model used in the rabbinical school might prepare one for an academic career, but has not adequately included considerations required by the contemporary congregational rabbi. Rabbis often enter the field feeling inadequately prepared to face the demands of the careers on which they embarked. Much of what they have learned about functioning as rabbis is self-taught.[6] The rabbi should know how to teach both adults and children, which are a special skill requiring training. He or she should have experience in pastoral counseling. Becoming expert in these skills could begin in rabbinic school with intense study and continue into post-rabbinic school years. In an active rabbinate there are many challenges that are not appreciated until the rabbi enters congregational life. Offering post-graduate courses in the many aspects of the rabbinate would be of benefit to the rabbi, members of the congregation and the larger community. When the rabbi does not pursue study individually and in offered classes, there is early burnout. Among the courses, that I feel are essential would be Jewish Feminist Thought. Through the work of Judith Plaskow, Rachel Adler and others in this field an appreciation for the Other is essential in an effective rabbinate.[7]

Here I am referring to an awareness of the I-Thou relationship described by Martin Buber.[8] Jewish Feminist Thought goes even further, and our rabbis need exposure to these ideas.[9] Because of the historic subjugation of women in the in Jewish society and society in general, women are especially well qualified to speak to the issue of

6   Zachary I. Heller , Ed. *Re-envisioning the Synagogue* (Hebrew College, 2005) 156.
7   Rachel Adler, *Engendering Judaism: An Inclusive Theology and Ethics* (Beacon Press, 1998).
     Judith Plaskow, *The Coming of Lilith, Essays on Feminism, Judaism, and Sexual Ethics, 1972-2003*, (Beacon Press, 2005). Judith Plaskow, *Standing Again at Sinai* (Harper Collins, 1990).
8   Martin Buber, *I and Thou*, (Gregor Smith trans.) (Scribner, 1958/86).
9   James W. Walters, *Martin Buber and Feminist Ethics: The Priority of the Personal* (Syracuse Univ. Press, 2003).

transforming an I – It relationship to an I – Thou relationship. This means showing respect for every living human being at the deepest level. "And you should love the stranger for you were strangers in the land of Egypt."[10] This should be the essence of every rabbinate. Praying, teaching, and being involved in social action begin with this awareness. A rabbi who does not observe this precept with all its implication will have a fundamentally flawed rabbinate.

The successful rabbi, just like the successful physician, requires a strong knowledge base, which he or she is continuously updating. Just as important is the ability to listen. What the physician and the rabbi need in their training is to learn how to listen not from the doctor's or the rabbi's frame of reference, but what the meaning and significance is to the patient or, in this case, the congregant.[11] If the rabbi continues his quest for greater knowledge after his or her years in rabbinical school and then applies that knowledge being sensitive to the needs of the community in which he or she serves—to each individual and collectively—he or she will have a successful and fulfilling rabbinate.

I have had many rabbis in this journey through life. Our small town congregation would get rabbis immediately out of rabbinical school, before they moved on to a larger congregation. Most of them were outstanding. Of them all there was one who, for me, stood out above the rest. I remember him well to this day, even though he was only with us for two or three years. Rabbi Hayim Halevi Donin, ז"ל, came to our congregation the year after my bar mitzvah. I am sure he was formulating his first book, *To Be a Jew*, at that time, because almost everything in the book was in the classes that he taught. I remember him as an extremely knowledgeable person. But what has made him standout, in my mind, was his approach to us students. Rabbi Donin had a quality of being, respecting us as students and as young people. This quality is something that is innate in those who have it. It can also be learned. Even for those who are naturally sensitive to others, studying Jewish feminist thought will enhance this quality.

---

10 Deuteronomy 10:19.
11 Robert K. Greenleaf, *Servant Leadership; A Journey in the Nature of Legitimate Power and Greatness* (Paulist Press, 1977) 274.

Post-graduate courses must be learning experiences in every sense of the word. This includes assigned reading, presentations and evaluation of the post-graduate rabbinic students mastering the material. With current technology, such courses can be offered through distance learning, allowing the rabbi to work the course into an already busy schedule, decreasing costs and time away from the congregation. This approach is already being used effectively in some rabbinical schools.

In 2008, the Alliance for Continuing Rabbinic Education (ACRE) was formed. This organization has brought together all of the rabbinical schools, all of the rabbinical organizations and independent providers to address the need for continuing rabbinic education. Today there are more schools providing continuing rabbinic education and more programs. Through ACRE, a research study is being conducted by Rosov Consulting, LLC to develop the metrics to determine the impact of continuing rabbinic education on the community in which the rabbi serves. This study will, in addition, help to determine areas of need and help individual programs adjust to attain better outcomes in addressing the needs of the Jewish community.

At ACRE's first conference in September of 2008, Rabbi Hayim Herring addressed the more than 100 attendee providers of rabbinical education. The title of his address was, "Study Leads to Action: Energizing Rabbinic and Congregational Growth." He outlined what might be accomplished through broader collaboration among the providers: developing the rabbi's role as a cultural mediator; educating in multimedia, multigenerational environment; and, cultivating faculty who are well matched for this kind of work.

A multi-year rabbinic curriculum, with concentrated study in the rabbinical school and continued study during the rabbi's engaged years, will address the rabbi's need for growth in his or her desired effectiveness in their community. It will, to some degree, decrease the isolation that the rabbi feels from the environment in which the rabbi works. It will foster the self-care for the rabbi and his or her family, which is too often neglected. The rabbi's continued learning, growth and competency in his rabbinate will be the result of his or her continuation of study. This is not conjecture. Through continuing education in other fields—medicine, law, teaching—the individual attains a level of self-confidence in knowing that he or she is achieving that which he or she had set out to do.

With this justified confidence, the rabbi presents herself to her board and congregation knowing that she is up to the performance for which she was engaged. The rabbi's congregation will appreciate her competency and her ability to lead. Through continued study and learning, there will be no need to present herself as anything other than that which she is. She will exude *k'dushah* as Hayim Herring addressed it in 2008.

Realistically, continuing rabbinic education does not mean that the rabbi will solve all the problems of his or her congregation; nor will a re-invigorated rabbinate alone guide us through the changes and challenges that are taking place in the Jewish world in the early 21st Century. What it will do is help the rabbis more confidently evaluate who he or she is and what he or she can provide to the community. This will enable the lay leadership and the rabbi together to maneuver the many rapid changes that are taking place in American Judaism.

The Jewish world is in the midst of a great paradigm shift, perhaps, as great as the paradigm shift that occurred almost two thousand years ago with the destruction of the Second Temple. If it were not for the rabbis at Yavneh, who transformed a Judaism centered on the Temple cult to the rabbinic Judaism that we know today, the Jewish people would likely have disappeared.

Essential to this new world is that the rabbis and the lay leadership must work together to create a new future. A rabbi who can inform his lay leadership of the importance of his continued learning for the benefit of the congregation will help to move the community toward increased Jewish engagement and community building.

In 2001, Rabbi Richard Hirsh led the Reconstructionist Commission on the role of the rabbi. The result was a publication: *The Rabbi-Congregation Relationship: a Vision for the 21st Century.* The report states that the sustainability and advancement of a successful community depends on *k'vod-harav* (the honor due the rabbi), and *k'vod-hatzibur* (the honor due the congregation). Rabbis and congregants are equally deserving of *k'vod*, and should express and live that honor towards each other and all members of their communities as a contemporary manifestation of the "tangible Presence of the Divinity."[12]

This *kavod* begins with the rabbi's own self-respect which will come about by the rabbi's continual growth, then by the community respecting the rabbi for his knowledge, insight, vision and support of community matters. The congregation should, with the rabbi's support, respect each and every member of the community and appreciate the leadership that a well-informed rabbi provides.

Our rabbis will lead us through these exciting and challenging times. They will do this having obtained a strong foundation in rabbinical school, which will be supplemented with a multi-year curriculum developed by talented and dedicated providers of rabbinical education. This is the formula for our continued march through history.

Dr. Maury Hoberman *is a retired Otolaryngology-Head and Neck Surgeon. He served in the U.S. Air Force in Germany. Dr. Hoberman has held leadership positions in the Jewish and communal world for over forty years. He is a founding member of ACRE, the Alliance for Continuing Rabbinic Education and is involved in new approaches to Jewish Education in synagogue schools. Dr. Hoberman is currently in the ALEPH Rabbinic program. Dr. Hoberman shares his life with his wife, Joyce, in West Chester, Pennsylvania. They have two sons and four grandchildren.*

---

12   Richard Hirsch, The *Rabbi-Congregation Relationship: a Vision for the 21ˢᵗ Century*, (2001) 11.

The New Jewish Neighborhood

By Daniel Cotzin Burg

Jews wander. Jewish communities migrate. Half a century ago these communities drifted on various wheel spokes outward, their institutional identities and Torah scrolls in tow. In recent years, a new pattern has emerged, and America's cities are bursting again with Jewish life.

The Old Jewish Neighborhood

I live in a Jewish neighborhood—or at least it used to be a Jewish neighborhood. If you watch Barry Levinson films like *Avalon* or *Liberty Heights*, you will see my neighborhood. It's called Reservoir Hill, but in those days it combined two communities: Eutaw Place, the grand boulevard with its elegant town homes and Lake Drive, which included several blocks east of Eutaw with still beautiful, but more modest row houses. I have congregants who still wax poetic about Manheimer's, the corner drug store, or Surosky's Deli on Whitelock, or playing stickball in the vacant lot at Linden Avenue and Brooks Lane, or sleeping in Druid Hill Park on hot summer nights.

For a number of reasons, including a mixture of opportunity and fear, plus racist and anti-Semitic housing policies, Jews moved away from Reservoir Hill and toward Baltimore County. By the 1970's, when Beth Am was founded in the old Chizuk Amuno building, much of the nascent congregation was still living in the city, but elsewhere. The neighborhood was now predominantly African American and increasingly poor. By the 80's, crime had become endemic and sidewalks abutting the former Jewish shops played host to open-air drug markets. By the 90's, two blocks of Whitelock Street—the entire commercial center of the neighborhood—were demolished. Reservoir Hill now resembled a bagel with a gaping hole in the middle.

The New Jewish Neighborhood

In recent years, Reservoir Hill has enjoyed a general resurgence and modest Jewish renaissance: young Jewish singles, couples and families have begun to move back. Crime is down, and vacant properties are at their lowest numbers in decades. A team of 350 volunteers built a new playground in 2011—the community's first clean, safe play space in years. Whitelock boasts an urban farm and farm stand, a community garden and a new park—the community's core, empty lots now an emerging green space. The school, remembered fondly by numerous congregants, is again on the upswing and slated for a total redesign next year. Druid Hill Park across the street, Baltimore's grand Central Park, once filled with shul-goers from dozens of nearby synagogues on Rosh Hashanah afternoon, boasts a refurbished zoo and conservatory, a new playground and swimming pool, a farmers market and weekend festivals from art fairs to dog-walkers and various ethnic celebrations.

But Reservoir Hill has been slow to transition. Poverty persists as do drug sales and use—though not near the levels of decades past. While adjacent communities like Hampden, Bolton Hill, Station North and Remington have prospered with restaurants, hip wine bars and cafes, our neighborhood's only commercial venues are a couple of corner stores and a liquor store. Beth Am remains the strongest anchor institution and the largest house of worship by far.

Those who crave gentrification might despair at our sluggish renaissance, but there are opportunities, too. Beth Am flourishes for many reasons including the neighborhood's great promise and potential. How many synagogues get to do social justice and community development on their front doorstep? In a provincial and still largely segregated city like Baltimore, Reservoir Hill is teeming with otherness. We are diverse ethnically, racially and socioeconomically. We are young and old, Jewish, Christian and

Muslim. This is our strength and our great challenge—to harness the energy of such a community to help refine and improve urban living.

From my perspective this requires us, the Jewish community of Reservoir Hill and the many synagogue members who live elsewhere, to reframe the entire notion of a Jewish Neighborhood. Where once a Jewish neighborhood was defined by a preponderance of Jews and Jewish institutions, we at Beth Am are focused less on Jewish quantity and more on quality, on a community infused with Jewish values like education, pluralism, *derech eretz*, social justice and sustainability.

What I Didn't Learn in Rabbinical School

Seminaries prepare their students primarily for two things: life-long learning and Jewish institutional leadership. These are good aims. Rabbis must be agile and imaginative, mining ancient books for new insights. Good schools impart resourcefulness along with knowledge. But institutional agility is harder to teach. The Jewish communal landscape, teeming with innovation, has largely sidestepped the synagogue. Organizations like STAR and Synagogue 3000 taught congregations to be welcoming, creative and compassionate, to transcend their static buildings. But they are no more and movement-based umbrellas are struggling to provide the infrastructure they once could.

The bulk of philanthropic dollars and attention in recent years have gone to synagogue-alternatives: Indie-minyans or pop-up shuls, Jewish farming, and novel programs, the bulk of which are targeted to specific constituencies. Ingenuity abounds. But this presents many graduating rabbinical students with a conundrum: innovate or surrender, avoid the congregational world and seek soul-stirring alternatives, or settle for synagogue life. Both synagogues I have had the privilege to serve have proved this a false dichotomy.

Why the Synagogue?

Synagogues are as essential today as sixty years ago. While other Jewish experiences may focus on education, prayer, community, or social action, what makes synagogues unique is that we do all of these with every kind of Jew. Our target demographic is Jews—not young

Jews or older Jews, Jews in traditional families, Jews in interfaith relationships, Jews by Choice, single moms, gays and lesbians or Jews of Color. We are here for any and all of these and that is what makes us absolutely vital, the central address in the landscape of Jewish life and living. The synagogue is the only truly cradle-to-grave Jewish institution where we can pray and serve, engage and learn.

Jewish Values Re-Imagined: The New Jewish Neighborhood Perspective

When people ask me the inevitable question, "Why do you live in Reservoir Hill?" I respond with three primary reasons:
- Shabbat observance
- Diversity/social justice
- The intrinsic value of living near my shul

The first two are fairly straightforward. The third, however, is hardly self-evident. Lots of people, the vast majority of people, live far from their jobs. City living helps some to cut their commute time down, but there are plenty of urban residents who drive regularly to the suburbs or distant parts of the city. Cities across the country, though, are creating incentives to live near work. Decreased fossil fuel use and increased alternative modes of transportation (like biking, walking and public transit) are an obvious advantage. But what about the simple value of contributing to one's own community—financially, ecologically and interpersonally?

The question is not only whether we rabbis and observant Jews ought to live near shul, but whether Jews in general ought to give this serious thought. Leaving aside the particulars of whether one should drive on Shabbat, I think the more salient question is, "What does it mean to commute to community?" Urban life is, at least partially, about wanting to shrink the geographic radius of daily living. City residents like the idea of walking to parks or neighbors' houses, cafes or the dry-cleaner. Might urban renewal offer a chance to rethink the value of walking to shul?

Otherness as Opportunity

"Because God is Other, God creates a world filled with difference.
Because God is Partner, all difference is filled with holy possibility."
– Rachel Adler, Engendering Judaism

The conventional wisdom about today's younger Jews is that they shun tribalism, but this is not really true. Jewish pride is at an all-time high, and young Jews appreciate Jewishness, if not always religiously. Jews in their teens and twenties come of age in a world where Adam Sandler's Hanukkah Song, The Hebrew Hammer, J-Vibe and *Heeb* Magazines are things of the past. They watch shows like Glee where central characters are Jewish and flawed, but where Judaism isn't a punch line. In the fourth grade, Mrs. Christiansen informed me that the word "Jewish" was fine, but the word "Jew" was a slur. It was perhaps true then, but not anymore.

Once, Jewish families looked to settle in comfortably contained neighborhoods and sought refuge in kosher markets, synagogues and organizational structures transplanted from the Old Country. Later, we trended toward assimilation, eager to move beyond provincial neighborhoods of immigrant parents. These days, Jews are looking to reclaim a place not of difference, but of distinctiveness within the whole. This is why public-space Judaism works so well, why so many are drawn to our services in a park, Israel-themed bar-parties or children's story time at Barnes and Noble. Fitting in no longer means blending in.

The New Jewish Neighborhood should be a place of Jewish pride, where being a Member of the Tribe means belonging and does not require you to compromise your values like pluralism, service or sustainability. Today's Jews are increasingly comfortable with who they are, more at ease in a world that is bigger than their own. Sometimes that world offers trends and tendencies in conflict with Judaism. But encountering otherness is also an opportunity to apply particular Jewish values in a universal context.

Prepositional Judaism: In, For, and Of The Neighborhood

Cities are where Jewish interactions with the other are most ubiquitous and obvious. When I first came to Beth Am, I learned of a post-N'ilah Yom Kippur tradition: taking the lovely potted flowers which adorned our synagogue steps throughout the High Holy Days and leaving them in front of our neighbors' homes. In fact, the first year I was here I completely forgot to remind people to do this. Some didn't, and folks from the neighborhood who had received a plant for years came up to me and said, "Hey Rabbi, how come I didn't get my plant this year?"

Leaving a plant on the same doorstep each year for several years is a beautiful tradition. But this tradition, thoughtful though it is, begs the questions: How many Beth Am congregants know the people who live behind the door? How many go beyond the initial and lovely gesture to hear someone's story? To tell his or her own story? To see the other face to face?

These questions led us to create the "In, For, and Of" leadership development initiative. In Beth Am's early years, while so many other congregations fled, it was a point of pride to remain in the city. But during those early years, when the neighborhood faced significant challenges, the posture was defensive, the synagogue a fortress. At some point it became clear that we needed to do more than just exist in Reservoir Hill. We had to assist, to volunteer, to be for the neighborhood. A Social Action Committee was founded, and a relationship with the local elementary school developed. Beth Am ran book and clothing drives, planted trees and helped to organize the Reservoir Hill Improvement Council and the Lakeside Neighbors Coalition.

But the questions remained: How might we move beyond seeing the neighborhood as a project and problem to be solved? How might we build relationships, soften boundaries of race, religion and class? How might we, in our own modest way, begin to undo Baltimore's sordid legacy of segregation? In other words, how might we be increasingly of our neighborhood?

The real paradigm shift, though, wasn't for those who live in the community; it was for the entire shul. We asked ourselves, "What is our individual and collective responsibility to a neighborhood in which we pray, eat and learn? How might we transcend the walls of our historic building and engage our neighbors? And how might we welcome them in?"

These questions have set us on an exciting path of strategic engagement with our neighbors. There have been big programs: 350 people coming together to hear the Afro-Semitic Experience, a Jewish/African American fusion ensemble. And a visit from best-selling author Wes Moore, planned collaboratively with half a dozen community organizations. There have been smaller, subtler achievements. We have congregants serving on the RHIC board, others on the design team for the soon-to-be rebuilt elementary school. Students in our Jewish Discovery Lab (project-based supplementary program) volunteer at the urban farm. We've hosted college students from out of state and Jewish groups from near and far. We created a program for USY teens moving them beyond typical youth-group volunteerism. They learned about the history of the neighborhood and then sat in neighbors' homes where black and Jewish residents told their stories. By the time the kids went to clear fieldstones from the farm expansion site, they had a sense of the community they were serving. They had, in their small way, become of the neighborhood.

Beyond Baltimore

Plenty of Jews live in suburbs where plenty of synagogues continue to thrive. Can any neighborhood be a New Jewish Neighborhood? Yes. While there are clearly differences between cities and suburbs, there is a critically important similarity—the vast majority of American Jews live and work among those who are demographically dissimilar.

Jewish tradition has always existed in the tension between the universal and particular, between understanding ourselves as simply in relationship with the other and casting our lot with the whole of humanity. Our sense of chosenness has sometimes meant a proclivity for the parochial. Even when Jewishness inspires outward action, being a light unto the nations has found us at times bordering on the triumphal. Such is the case in the realm of social justice where our posture has often been more about doing for others.

At Beth Am, we have begun to reframe and broaden Jewish tribalism. Where once the Jewish people consisted of twelve distinct tribes, now we are one tribe among many. And our tribe, looking at once to thrive as a distinct entity and actualize our universalistic values, must better understand itself in relationship with the other.

Rabbinical schools have an opportunity before them to help students transcend the false dichotomy of innovation vs. surrender. Synagogues are in crisis, and Jewish institutions are widely viewed as out-of-touch or irrelevant. This generation of rabbis has a critical choice before it: save the synagogue for the sake of the synagogue and fail or save the synagogue for the sake of the Jewish people and succeed. Congregations grapple with differences within such as inter-faith marriage or LGBT Jews, but fail to recognize the semi-permeable membranes of every day life and how those relationships affect the way average Jews think about their Jewish faith. It may very well be that the future success of Judaism in America will depend, in part, on whether we can overcome the mindset of the old Jewish neighborhood in favor of the new.

Daniel Cotzin Burg has been Rabbi of Beth Am Synagogue since July of 2010. Previously, he served at Anshe Emet Synagogue in Chicago. Ordained by the Ziegler School of Rabbinic Studies at the University of Judaism in Los Angeles (now American Jewish University), he holds M.A.s in Rabbinic Studies and Jewish Education. He earned a B.A. in Hebrew Studies and Anthropology from the University of Wisconsin and spent two academic years studying in Jerusalem. Rav Daniel is a recipient of the STAR PEER Rabbinic Fellowship, is a contributing author to Celebrating the Jewish Year: The Spring and Summer Holidays, *and blogs at www.theUrbanRabbi.org. He is a trustee of the Institute for Christian and Jewish Studies (ICJS) and was featured in the* Conservative/Masorti Judaism's *international quarterly publication and in* Baltimore Magazine. *Rabbi Burg recently served on Baltimore's Comprehensive Economic Development Strategy (CEDS) committee and lead Beth Am to create the New Jewish Neighborhood Project and "In, For and Of, Inc." a 501(c)3 organization affiliated with Beth Am. He supports pro-Israel legislation, traveling to Israel regularly, and has been a vocal supporter of Marriage Equality, Education, and legislation to restrict gun violence and raise the Minimum Wage in Baltimore. Rabbi Burg lives in the Reservoir Hill neighborhood with his wife, Rabbi Miriam Burg, and their two children, Eliyah and Shamir.*

Living the Liturgy:
An Authentic, Personal Path to the Rabbinate

By Rabbi Steven C. Wernick

Belonging to USY as a teenager set me along the path to the rabbinate. I belonged to the Emtza region (serving the middle states) whose motto was a paraphrase of a series of infinitive verbs in the *Ahava Rabbah* prayer—*lilmod, l'lamed, laasot*—"to learn, to teach, to do." As a teen, you don't often pay attention to words, unless they're in a rock song, but these three words spoke to me even then and later became the foundation of my rabbinate.

During my teenage years, I was profoundly shaped by the painful loss of my father's second wife, Judy Epstein Wernick, the only mother I ever knew. After her passing, I watched the words, "to learn, to teach, to do," take on new dimensions of caring and support through a *k'hilah,* a Jewish community that embraced me in this time of great sadness and trauma. It was this embrace of community that carried me through incredibly difficult times. In hindsight, I now understand that my many moments of personal introspection, of caring that I received from others and the Jewish learning they shared, were unconsciously directing me along a pathway and journey toward the rabbinate. A passion to "pay it forward" continues to motivate me each and every day.

Through my formative academic years as a rabbinical student, I came to believe that the essential task of rabbis is to be learning constantly so that the narrative of our tradition, its history and applications are always at our fingertips to teach and translate. My current role as Chief Executive Officer of the United Synagogue of Conservative Judaism (USCJ) has further reinforced my vision of the kind of rabbinical leadership needed for today. Frankly, in the name of that vision of Jewish leadership, we need to make some significant changes in rabbinical education.

Today, most students in Conservative rabbinical schools are on a six-year track. The length, coupled with the investment of money to graduate does not yield an appropriate return on investment. By the time our students receive their rabbinical ordination they are saddled with debt, which influences their ability to learn, to teach and to do. We could consider having a higher bar of entry, requiring incoming rabbinical students to have met certain requirements in Talmud, Bible and Rashi, through a gap year program in Israel or by enrolling in one of many stellar Jewish learning institutes, such as Yeshivat Hadar, to gain a basic introduction to rabbinic texts and methodology.

We could reduce rabbinical school from six years to four years, and emphasize learning a basic knowledge of Jewish history, ideas and practical rabbinic skills. Following ordination, we could implement a two year mentorship program with a rabbi who is specially trained and then suggest the academic institutions grant an additional certificate to a rabbi after he has completed a mentorship program that gives him or her additional credentials.

Indeed, rabbinical schools can learn a lot from the medical school model. For instance, there should be a continuing education requirement that employers support, demonstrating their belief in the ideal of continuing education as a priority for their rabbis. Primarily, there is a need for advanced learning in skills, such as leadership, board development, fundraising, pastoral care, use of technology and practical rabbinics. The need for the acquisition of these advanced skills are often sidetracked or take a back seat to knowledge of classical Jewish texts once rabbis are working in congregations.

We should also make sure rabbinical education has an additional focus on self-care. Rabbis make sacrifices when entering the rabbinate. However, rabbis can learn how to create their own boundaries so that the sacrifices they make are not self-defeating or, even worse, harmful to members of the communities.

Rabbis need to learn how to lead collaboratively. A flatter, non-hierarchical view of leadership is more effective as a model for today. The "grand conversation" that United Synagogue introduced at our Centennial celebration in Baltimore in the fall of 2013 was built around this concept. By learning the value of collaborations that empower others, a rabbi can provide more value to his or her congregants.

Also important is our work on inclusion across the spectrum of need and lifestyle. This work is as holy as our ritual observance. At United Synagogue, we put a lot of effort, thought and care into the creation of safe spaces within our synagogues, and our youth organization to this end.

The face of our communities has drastically changed since I first became ordained. The conversations that are taking place in our congregations never could have been imagined even five years ago. The conversations we convene through USCJ with our k'hilot address key issues such as equality and job fairness. However, more discussions need to occur. We still have a dearth of qualified women within pulpit life, and we need to find ways to encourage women's voices to be heard throughout our congregations. Also, issues of gender and sexuality are ripe for discussion. USCJ is now partnering with Keshet, an organization that advocates for gay, lesbian, bisexual and transgender Jews. Sexuality and gender, and the new make up of what constitutes a family is creating new communities.

By adding opportunities for rabbinical students to learn about the diversity of the Jewish community in rabbinical school, rabbis will start teaching about it sooner and doing the work of changing synagogue models to reflect it. We have to challenge ourselves to expand our focus and serve the real, diverse, complex communities we are living in. Let's learn, teach and do—actively work to bring about living, breathing, authentic Jewish communities. Let us lead our lives as rabbis so that we might be *dugmaot*, role models for others on their spiritual paths.

Rabbi Steven C. Wernick serves as the Chief Executive Officer of the United Synagogue of Conservative Judaism (USCJ), leading the organization through a momentous transformation. A force for religious pluralism in Israel, gun control, youth engagement, relational Judaism and the revitalization of synagogues—among other causes—he has been named one of Newsweek's 50 Most Influential Rabbis in America *and was included in* The Forward's 50 List of Influential Jewish Leaders. *He has invigorated and expanded USCJ's national programs, like Sulam for Emerging leaders, focused on strengthening and transforming kehillot. He has also built successful partnerships with organizations like PJ Library, as he continues to redesign the leadership, membership, participation and governance paradigms for the United Synagogue. A contributor to* The Huffington Post, The Jewish Week *and other publications and author of the blog* Rabbi@theEpicenter, *Rabbi Wernick is married and the father of three daughters.*

Preventing Clergy Sexual Abuse

By Rabbi Ellen Lewis

Clergy sexual abuse is a problem that just will not go away. The news media inform us that Vatican officials had failed to report sex abuse charges properly and had moved priests rather than disciplining them. The Catholic Church suspends a local pastor for allowing a priest with a history of groping boys to attend a church-sponsored family festival. A rabbi allegedly took nearly half a million dollars from synagogue funds and congregants to hide an illicit relationship with a teenage boy. The problem of clergy who commit sexual abuse crosses denominations, geography and social class. The Rev. Marie Fortune reports:

> Research on sexual involvement between clergy and congregants is sparse, but research and media reports of charges and civil or criminal actions suggest that between 10 and 20 percent of clergy violate sexual boundaries in their professional relationships. Although the vast majority of pastoral offenders in reported cases are heterosexual males and the vast majority of victims are heterosexual females, neither gender nor sexual orientation excludes anyone from the risk of offending (clergy) or from the possibility of being taken advantage of (congregants/clients) in the pastoral or counseling relationship.[1]

---

1   Marie Fortune, "Sexual Abuse by Religions Leaders." *When Pastors Prey Overcoming Clergy Sexual abuse of Women*, ed. Valli Boobal Batchelor (World Council of Churches: Geneva, Switzerland, 2013) 15.

Reading about these cases, we respond with surprise and revulsion. Each time, we express shock that someone in a position of religious authority can violate the trust we place in him or her. Each time, we rightly call for swift exposure, condemnation and punishment, but all that is after the fact. While there are no quick fixes, there are steps we can take to make clergy safe for those they serve.

What makes clergy unsafe? In my experience as a rabbi and therapist who works with clergy, clergy are no different from other abusers in motive, just in opportunity. Although we might resist admitting it, we possess all the same human weaknesses as everyone else. We are insecure, desirous of being loved, anxious about doing the right thing, depressed about the state of the world, over-worked, confused about power and unclear about personal and professional boundaries. It isn't that we don't possess intellectual knowledge of the difference between right and wrong. What we often lack is emotional self-awareness and the usual outlets for talking.

It seems counterintuitive to think of clergy as people with no opportunity to talk. We commonly joke about clergy whose sermons drone on endlessly. Clergy talk all the time in all kinds of settings: from the pulpit, in the classroom, on television, in boardrooms and in hospital rooms. We speak as experts in those contexts. People look to us for words of truth and solace in hard times. We struggle to find just the right word in the right moment. But whom can we trust with our own deepest fears and doubts? We who live with this dilemma are a paranoid lot; we know we need to share our personal stories, but if we confide in a board member, we can't be sure our intimate details won't become grist for the congregational mill. And how can we be sure that that very act of confidence does not, in itself, constitute a boundary violation? And so we face the challenge of where to find friends if not within the community to which we are devoted day and night.

To further complicate the picture, people unknowingly project their own fantasies onto us. When I first started out in the congregational rabbinate over thirty years ago, one of my senior rabbis liked to repeat a story he thought was funny but couldn't explain. Every time he visited congregants in the hospital, he would walk into one patient's room and the patient would greet him by saying, "Rabbi, you look wonderful—so rested and relaxed. You must have had a great summer vacation." Then he would walk into the room of the next congregant, who would say, "Rabbi, you look terrible—so drawn and gaunt and tired. Didn't you get to take a vacation this summer?" People see us the way they need to see us based on their own personal history and psychology.

We clergy sometimes become confused by these projections. If someone in our office or in the hospital room confesses their love for us, how do we understand and receive that love? We need to acquire the skills to distinguish what we psychoanalysts call transference love from true interpersonal love lest our own loneliness and lack of emotional self-awareness lead us to look for love in all the wrong places. We fall victim to our own needs. That is how easy it can be for those who trust us to become the victims of our darker impulses. The clergy role itself invites our entrance into this dangerous arena. "The clergy role is *sui generis* for it is the only profession that wraps personal identity, professional identity and religious all in the same package."[2] The daily emotional demands alone can be dizzying. We spend the day switching emotional gears, moving from counseling a premarital couple to teaching seventh graders to consoling a bereaved family. Our own needs can get lost in the congregational shuffle.

And then there is the loneliness. Members of the clergy often enter the profession because they consider themselves to be people persons and yet end up feeling lonely and isolated. As Mark Brouwer writes:

It's ironic that pastors, who talk the most about the need for community, experience it the least. Our days and nights are filled with calls, meetings, and interactions with people. But despite lots of people contact, we have few trusted peers. We have too many relationships and too few friends.[3]

He goes on to point out the dangers of this kind of isolation: isolated leaders are more susceptible to feelings of sadness and loneliness, anxiety and stress, discouragement, temptation, and doing stupid things. We clergy, the very people who listen to the feelings of others and counsel them in an attempt to prevent them from

2   Lloyd G. Rediger, *Beyond the Scandals: a Guide to Healthy Sexuality for Clergy* (Minneapolis: Fortress Press, 2003) 22.
3   Mark Brouwer, "The Friendless Pastor," *Christianity Today* online, Accessed March 25, 2014.

doing stupid things, often are unaware that we are subject to those same feelings and temptations. Our isolation encourages an even greater danger of acting inappropriately. At times, we grandiosely and piously convince ourselves that we should be above having these feelings. Yet feelings do not just go away, however we might wish it; there are consequences to having no healthy outlet for their expression. Some of us are inclined to act in. We overeat, don't exercise, don't sleep enough, swallow feelings, and are susceptible to stress-related disease. We only hurt our families and ourselves. Others of us act out. We run from our feelings into the embrace of drugs, alcohol, and worst of all, vulnerable parishioners. The cycle becomes addictive. When you don't know what you feel, you are more likely to act on impulse. When you act on impulse, you avoid experiencing uncomfortable feelings. And that is what gets us into trouble. We lose sight of the difference between a loving relationship and an abusive one.

People often assume that those of us who enter the rabbinate do so because we love people. We're the only ones who know the complicated truth, that we enter the rabbinate because we love people who can then drive us to distraction. It's ironic in a way; it's not until we enter the rabbinate that we discover that the rabbinate is a great place for avoiding intimacy. Rabbi James Bleiberg makes the case that our entrance into the rabbinate and its conflicts is not an accidental one. "Broadly speaking, clergy lurch toward maturity driven by a deep hunger for connection with others. This movement is balanced by a strong aversion to uncomfortable intimacies rooted in our earliest experiences."[4] He offers an analogy that he frames as a contemporary *mashal*:

> To what is the inner life of the rabbi similar? It is like someone who is afraid of the water. At times, this person will carefully enter a pool or lake but prefers to venture no farther than knee deep. Avoiding water or making special accommodations to feel safe in the water becomes an underlying postulate of life. When choosing a profession, this person selects a field

---

4   Rabbi James Bleiberg, "A Pathway to Wisdom: Three Stages in the Development of Clergy," *Congregations* (Alban Institute, January/February 2002, Number 1) 1.

that on the surface appears to eschew water entirely. But incredibly, a part of the person's job description turns out to include serving as a lifeguard![5]

We rabbis are not immune to the deepest of human paradoxes, that what we want is also what we fear. The problem is that rabbis cannot feel whole when they are confused about intimacy. We all think we want it, but we unconsciously do things to sabotage our getting it for reasons that are quite individual. And if we are confused about intimacy, that confusion can lead us to look for love in all the wrong places. In an extreme case, that confusion can lead us to act sexually inappropriately with congregants because we are not clear on the difference between their need for our rabbinic love and our own needs for gratification. At those times, we must exercise enormous self-discipline. As Marie Fortune writes, "Even if it is the congregant who sexualizes the relationship, it is still the religious leader's responsibility to maintain the boundaries of the pastoral relationship and not pursue a sexual relationship."[6] We have to get our personal intimate needs met, but not from our profession. Our profession may bring us satisfaction and a sense of professional achievement. The appropriate way for a congregation to show its love is to pay us well and treat us well; it is important for congregations to do their own emotional work so that they can treat each other and their clergy in healthy ways. The appropriate way for clergy to love congregants is for us to take care of ourselves so that we can do our job.

Clergy need to talk, not just in sanctuaries or classrooms, but in environments where we can feel safe, with professional supervisors who understand the sacredness of the task. Supervision isn't a place where someone gives you answers and tells you what to do; it is a process of emotional education and self-discovery that requires an ongoing commitment. It can be a therapeutic experience, and it can supplement personal therapy. Among its benefits are the following:

1. Setting aside and protecting one hour a week is a great accomplishment for any rabbi. An enforced way of taking care

---

5   Rabbi James Bleiberg, "The Seasons of a Rabbi's Life: A Psychological Portrait," (*CCAR Journal*, Winter 1999) 3-4.
6   Marie Fortune, 19.

of yourself emotionally, it is an hour that is all yours. Once you get into the habit of doing something that is good for you, you might go on and do something else that is good for you.

2. It is important for the rabbi to get the view from the other side of the couch. It makes you more aware of how your congregants or clients experience coming to you for help. Rabbis need to have the experience of being listened to in order to listen well to others.

3. It supports your being helpful and compassionate without taking on other people's problems as your own.

4. The very contract of a supervisory relationship requires the setting of boundaries—when do we meet, where do we meet, for how long do we meet, how much do I pay, what if I cancel at the last minute, can I call between sessions. If you experience how someone else handles setting boundaries, it will help you figure out how to do so with others.

5. Talking in supervision and therapy makes people less likely to act out. Acting out can range from yelling at a recalcitrant bar mitzvah kid to going home to kick the dog to violating sexual or financial norms. Acting out happens when you have reached your breaking point and rarely results in anything constructive.

6. Talking helps you to become aware of all your feelings, including feelings you might not have been aware you had. It can help you tolerate feelings you might not like having. If you can tolerate your feelings, it goes a long way towards helping others to tolerate theirs. Even better, if you can learn to enjoy all your feelings, it will help others to enjoy theirs.

7. Being in charge of everything is vastly overrated. Rabbis have to have something they are not in charge of. Even Moses figured out that he couldn't be in charge of everything all the time. In supervision, someone else is in charge. We all have to have a place where we can regress and act like a baby without there being any adverse consequences. Your supervisor's sole job is to help you get what you want irrespective of the supervisor's needs.

8. Working in any group, whether congregational, Hillel, organizational, chaplaincy or anything else, recreates the emotional environment of a family and raises whatever old feelings you have about being part of a family. It is important to

get some distance from these feelings so that you can evaluate whether you are reacting appropriately to a situation in the present or to your old family in the past.

9. The rabbinate is a hard job. We are surrounded every day by people who hate us for no apparent reason and who love us for no apparent reason. Supervision helps.

10. If we expect our congregants, clients and coworkers to grow, we have to grow as well. Spiritual leadership demands continual transformation.

Putting feelings into words on a regular basis builds the emotional resiliency necessary to be a whole person whose internal security allows us to be safe with those we serve. It allows clergy to enjoy the satisfactions of an engaging and meaningful profession while enabling our constituents to benefit from our efforts.

It is important for our seminaries to train clergy in the ethics, texts and homiletics of our respective traditions. It is more important that our seminaries offer instruction about the nature of sexual boundaries and the right codes of conduct. It is that much more important for our institutions to encourage students to develop good mental health habits while in training in order for therapy and professional supervision to develop into a habit. And it is most important for clergy working in schools, hospitals, synagogues, churches and mosques to be in ongoing therapy and supervision, mandated and funded by those very institutions. To be sure, we cannot prevent all abuse. We can, however, do a better job at making clergy safe.

Rabbi Ellen Lewis has the distinction of serving both as a practicing clinical psychotherapist and congregational rabbi for over thirty years. After her ordination at Hebrew Union College in 1980, Rabbi Lewis served congregations in Dallas, Texas, Summit, New Jersey and Washington, NJ (named Rabbi Emerita). She works with rabbis and cantors in therapy and professional supervision to develop the emotional resiliency and flexibility required for contemporary congregational and organizational work. She has been a guest lecturer at the Wexner Fellowship, The Jewish Theological Seminary and the Hebrew Union College in numerous leadership programs. Rabbi Lewis, a Fellow in the American Association of Pastoral Counselors, was trained at the Center for Modern Psychoanalytic Studies and has served on the faculty of the Academy of Clinical and Applied Psychoanalysis.

Rabbinic Education:
More than an Academic Exercise

By Dr. Ora Horn Prouser

Any discussion of rabbinic education needs to take into account that it is by its nature different from most other graduate educational systems. Our thinking about rabbinic education has to take into account the needs of the individual student, the needs of the contemporary Jewish community, our responsibility to past generations, and our responsibility to the future. Each of these stakeholders may not have equal weight in every decision, but it must be recognized that each plays a role in determining what a rabbi needs to know how to function as a truly responsible spiritual leader.

I bring to this discussion my own experience as Dean and Executive Vice President of The Academy for Jewish Religion (AJR), a pluralistic rabbinical and cantorial school approaching its sixtieth anniversary. We take very seriously the *shalshelet haKabbah*, the chain of tradition. We recite the following to our rabbinic graduates at their ordination ceremony:

> Moses received Torah from Sinai and transmitted it to Joshua. And Joshua transmitted it to the Elders. And the Elders to the Prophets. And the Prophets transmitted it to the Men of the Great Assembly. And they raised up many students. And from their students to their students, to the teachers of Torah in every generation. And they transmitted it to us, and we have transmitted it to you.

This passage expresses that we as an institution, and our ordinees and alumni as rabbis, should remember their place in this chain of tradition. They should remember that they are links in that chain, and not solo practitioners only acting on their own desires and personal visions.

What does it mean, however, to be a link in that chain? A core value at AJR is that our students need to learn traditional approaches, and they need to learn the importance of creativity and interpretation of these traditional approaches. Creativity without depth and knowledge causes us to lose sight of our connection to others, those who came before us, and those who will follow us. At the same time, a rigid interpretation that does not leave room for creativity can lead to stagnation and spiritual loss. Our emphasis on both elements attempts to reach backwards and forwards along our chain of tradition. It shows respect both for those who came before us and for those who will follow us.

While this may sound logical, how does one actually accomplish this even in five years of rabbinic education? Our philosophy entails developing in students deep knowledge, respect for tradition, a humble understanding of their role as leaders, an understanding of what it means to serve, and a thoughtful acceptance of the responsibilities inherent in leadership. I would like to offer some thoughts based on what we have learned at AJR, and how we think about these issues. We work to accomplish our task through a combination of a deep philosophical commitment to pluralism, careful curricular design and refinement, and establishing an environment as a community of learners.

Pluralism

An overarching value of AJR is that of pluralism. Pluralism has become the buzzword of our time, used even by many within the denominations. In the denominational context, the word has been used to express a range of acceptable opinions, though that range is carefully constrained within movement parameters. Alternatively, it is used to express an approach designed more effectively to draw people in, or better to serve those with different viewpoints. In some cases this is similar to the *keruv* approach, meaning that the aim is to draw others in to the world view of the movement. While such pluralistic elements of rabbinic education among the denominational movements of Judaism allow for differences of opinion, the approach is still within carefully defined parameters.

Rabbinic education within a truly pluralistic, non-denominational environment is unique. The foundation of this education is its pluralistic approach: its appreciation of, and principled commitment to diversity. This finds expression in the educational system in a range of ways. First and foremost is the range of opinions and voices one hears in every class on a daily basis. This occurs not only through the variety of religious perspectives represented by faculty, or by the requirement that class instructors present a range of perspectives. This occurs because students naturally and instinctively bring a variety of views and approaches into the classrooms, into their *chevruta* study, into the hallways, and into all of their interactions. This range of and respect for opinions generates an organic and continuous communal conversation, in which people don't feel the need to dig their heels in to convince others of their points of view. Rather, they question, struggle, interact, and discuss, leading to a deepening, and often a rethinking, of each person's individual perspective and approach.

An atmosphere which includes such robust diversity also naturally includes training in expressing that diversity. Students learn to share their approaches to Jewish law, and their theological and spiritual journeys, and to listen appreciatively to the approaches and journeys of others. What is respected and, more critically, expected, is honesty and passion. No one is expected to have dogmatic answers to what a Jewish life must be, but rather to be able to explain their own approach to Jewish living. Students do not feel the need to defend their own approaches as exclusively correct or authentic, since multiple paths are the norm. This makes it possible for students and faculty from all parts of the rich spectrum of Jewish life to study and learn together. Individuals from the "right" and from the "left" who feel attacked or alienated by their own movements when they don't fit perfectly into the normative approach, find that they fit at a pluralistic institution because of the emphasis on passion and the desire of each individual to appreciate and understand the Jewish lives of others. This type of empathetic listening and deep appreciation entails viewing everyone as individuals worthy of attention and respect.

The approach to prayer at AJR is a good example of this philosophy in action. Praying in a pluralistic environment is necessarily complicated. The approach at AJR is that when we pray as a community, we all agree to follow the individual leading the prayer service. The prayer leader can decide to make the service traditional, creative, meditative, or an eclectic combination of styles. The prayer leader, for example, might decide to follow a liturgy that includes matriarchs or one that does not. Each member of the minyan experiences the prayer service as presented. Although this means that there are times that people feel comfortable, and other times that they do not, we are committed to this concept as a community. It supports our pluralistic ideal. It causes individuals to experience prayer services that are not their norm, and thus to confront their own approach and understanding of prayer. Many people discover that once they experience a form of prayer that they are not used to, they see it as meaningful, and absorb elements of this style into their own prayer practice. This is an example of how a pluralistic approach leads to a widening of perspectives, causes individuals to struggle with their own ideas, and ultimately leads to appreciation and understanding, and to personal spiritual and professional growth.

Curriculum

Rabbinic curricula include many different areas and elements. Students need to learn a wide range of sacred literature including biblical, rabbinic, and liturgical texts, history, philosophy, Hebrew, pastoral skills, education, and synagogue skills. At the same time, the student needs to develop as an individual, as a Jew, as a member of the larger Jewish community, and as a leader. This range of material is daunting. Interestingly, when AJR students are asked what the hardest part of rabbinical school is, one may expect the answer to be the study of Talmud or learning Aramaic. The answer most often given, however, is that the hardest part of rabbinical school is the work each student needs to do on him or herself. To develop into a rabbi who can fulfill all of these various responsibilities entails tremendous personal work and development.

Curricular decisions are made at AJR with all of these issues in mind. The curriculum reflects a desire that students should be steeped in sacred literature, learning a wide variety of texts in their original languages. There is a great emphasis on giving students the skills to continue the learning on their own. Thus, a major part of Talmud study involves learning the structure of the Talmudic argument, so that students will feel the accessibility of rabbinic texts, and acquire the tools to tackle texts on their own.

A major part of the curriculum includes courses on professional skills with students learning counseling, life cycle skills, homiletics, and the management and dynamics of conversion to Judaism. Each of these classes emphasizes that Jewish communities may differ in how they approach these issues, so students need to be prepared to serve a wide spectrum of the Jewish community. Differences do not only come from denominational and philosophical differences, but also because family constellations are different, and students need to have the sensitivity to address all of these types of individuals carefully in their work.

One characteristic that distinguishes MA or PhD graduate courses from rabbinical school courses is the importance of the spiritual and professional elements in rabbinic education. Rabbinic education properly includes not only the study of the text, but an understanding of the spiritual elements involved in that study, and thoughts about how to use this material in serving the Jewish People. Some professors are able to cover both parts of this mandate. At times, to cover all of these elements, courses should be team taught, or, less optimally, the material is covered in two separate courses.

A good example of AJR's curricular work is our Sacred Arts Initiative. This program brings together sophisticated text study and real work in the arts. The arts are used as a means of processing text. At AJR we have done this using biblical and rabbinic texts. While many people use the arts to study an interpretive gem, we try to take this to another level. For example, we have used the arts to study the *p'shat*, the contextual meaning of sacred text. We have shown that the arts are not only helpful in delving into interpretive material, but even in processing the tools used in contextual interpretation. Similarly, in studying rabbinic texts, we have not only focused on interpreting aggadic texts, but we have used the arts to express and process the structure of the rabbinic argument in the Talmud. AJR is probably the only institution in history to have used circus arts to analyze the structure of the argumentation comprising a Talmudic *sugyah*! This creative approach, however, in no way lessens the academic rigor of the enterprise. The arts are approached as a legitimate mode of interpretation subject to critical analysis, not unlike hermeneutics of the medieval Jewish commentators. They are not merely personal expressions that are only meaningful to the individual.

Studying through the arts serves several purposes. It provides for different types of learners, recognizing that people can learn differently and all study sacred texts. At the same time, it recognizes that those whose approach to life is through the arts often feel alienated from Jewish life and Jewish study, which have often emphasized the analytical and discouraged graphic representation. This type of approach opens the door to all Jews and all types of learners. This initiative brings together AJR's pluralistic philosophy, inclusive approach, and emphasis on diversity. At the same time, it epitomizes AJR's approach that we combine traditional study and text, and combine it with creative approaches.

Community of Learners

The AJR community experience serves students well as they go out to work in the Jewish world. The appreciation that they develop for the individual enhances students' ability to work with the Jewish community with respect and openness. AJR's enthusiastic inclusion of second career students is in keeping with this philosophy. The role of second career students goes back decades. An institution founded on diversity and pluralism not only accepts but cherishes the role of those who come to spiritual leadership as a second career. These students enhance the diversity of the community by virtue of their various religious viewpoints, ages, occupations, interests, and family dynamics. Students learn that they can't make assumptions about anyone else. They learn that each person needs to be treated as an individual with his or her own needs, desires, and aspirations, which can't be strictly or reliably categorized by mere age, profession, or prior life experience.

A further element of the AJR community is the non-competitive atmosphere within the student population, and the warm and supportive relationships among all members of the community: administration, faculty, and students. Students who operate within this type of supportive environment learn that true engagement can occur when each person is not only looking out for him or herself. They discover that communal support, encouragement, the value of the individual, and constant respect for the dignity of the other provide the safe atmosphere for true personal growth, leadership development, and mutual attentiveness.

The principles shaping this community of learners is not only helpful during the time when rabbis are studying toward their degrees. It serves them well throughout the careers for which the Academy prepares them. A rabbinical program should create an atmosphere that models that which rabbis should work toward in their own communities and institutions. The institution of learning should model concern for each student as an individual. That means not only caring for their educational needs, but recognizing that each individual comes to school with a full array of other issues, including professional obligations, family commitments, personal concerns, and more. By showing our concern for the whole person, and recognizing the uniqueness and individuality of each person, the rabbinical school models an approach to creating a caring and attentive community.

Each student needs to feel that he or she is part of the larger community of learners. They have a community to lean on and, at the same time, they have a responsibility to the community as a whole, and to their peers. Each member feels the joys and responsibilities of being a part of that group. The training of rabbis at the Academy for Jewish Religion thus models our vision of the Jewish community our graduates are charged with leading: a system in which individuals know that they are an indispensable part of something greater than themselves. They are links in a chain: each indispensable to those to their right and left, none sufficient or particularly effective outside of a principled bond with an extensive variety of counterparts:

Moses received Torah from Sinai and transmitted it to Joshua. And Joshua transmitted it to the Elders. And the Elders to the Prophets. And the Prophets transmitted it to the Men of the Great Assembly. And they raised up many students. And from their students to their students, to the teachers of Torah in every generation. And they transmitted it to us, and we have transmitted it to you.

Dr. Ora Horn Prouser *is the Executive Vice President and Academic Dean at The Academy for Jewish Religion, a pluralistic rabbinical and cantorial school in Yonkers, New York. She received her BA and PhD from The Jewish Theological Seminary, as well as a BA from Columbia University. She has published widely on the Bible focusing on gender issues and literary analysis. She has also worked with the Melton Center for Jewish Education, the Davidson School of Education at JTS, and various educational institutions to develop curricula and approaches to Bible pedagogy for all levels and learning styles. Her recently published book,* Esau's Blessing: How the Bible Embraces Those with Special Needs *was recognized as a National Jewish Book Council finalist.*

The Engaged Rabbi

By Rabbi Joseph S. Ozarowski, D. Min., BCC.

Everything I needed to know as a rabbi, I did not learn in yeshiva, but I did get some good things there. My yeshiva years in Israel and Chicago during the late 1960s and 1970s were fruitful ones. I spent time learning Torah for its own sake as well as picking up textual skills, studying how to paskin halachah, and picked up a lot of Talmud and a passion for Jewish texts. I was able to study with a variety of major and minor figures in the yeshiva end of the Modern Orthodox World. They did not all get along with each other that well, but I was able to pick and choose from all of them. I took a variety of other courses including Jewish Education—a little bit of high-level this and a little bit of high-level that. In addition, I had opportunities to shadow various pulpit rabbis in their work over a period of time. We did not call it "internship" at the time but in retrospect, that is what it was. My relationships with senior colleagues continued into my own pulpit years while serving in smaller and larger communities; these served me well as a young rabbi. All in all, it was not a bad rabbinic training education for its time.

Now that I am well into my fourth decade of rabbinic service, I have found that the field, the Jewish community, and the world at large have changed dramatically. Torah is still Torah and people are still people, but the structure continues to evolve, and evolve at a much quicker pace than before. The rabbinic landscape looks quite different than it did when I started as a newly minted Orthodox rabbi in the late 1970s. At the time, there were a few major "denominations," each with its own institutions, plus the secular world of Jewish institutions, such as Federations, Jewish social service agencies, and community relations groups. My world was the Orthodox one, both in terms of my beliefs and practices, as well as the basis from which I approached the rest of the world. Since then, the growth of Chabad, Storahtelling, independent (so-called "Indie") minyanim, online communities, Jewish Healing Centers, and Jewish Spiritual Direction has changed both the structure and nature of rabbinical work. As a personal example, the job I am in right now was not even a dream when I started my career and calling. I currently serve as Rabbinic counselor and chaplain for Jewish Child and Family Services. I do pastoral and spiritual counselling, hospice chaplaincy, work with Jews in recovery, help lead support groups, teach Torah to Mental Health professionals on topics of concern to them, write, research issues connecting Judaism and spiritual care, and serve as a rabbinic resource to the entire agency. Even the idea of a secular Jewish social service agency employing a rabbi to do "spiritual work" was completely foreign at the time. In order to do the work I developed towards and currently do, I had to equip myself over the years with other non-yeshiva training, including early undergrad training in psychology (from a Jesuit college!), a Doctorate in Ministry (from a Protestant Divinity school!), and I also became a Board Certified Chaplain. I still live in the Orthodox Community, and I still believe and practice Orthodox Judaism, but my work requires me to address the needs of the hour in the broadest definition of Jewish community.

The fact that the secular and Jewish worlds are far more open to spirituality and spiritual issues is a remarkable change. But ironically, it is accompanied by a distancing of increasing number of Jews from their tradition, faith and texts. Much has been written about the need to communicate these in high tech fashion. While I agree with this, it is not the subject of my essay. Rather, I wish to deal with what we need to communicate to our fellow Jews, and some aspects of how we ought to convey that content.

A Ridiculously Brief History of Rabbinic Text Training: My View

Rabbinical training has always been text based—from the Written Torah of Moshe Rabbenu, through rabbinic literature of the Oral

Torah, codes, commentaries, mysticism, and all the other rich aspects of our tradition. As the rabbinate became professionalized in the last few centuries, training has focused on text mastery. In the Yeshiva world of Orthodoxy, this has meant a deep knowledge and ability to teach Talmud, along with Codes and other sacred texts. In yeshivot, Talmud has been taught primarily via the "Brisker Method," a means of using conceptual logic from outside the text to clarify issues in the text. The critique of "Brisk" is that while its clarifications work, often brilliantly, they are not necessarily what chazal, the Talmud's authors, intended. Recently, there has been movement in the world of Orthodox yeshivot and among many teachers away from the "Brisker method" of Talmud study.[1] In addition to Brisk, Talmud and commentaries are studied in Orthodoxy to find the path to practical halachah, Jewish Law, which is based on the Oral Tradition. Both of these methods are used in "Modern" Orthodox as well as "Chareidi" (so-called "right-wing") Orthodox institutions.

In the main Non-Orthodox rabbinical schools such as Hebrew Union College and The Jewish Theological Seminary, the academic approaches to both Oral and Written Tradition have been taught. These involve source and literary criticism. I did not have this training in my early years, but I have picked up aspects of it on my own over time.

There has been some movement (though one might call it a synergy) in these two trends. One will find courses in Biblical and academic approaches to Talmud and Torah at Yeshiva University, and the non-Orthodox schools will encourage (or at least allow) students to study at Israeli yeshivot such as Pardes which, while liberal and/or non-denominational, teach more traditional methods of text study.

Both approaches suggest that one needs to understand that our Tradition is rooted in the past and connected to the present. The Rav, Rabbi Dr. Joseph B. Soloveitchik years ago[2] gave a most wonderful

---

1   Yakov Nagen, "Scholarship Needs Spirituality, Spirituality Needs Scholarship: Challenges for Emerging Talmud Methodologies," *The Torah U'Mada Journal* (2013) 101-133. Also Joseph Ringel, "A Third Way: Iyyun Tunisai as a Traditional Critical Method of Talmud Study" *Tradition* (Fall 2013) 1-23.

2   Audio of the original talk, given on January 1, 1974, is available at www.yutorah.org. Besdin, Abraham. "The First Jewish Grandfather," *Man of Faith in the Modern World: Reflections of the Rav*, Volume Two (Hoboken, 1989) 15-24.

talk at a simcha where several generations of the family were his students. In it, he envisioned himself as the elderly Rosh Yeshiva trying to teach eager young students. As he described beginning his *shiur*, he envisioned other sages of the past walking into the classroom, including his grandfather (who created the Brisker approach), the great Rishonim and codifiers, and chazal. They all participated in, through his teaching, a dialogue that transcended the ages. I have always been inspired (and continue to be so) by this story. It lets us know that we are part of something greater than just ourselves, that our study is part of a great chain that stretches back thousands of years. But along with the reverence I give to the Rav and his teaching, I have to say that it may not be enough in this day and age, at least not for students who are not already part of the system of learning.

Rabbis need deep knowledge of these approaches. And these approaches are certainly interesting to lay people who have 'Yeshivish' or academic training. But they are not enough to reach the thousands of Jews who have neither, are not seeking either, but are interested in what a Jewish text might teach them. They are looking for personal meaning in their lives, and they are or could be willing to study a classic text if it speaks to them. There are many critiques of the self-absorbed nature among contemporary Jews. But whether this is a good thing or a bad thing, it is the reality today. How can we teach Torah to our people today? How do we reach them *baasher hu sham*—where they are right now?

While it was not my experience, for the last generation, some rabbinic schools have tracked their students into pulpit, education, or chaplaincy tracks. Certainly each of these areas, if one enters these specialized fields, requires focused training. But more and more, as pulpits decline and rabbis are called upon to do a variety of tasks (either within their jobs, or to hold multiple jobs just to make ends meet), rabbis need to have a variety of skills at their fingertips. Pulpit rabbis need to also be educators and both educators and community rabbis need to have excellent pastoral skills. In the following sections, I suggest several ways that these can be applied while reaching people *baasher hu sham*.

"Playing Ball Mit Abaye and Rova:" Engagement with the Text

One of my sainted teachers was Rav Zelig Starr, zt"l who taught at the Hebrew Theological College in Chicago, Illinois for over fifty years. He signed my father in law's *s'michah* in 1940 and mine in 1977. He was a product of Pre-World War I Slabodka Yeshiva (in Yeshivish terms, a "non-Brisker"). He also had a Masters from the University of Chicago, and always enjoyed affixing that MA to our semicha certificates. Most of all, he had a pithy wisdom which many of his students still keep with us. He used to say, in his "Litvisheh" Yiddish accent, "Vell yes, you have to play ball mit Abaye and Rova, und you have to toss dem ball fort und back und fort und back; and if dem ball bounces from dem ceiling, it's vonderful!" He was teaching us that we have to be engaged with the text. We have to let the text speak to us, to toss it around, see what it means to us, how we react, discuss with others in class or havruta. And if it comes down "from dem ceiling," that is good too! He was suggesting that we indeed let the text speak to us as we wrestle with it, without preconceived notions about conceptual approaches or where layers of the text may have arisen. Those approaches are helpful to know in other contexts, but not as we try to present an ancient and relevant tradition to a modern mind. Jews today want to know how Torah can help their lives, for the big picture issues of life and death and the day to day issues of offering wisdom to raise families, in work, relationships, as well as in dealing with culture, technology, politics, and world events.

Here is an example of how I now teach a text:

R. chama said in the name of R. chanina: What does it mean, "You shall walk after the Lord your God?"[3] Is it possible for a person to walk and follow God's presence? Does not (the Torah) also say "For the Lord your God is a consuming fire?"[4] But it means to walk after the attributes of the Holy One,[5] Blessed be He. Just as He clothed the naked, so you too clothe the naked, as it says "And the Lord made the man and his wife

---

3   Deuteronomy 13:5.
4   Deuteronomy 4:24.
5   See also Maimonides, (12th Century Spain/Egypt) *Yad HaChazaka* (Code of Jewish Law), Laws of Knowledge, 1:5, who codified, "Walking in the way of the Lord," as the "Middle Way" or "Golden Mean."

leather coverings and clothed them."[6] The Holy One Blessed be He visits the ill, as it says, And God visited him (Abraham) in Elonei Mamreh;"[7] so you too shall visit the ill. The Holy One Blessed be He comforts the bereaved, as it says, "And it was after Abraham died and that God blessed his son Isaac...," so too shall you comfort the bereaved. The Holy One Blessed be He buries the dead, as it says, "And He buried him (Moses) in the valley,"[8] (Deuteronomy 34:6) so you too bury the dead.[9]

I teach this in classic Talmudic fashion, sometimes using "Yeshivish" intonations. I also often give a two-minute explanation of what is the Talmud. I cover the meaning of the text, the Biblical references, and note how this is legislated into Jewish Law citing the appropriate texts. But I also ask them what they—the students—see in the text. We discuss how "walking in God's ways" actually means being human, interacting with and supporting the most vulnerable members of society—the needy, the sick, the bereaved, and the dead. I ask them how they have experienced these situations, and how the text might inform them in the future. My goal to show them that the rabbis have a formula to becoming God-like, and it is not esoteric or other worldly. In the eyes of the rabbis, God wants us to be as human as possible. I try to show them that things they may already be doing are God-like, allowing them to Walk in God's Ways. There is also another benefit to teaching this way: I always learn something new from my students. They never fail to challenge me, to teach me new insights and ways I had not previously considered looking at in a text.

Lessons from CPE: Engagement with the Person

About fifteen years ago I proposed a course at Yeshiva University's rabbinic school (RIETS) that was meant to be a very basic introduction to actual pastoral work. Unlike what was being taught at the time, a primarily classroom approach, it was meant to be interactive. It was rejected by a high RIETS official with, "You see, Joe, we have the burden of being a Litvishe Yeshiva as well as an academic university,

6   Genesis 3:21.
7   Genesis 18:1.
8   Deuteronomy 34:6.
9   *Talmud Bavli* (Babylonian Talmud), *Sotah* 14; also *Midrash B'reishit Rabbah* 8.

and this is just too touchy-feely." But people who suffer in real life, who struggle with life's large and small issues already come to clergy for support, whether we seek those visits or not. There are several reasons why this is so:

1. Clergy have a rich tradition of serving their people's needs, and generally continue to maintain that tradition.

2. The various religious groups embody powerful symbols and literature offering comfort, hope and healing to people in pain. Theological themes, which assist those in need include faith, a prophetic context, ethics, the power of blessing, as well as the religious community's own resources.

3. One of religion's basic purposes is to foster love of God and neighbor, and thus love of one's self. Counseling helps a person in this direction and thus implements religion's intent.

4. People's expectations of clergy, clergy's context and setting within a religious institution, and clergy's goals of fostering spiritual growth all add to the uniqueness of their pastoral role as counsellor.

5. People with any type of religious instinct (even if not religious by any formal affiliation or practice) will generally trust clergy to be caring.

6. Finally, clergy are constantly available, and they are generally cost-free.[10] As a result, people will inevitably come to clergy for help whether clergy desire it or not. Therefore, it is important for clergy to possess training in this area. But more often than not, we do not have this training beyond a surface introduction. If at all, rabbinic schools will offer a course in pastoral counseling. However, one cannot learn how to do this kind of work in a course. Pastoral counseling and care have to come from engagement with real people, having a spiritual basis.

Spirituality and spiritual language is much more a part of society now than in the past. This is true of health care, where big picture issues of life and death are present all the time.[11] It is also true of

---

10 For a fuller treatment of this theme, see Chapter 1 of my *To Walk in God's Ways: Jewish Pastoral Perspectives on Illness and Bereavement*, Lanham, MD (Rowman and Littlefield, 2004).

11 See social ethnographer Wendy Cadge's book Paging God (Chicago, University of Chicago Press, 2012) for a deeper look at this subject. While Cadge's book could have used better editing and proofreading, it is a much needed study of the lives of chaplains, the history and effect of CPE, and, especially, how other health care professionals including doctors, nurses and social workers deal with spirituality in their work.

work with people in recovery. So much of addiction is tied to a lack of spiritual life and in so much of recovery, such as in the twelve-step movement, has a core of spirituality.[12]

At the outset that spirituality, as it is defined by both clinical work in the field as well as Western Pop Culture, is not the same as organized religion, but often draws from it. It is possible to be spiritual without being religious as well as vice versa.[13] Increasingly in the rabbinate, we are called upon to serve and teach Jews who claim to be spiritual but who are unaware of the spirituality within their own faith and tradition. One approach involves teaching texts spiritually, as I have outlined above. But there has to be more than just text teaching to touch people at the spiritual level.

In order to do pastoral work more effectively, I took several units of Clinical Pastoral Education (CPE), the accepted and accredited training for chaplains. Besides the professional lessons which have become essential to my work, and aside from the benefits of professional accreditation, I learned several other lessons which have enhanced me as a rabbi, and which, in my opinion, should become standard for all rabbinic training.

1. The person as a text: This term is not mine, but is traced back to Anton Boisen, founder of CPE. Just as we see sacred texts as guides for life and living, so too can we see other lives and stories as guides for us. This requires empathy and deep listening skills. *Mipnei seivah takum*,[14] as the commentaries explain, does not only apply to the aged, for whom we rise in respect, or even scholars, to which many commentaries apply the verse. It also applies to people with life experiences. We are bidden to listen and learn.

2. Flipping the rebbe-talmid model: This is the Jewish application of Boisen's model. Most of us were trained to listen and learn from our Rebbe-im, Roshei Yeshivah, professors and mentors.

---

12 Much of the literature on recovery terms it a "Disease of the Soul" and thus needs addressing via spirituality. The AA "Big Book," which is the basic text of Alcoholics Anonymous, has this as major theme (Alcoholics Anonymous, The Big Book, 4th Edition, New York, AA World Service.) Also see Keven McClone, Psy.D., "Psychospirituality of Addiction, in Seminary Journal, Volume 9, Winter 2003.

13 While there are a variety of definitions of spirituality present in both clinical work as well as American society, they all appear to center on issues of meaning, purpose, hope, often a "Higher Power" (which could be and frequently is seen as God but not necessarily), and an awareness of something/someone beyond ourselves.

14 See *Vayikra*/Leviticus 19:32, and commentaries of Rashi and Ramban.

We still do drink from their wells of wisdom. But to be effective today, we also should adopt the CPE model of learning from our clients and patients. In reality, this is a very ancient Jewish model.[15] In our case, the patient becomes our teacher on life and suffering. We come in with humility, a non-judgmental presence (very hard for most rabbis!) a listening ear and an open heart. We usually cannot fix their problem. But with presence and support we can help them by supporting them and walking with them. One can say we are "walking in God's ways" as we turn the teacher-student model in its head, by listening to and becoming students of our congregants, patients and yes, our students.

3. Reflection: Because our training is so based on learning, whether of the Yeshivish or academic variety, many of us are not trained in the art of reflection. What does a text mean to us? What do our experiences mean to us? This is not just a mere exercise in personal thought. We cannot be called upon to support people struggling with life unless we can reflect on life, its nuances, or its ups and downs.

4. Group Process: One of the great lessons of CPE is the need and ability to discuss and make decisions as a group. This means give and take, negotiations, constructive confrontation as well as conflict resolution. We actually have the Jewish version of model in *chevruta* and dibbuk chaveirim/chaveirot. My sense is that many of us, once on the pulpit, let our egos take a leading role. Being part of a group and allowing a group dynamic to function can help ameliorate this.

5. Less didactic, more presence: As rabbis, we are used to making judgments, being instructive, offering guidance, paskining Halacha. We do not always understand that people are not always coming to us for instruction. I recently spoke to one prominent and generally excellent rabbi who could not understand why some folks in his shul were not accepting of his advice. "Why are they not coming to me for guidance?" he asked me. I suggested that, in some cases, maybe they wanted to share things with him. The

---

15 Think *Pirkei Avot* 4:1 – "Ben Zoma said: Who is wise? One who learns from all people." Also Rabbi Chanina's dictum in Babylonian Talmud *Taanit* 7a: "Much I have learned from my teachers, more from my peers, but most from my students."

rabbi-student/congregant/patient relationship is not meant to be one way. Sometimes we need just to listen, to be there. We may even learn something along the way.

6. How to listen deeply: This is easier said than done, and it means using a variety of listening skills—including noting the surroundings, the person's body language and non-verbal cues, using mirroring skills (repeating the last few words of occasional sentences to let the person know we are hearing them) and actual reflective listening (reframing the words we have heard and saying them back) to let them know they are being heard. My own clinical experience is that when people in suffering ask painful and profound questions such as, "Why is God doing this to me?" they are not really looking for theological answers. They are looking for presence, for someone to be with them, to walk this path with them.

If I were designing rabbinic training curricula, I would require every potential ordainee to have at least a minimum of CPE training, even if they had no interest or intention to go into chaplaincy. The skills offered are immeasurably helpful.

Buck, Buck, Buck: Engagement with the Children

Reaching children is worth a whole separate work in and of itself. I am not even aware of courses in rabbinical school about children's storytelling. But I do know that rabbis need to engage young children more, to share a love of Torah and Judaism. There should be such a program.

Following the model of *baasher hu sham*, my own experience involves reaching children at their level. Aside from my teaching and pastoral work, I have created a whole series of (as yet unpublished) children's stories. Using talking animals and always based on a text or message, I have found this to be a great way to reach young kids where they are. I often use stuffed animals as helpful props. For example, my story *How the Chickens Helped God Give the Torah* is about how God asked the chickens, who were special friends, to help by waking up the Jewish People early prior to *Maamad Har Sinai*.

"Buck, buck, buck, please get up, *hashem* has a special present for us. No, I'm sorry, sir, I do not know exactly what the Torah is. I'm a chicken."

Of course they could not get everyone up and sadly some slept in; this is a root of our tradition of late night/all night Shavuot Torah study. When people came late they had to ask the chickens what was said at the Mountain.

The responses: "Bu-u-uck... *hashem*..... bu-u-uck... *Shabbos*.... Bu-u-uck... parents."

Of course being able to do animal noises helps. It is not important that everything be academically accurate or theologically pure. It is important that there is a basis and a message. It is equally important that stories are told in a whimsical, fun-loving fashion. The latest research suggests that training at the youngest levels has an effect on adult success.[16] Why should we not include appropriate skills toward this end in rabbinic training? Young children who share a positive engaged relationship with their rabbis are likelier to maintain those relationships later in life.

None of what I have written is meant to suggest that we should deny classic forms of rabbinic training. Rabbis need to be deeply aware of and passionate about the basis of sacred texts and have the skills to deeply study them. However, without the skills to convey them to folks who lack our training, and without the pastoral (and child-centered) skills to engage people where they are, we risk losing them. I pray it is not too late. We need to be engaged with texts and with people, as we help them get engaged.

Rabbi Dr. Joseph S. Ozarowski is Rabbinic Counselor and Chaplain for Jewish Child and Family Services of Chicago, co-leader of the Jewish Healing Network of Chicago and Jewish Chaplain at Skokie Hospital. Rabbi Ozarowski is Board Certified by the National Association of Jewish Chaplains. An engaging, nationally known teacher and speaker, he has served congregations on both coasts and currently is Visiting Rabbi at Congregation Darchei Noam in Minneapolis. He received his undergraduate degree from Loyola University of Chicago, his rabbinic ordination from Chicago's Hebrew

---

16 There is a plethora of research noting positive outcomes after Early Childhood Education. For example, Cambell, Frances A., Ramey, Craig T., Pungellos, Elizabeth, Sparling, Joseph, Miller-Johnson, Shari. "Early Childhood Education: Young Adult Outcomes From the Abecedarian Project" 42-57. Online at www.tandfonline.com.

Theological College and his doctorate from Lancaster (PA) Theological Seminary. A prolific author and member of the editorial board of the Journal of Jewish Spiritual Care, *his volume,* To Walk in God's Ways—Jewish Pastoral Perspectives on Illness and Bereavement, *is a standard in the field of Judaism and Pastoral Care. As a local and national leader, he has served as an officer of the Rabbinical Council of America, Executive Director of the Chicago Rabbinical Council and is currently First Vice President of the Chicago Board of Rabbis. He was cited by the Chicago Jewish News as one of the "Top Jewish Chicagoans of 2013." Rabbi Ozarowski is married to Chicagoan Ashira (nee Rapoport) and is the father of four children and twelve grandchildren.*

Training Adaptive Leaders

By Robert S. Karasov, MD

I was raised in a large Conservative synagogue, joined a small Orthodox shul during my medical residency and another large Conservative shul when we moved back home, then had dual memberships as I drifted over to the centrist Orthodox shul. Nine years ago I was part of a group that broke away and started a small modern Orthodox shul of which I am currently president. I have studied regularly, frequently one-on-one, with Reform, Conservative and Orthodox rabbis. I am also a mohel and perform brises with rabbis from all denominations. I have worked with rabbis on Federation boards as well as at Camp Ramah, where I was a doctor for twenty years. It is my interactions with rabbis in these many contexts that inform my views.

Is there one rabbinical educational model that would best prepare rabbis for the multiple career paths they make take? The answer is obviously not. However, as a physician, I think the medical model can provide guidance on how to educate rabbis who will pursue varied career paths. Just like a pediatrician and surgeon need different training, so do a congregational rabbi and a Hillel rabbi.

Doctors' postsecondary education consists of three steps: undergraduate, medical school and residency. Doctors all get the same basic education in their pre-med college classes and medical school. This is partly because we all need to know the same fundamental information and partly so that we can communicate with each other during patient care with a shared vocabulary and basic knowledge of each other's discipline. The same model can be applied to rabbinical education in all but perhaps the chareidi community where frequently getting *s'michah* doesn't necessarily mean one plans a career as a rabbi.

Rabbis all need to have facility with Hebrew. When they don't, they sound uneducated. This doesn't mean they need to be fluent Hebrew speakers but should have reasonable conversational Hebrew and definitely be able to read Hebrew well. It is painful for me to participate in life cycle events with rabbis who struggle to read a Hebrew text. One might argue that with almost everything available in translation, this is not necessary. But to me, fair or not, it is a credibility issue. Rabbis should pass competency tests and be offered the opportunity to test out of these classes prior to or during rabbinical school if they are able.

All rabbis need a thorough grounding in *Tanach* (Bible), prayer, and ritual. No matter what role a rabbi serves, lay Jews expect that a rabbi can give them guidance on these matters. It is more difficult to make generalizations about Talmud skills. All rabbis should know the structure of the Talmud, know the main commentators and be able to lead a class on a section of Talmud even if it is done with the help of English translation. This is another credibility issue and is a very low bar to achieve. How much additional fluency they need depends on their career path and denominational expectations. Other minimal educational requirements should include introductory training in pastoral counseling, leadership development and project management skills.

Just as medical students complete pre-med requirements, many of the skills I describe could be gained prior to entering rabbinical school. The number of years in rabbinical school needed to complete this required core curriculum could vary based on individual proficiency. Students could then graduate to a post rabbinical school residency of sorts where they specialize in their chosen field such as: congregational rabbi, elementary education, high school education, Hillel, camp rabbi, nonprofit management or an academic career.

Each of these specialties would have basic requirements of classroom learning and real world hands-on experience. Rabbis could complete the requirements of more than one track just as doctors sometimes complete more than one residency. Rabbis could also return to rabbinical school mid-career to complete the requirements of a different track.

Many of these tracks do not entail denominational differences and rabbinical schools could join forces to offer classes on education, non-profit management, and leadership. This would also help build bridges between denominations.

Leadership and management skills are important and earn elaboration. These two terms are frequently used together, yet they have very different meanings and require very different skills. Management refers to the skills needed to keep an organization running smoothly. These include strategic planning, finance, human resources and project management. In most large institutions, the rabbinic leader will be paired with a business partner such as the executive director, business manager or chief financial officer. However, as a co-leader, the rabbi needs to understand the basic concepts and vocabulary of management in order to manage effectively.

I define leadership as the ability to help guide a community through frequently painful changes. For a rabbi, this may be around halachic issues, changing the culture of the synagogue, restructuring staff or changing hallowed traditions. Not having training in leadership sets up rabbis for failure and disillusionment when change must occur.

Adaptive Leadership, a model described by Ron Heifetz and Marty Linsky at Harvard, is one example of leadership education that could be very useful. It describes concepts such as technical versus adaptive issues, leadership versus authority, self versus role, and how to regulate levels of distress.

The first concept is differentiating technical versus adaptive problems. Technical problems have a solution and there is an expert who knows the solution. Much of rabbinic education prepares rabbis to be technical experts, applying what they know to give the correct answer—knowing how to make a kitchen kosher or fix a Torah scroll that has an error. Adaptive problems, by contrast, do not have one correct solution. They are problems that often involve competing values, or force people to choose among competing loyalties. They often force people to question their identity and the solution often involves a sense of loss. Adaptive problems require others, and usually the rabbi, to go through changes. Therefore, rabbis cannot fix the problem. They can only orchestrate the conflict between competing parties, helping them to see the underlying issues and grapple with the values and loyalties that are in conflict. Rabbis must establish a culture or holding environment in which everyone feels safe enough to honestly and openly share their thoughts and feelings.

Deciding on a policy for whether members can bring home cooked food into the shul kitchen or deciding on the role of non-Jews in religious services are two examples that come to mind. If the rabbi just decides as if it were a simple technical issue, he or she may polarize the congregation and congregants' anger will come out in multiple inappropriate ways. An adaptive problem can be recognized if an issue keeps coming up despite multiple attempts to fix it or avoid it for several years.

This leads to a second concept: leadership versus formal and informal authority. Formal authority is the role the rabbi was hired to serve in. The rabbi is given money and power in return for fulfilling the congregation's expectations. Informal authority is the authority the rabbi derives from how well respected she or he is. Overuse of formal authority, by an authoritarian style, usually leads to a loss of informal authority and makes the rabbi less effective. Leadership, as stated above, is the activity of helping groups go through change. Leadership is also frequently exercised by those not in authority. Rabbis must learn how to nurture informal leaders in their congregations and consult with them on a regular basis. These informal leaders will be critical to changing the culture of a congregation or blocking the rabbi's efforts.

A third critical concept for rabbis is distinguishing between self and role. Unpopular decisions frequently lead to intense anger at the authority figure. The way the anger is expressed often feels very personal and sounds personal such as attacking the rabbi's character or family. The rabbi, as the authority, is the face of the decision or faction that the congregant is opposed to. In the heat of the moment, the attack feels very personal and rabbis run the risk of becoming demoralized or getting sucked into the fray if they can't separate self from role. They must learn to recognize that they are being attacked because of the role they play and not take it personally. This is easier said than done.

A final concept is learning how to assess and regulate levels of distress in different parts of the organization. For congregants to be able to go through change in a healthy way they must first be aware of the problem and feel invested in resolving it. Too often, those in authority positions know there is an issue and try to fix it, only to get pushback from congregants about why things were changed. Congregants want to avoid the work of change because they may not feel it is not worth the effort. Heifetz calls the process of getting people engaged "raising the heat."

Sometimes, though, the heat is already too high. Some issues are so toxic and scary that boards and congregants are afraid to deal with them. Pushing through a change in this environment will lead to significant push back. Congregants want to avoid the work of change because they are too stressed. Interestingly, work avoidance due to apathy (heat too low) and that due to stress (heat too high) can look the same with people checked out or arguing against change. But the rabbi's response needs to be very different in the two situations. Rabbis must learn to recognize work avoidance and assess and regulate the level of distress. For change to occur, they need congregants who don't feel overwhelmed, but are not so apathetic that they are not motivated to engage.

I have focused on adaptive leadership as an example of one model of leadership that can help rabbis navigate the difficult waters of leading congregations. Learning these principles of adaptive leadership and having the opportunity to practice them during training can spare new rabbis from learning all of these lessons the hard way. Shuls often hire new rabbis because of dissatisfaction with the status quo and there are usually competing factions and loyalties left over from the previous rabbi. Technical training such as rabbinics, halachah and public speaking won't prepare rabbis to deal with these adaptive issues.

By combining a flexible educational model, which combines core competencies with specialization, 21st Century rabbinic education can meet the needs of today's students, make mid-career retraining easier, build bridges between denominations and meet the widely disparate needs of the communities and institutions that will welcome our new rabbis.

Robert Karasov has been practicing general pediatrics in the Minneapolis area for 29 years. As a Mohel he has done several thousand brises, co-officiating with rabbis from all denominations. He is currently president of Darchei Noam Congregation, a modern Orthodox synagogue and has been active in the local Jewish community including serving on the Executive Committee of the Jewish Federation. After studying adaptive leadership at Harvard he now teaches this technique to physician leaders at St. Thomas University. Married to Hanna Bloomfield, MD, Dr. Karasov has 5 children and 3 stepchildren and recently completed the Boston Marathon.

Twenty Years After:
From Rabbinical Student to Dean

By Rabbi Danny Nevins

I write this essay at a propitious time, twenty years since my ordination, seven since I became dean of the school that ordained me. I first arrived at The Jewish Theological Seminary (JTS) in 1989, just after graduating college, following a decade of Jewish searching and study. That journey took me from my parent's wonderful Reform *chavurah* to a black-hat yeshivah in Monsey, NY, and then on to more modern yeshivot in New Jersey and Jerusalem, as well as to Conservative congregations, Ramah camps and our campus Hillel. Each community gave me a glimpse of the Holy, but I also felt fragmented and idiosyncratic in my Jewish identity.

In college I had grown uneasy with the bifurcation between my religious mind, which cherished textual prowess and consistent practice, and my modern mind, which valued critical inquiry and moral reasoning. On campus we protested South African apartheid in make-believe shantytowns, and I initiated dialogue between Jewish and Arab students. At a Lutheran church I volunteered in a homeless shelter, while at Hillel I read Torah and spent Shabbatot singing *z'mirot*. Present-tense political problems were becoming the most compelling theater of religious meaning. As a history major, I learned to examine the context and agenda of every author that I encountered. But in the realm of Torah, I continued to inhabit a pre-modern consciousness of revealed truths, unchanging norms, and a spiritual hierarchy that conveniently placed me, a Jewish heterosexual male, at the very top of God's order. There was growing tension between the way I observed the world and the way I observed mitzvot, between the lens used to study the humanities and the lens employed to study Torah.

As I sought a more integrated sense of learning and living, with mitzvot and common sense morality in constant dialogue if not perfect harmony, it became clear that I needed to engage more, not less, in my religious education, and that I had to find a place that would welcome and challenge my spiritual growth. I was required to adjust my grip on tradition in order to experience its vitality more fully. From one scholar I acquired the expression, "to find a usable past," which meant learning to segregate regressive elements of my tradition and highlight its redemptive ones, while looking honestly at the complex record of our religion, and seeking insights even in its less palatable features.

By the time I entered rabbinical school, the worlds of Talmud Torah, of Jewish history and theology were familiar to me, but the information had entered my mind hodge-podge, with no organizational principles and no overarching themes. When I arrived at The Jewish Theological Seminary in 1989, it felt too good to be true. There I was able to study our classical literature at the highest levels while inviting the independent and critical consciousness of the modern academy to guide my exploration. In an egalitarian setting, I could ask foundational questions about the covenant, and begin to ponder moral quandaries such as the untenable position of gay and lesbian Jews in the realm of traditional halachah. At JTS I would engage in Jewish literature that had barely registered in my yeshivah education: the Bible itself, the midrashic collections, Kabbalah, and also the secular literary products of modern Jewish experience.

I benefited from a graduate fellowship granted by the Wexner Foundation that brought me into contact with an all-star cast of Jewish leaders and peers from across a broad spectrum of the Jewish world. Pairing my JTS education with the semi-annual retreats of the Wexner Graduate Fellowship ensured that my rabbinic education would be both deep and wide. A program called Seminarians Interacting introduced me to Christian students and challenged me to consider my calling to become a rabbi. Sure, it was interesting to study Torah, and satisfying to practice mitzvot, but what was my purpose? What did God want from me?

For five years, mostly in New York, but also in Jerusalem, I explored the world of Jewish texts, becoming a better reader and a more nuanced believer. I was conscious of the professional side of my training, but it was never primary. For me, the goal of rabbinic education was to become a learned Jew, a generalist who could help contemporary Jews find guidance and inspiration in the Torah. Eventually I did take a few practical courses in developmental psychology and homiletics, and I completed brief field placements in a hospital and in a Brooklyn congregation. Moreover, I took jobs leading High Holiday worship, tutoring *b'nai mitzvah* and serving as a secretary for the Rabbinical Assembly's law committee. I continued to volunteer in nursing homes and homeless shelters, and came to see continuity between my religious and social selves. Fortified by my studies and by the rich friendships of those years, I began to assemble a rabbinic identity. Yet there was no forum for discussing the integration of these disparate elements of my Jewish identity. It was obvious to me that a good Jew would study Talmud by day and volunteer in a homeless shelter by night. But how did these aspects of being Jewish fit together? How would I prioritize them when things got busy? As a rabbi, where would I put my energies—into adult education or social justice work? What did the job require? What did the people desire?

Upon ordination, I took a rabbinic position in a large suburban congregation near Detroit. For the next thirteen years, I developed my rabbinic identity and also built a family with my wife and our three children. The concept of a servant leader was never explained to me, but I intuited the point. From early each morning until late into the night, I was involved in the lives of my congregants, and from them I learned what was needed. Becoming a father that first year in the pulpit was a radical transformation. Nothing shifts one's focus from self to other as dramatically as becoming responsible for a baby. We basked in the adulation of our family and congregation, but it nevertheless challenged us to transition from the self-centered lives of urban graduate students to the service mindset required of new parents and pulpit clergy.

There were days when my life felt balanced, but on others I was dizzied by the rapid reversals from sorrow to joy. I recall running one Sunday morning from a pre-marital counseling session after minyan to the cemetery for an unveiling, then back to the shul for a wedding, but en route stopping to say the final confession (*Vidui*) with a dying congregant, before finally performing the wedding; I ended that long day with a shiva call, and then trudged home, bewildered by the roller coaster ride of human experience I had ridden. Meanwhile, my wife and young kids had experienced a completely different Sunday filled with toddler birthday parties, errands and the sort of mini dramas that are hard to explain afterwards. By the time we reunited, there was no way to catch up.

Each one of my rabbinic encounters that day affected me deeply, but I needed to compartmentalize them from each other, and all from the experience of my family. The couple under the chuppah couldn't know that I had been holding a dying man's hand less than an hour ago, or that I was eager to get home to my own family. When I did walk into the house, and my young children would bowl me over with their eager embrace, it was never possible to answer their simple question of "Where were you?" Fortunately, my wife could and did support me through these emotional vicissitudes, but much of what I experienced was confidential and impossible to share. And how could I catch up on what she had felt all day?

In addition to facing the typical challenges of pastoral, professional and personal duties, I also wanted to continue my own Jewish learning. Each year I identified and attempted to fill gaps in my knowledge. I built relationships with rabbis of other denominations and also with clergy from other religions. I got to know the chareidi community through my Talmud *chevruta*, and I came to understand the nuanced differences between Presbyterians and Methodists from local pastors. From my remarkably knowledgeable and devoted lay leaders at the shul, I learned the budgetary and governance realities of a religious non-profit, the basics of fundraising, and the challenges of building new institutions, such as a community high school that I helped to organize.

Nothing in my JTS education directly prepared me for these experiences. I had received effectively no training in pedagogy, non-profit management, pastoral counseling, community organizing or entrepreneurial leadership. Yet I didn't fret over these blind spots. Thirteen years in a large congregation and a tight-knit Jewish community provided the best training I could imagine in all of these areas. I also benefited from continued professional training experiences with the Wexner Foundation, Clal, STAR, and other programs for young clergy.

Being a congregational rabbi gave me the chance to knit together a coherent narrative of Jewish meaning that might work not only for myself but also for other Jews. I learned to listen more than speak, and to ask questions before suggesting answers. My goal was always to help people find *sh'leimut*, or wholeness, in their relationships with each other and with God.

Still, when I returned to JTS in 2007 to become dean of our rabbinical school, I found that for many students, fragmentation was the norm. Few had charted a direct path through all the programs of our movement, and even those who had often felt the need to overcome many obstacles before embracing their path to the rabbinate. In many cases it was the strength of personal relationships with friends, teachers and mentors, more than the power of ideology, which brought them to the decision to become rabbis. Listening to their narratives of discovering that Jewish engagement and leadership needed to become the center of their career was exciting and humbling. I was eager to make their Jewish and professional education more systematic and supportive.

Fortunately, JTS had not stood still during my thirteen-year absence. My predecessor Rabbi Bill Lebeau and his team had introduced many enhancements to our field education and professional skills courses. In my first year as dean, our new chancellor and new provost both encouraged me to think big about curriculum, and I did. With the help of a faculty committee and input from students, alumni and lay leaders, I designed a two-stage curriculum which front loaded language and text skills, moved the Israel year earlier, and then dedicated the final three years to high level academic work and robust professional training.

In our new curriculum (which we have continued to revise nearly every year since), every student was required to earn a departmental

MA in place of the prior generic MA in Jewish studies from the Rabbinical School. Dual enrollment tuition was eliminated, and options were offered for every rabbinical student to earn a degree in Judaica from the JTS Graduate School, in Jewish education from the Davidson School, or in sacred music from our H.L. Miller Cantorial School. Moreover, the former succession of survey courses (medieval history, thought, and literature; modern history, thought, and literature) was eliminated, and in their place, students were invited to take electives in these disciplines. The goal here was to give students far more ownership of their academic experience, and less time marching in lock-step with their classmates for five years. By preparing for comprehensive exams or writing an MA thesis, the students would truly master a discipline and bring more value and marketability to their rabbinic careers.

An even larger agenda was to expand and integrate our professional and field education. We removed the peer-led course in life-cycle officiation from the first year seminar, and gave it to a practicing congregational rabbi to teach in the third year. We canceled the brief coaching sessions in homiletics (sermonizing) and created a full course on communications. We required courses in pedagogy, counseling, non-profit management and rabbinic leadership, and further developed our field education system with internships, seminars, and innovation grants for our students. We recruited younger and more diverse rabbis from the field to teach professional skills, and sought women and men to model rabbinic careers for our students.

One of the most exciting developments at JTS was the creation of a new Center for Pastoral Education. We were already encouraging our students to complete at least one unit of Clinical Pastoral Education (CPE), which typically involves 300 clinical hours and 100 hours of peer and mentor meetings at a hospital. Soon we had a licensed center of our own, only the third seminary-based CPE center in the country, and we began to require all rabbinical and then cantorial students to complete at least one unit. We also began to offer a certificate program in pastoral care that required a second CPE unit and twelve credits of course work. JTS began to attract seminarians from schools of other denominations and faith traditions to study CPE with us, and we developed a reputation for excellence in clinical education.

The landscape of American religion has been shifting rapidly, and it has been a challenge to remain true to our greatest strengths while also appealing to new styles of Jewish expression. Younger rabbinical students continue to crave the authenticity of deep immersion in traditional text study, yet many are also eager to move on to professional skills such as CPE that do not involve poring over the fine print in the back of the Talmud. There is respect for ancient normative traditions balanced by fierce defense of personal autonomy. We are supposedly in a post-denominational age, and yet the most active Jews remain affiliated, except perhaps during a brief stage of young adulthood. The JTS brand stands for serious engagement both with traditional text study and modern scholarship, as well as a balance between rigorous normative Jewish practice and a non-judgmental perspective. Like many learning communities we struggle to express consistent values and practices while also welcoming and encouraging diverse voices.

In this dynamic environment, JTS is changing. More of our faculty have welcomed a return to traditional styles of Torah study that use the informal environment of the *beit midrash* to establish an individual and collective learning culture. More classes include attention to questions about the personal and professional significance of the texts. Our worship space is now more inclusive of music and meditation, not just rapid-fire mumbling of the liturgy. We take time to process our emotional response to the experience of rabbinical studies and are in general a far more spiritual and supportive place than ever before. Still, students come to JTS looking for a rigorous academic environment and a diverse faculty, not just a modernized yeshivah, and this means that we value critical thought. Finding balance between the open atmosphere of the academy and the spiritual sensibility of the yeshivah remains the core tension of our Seminary. It is a productive tension, I think, and yet it is not always easy to manage.

One thing that has greatly helped in our quest for integrity and kindness is the increased openness to welcoming students of diverse backgrounds, including those from interfaith families, and those with different sexual orientations at JTS. As the student body becomes more diverse, our conversations become richer and our preparation to serve the evolving patchwork of Jewish life in America has greatly improved. Our general approach is to bring ancient wisdom into productive conversation with contemporary social realities, with the assumption being that this interaction, for all of its tension, can make us better citizens and Jews.

The winter of 2006-07 was quite eventful for us. The Committee on Jewish Law and Standards approved a responsum that I co-authored with Rabbis Eliot Dorff and Avram Reisner making a halachic case for normalizing the status of gay and lesbian relationships based on the demands of human dignity. We followed up with a 2012 paper on same-sex marriage and divorce ceremonies just in time for the spread of State and then Federal recognition of gay marriage. Soon after the 2006 CJLS vote, I was offered the position of dean, and JTS began to accept gay, lesbian and bisexual students. We worried that our gay graduates would struggle to find jobs but, with internal coaching and external interventions, they have been welcomed as talented rabbis and cantors bearing valuable gifts.

Little attention was paid initially to transgender issues, but with prodding from our students and extended discussion among faculty and staff, JTS announced that what had already been *de facto* would now be *de jure*: there would be no discrimination in either employment or admissions based on either sexual orientation or gender identity. We have a long way to go towards understanding the diverse forms of gender expression, but JTS had made great strides towards welcoming a more diverse student body and faculty. Classes on family law and life cycle officiation now include attention to the many forms of family arrangements in the contemporary Jewish community, and we are collectively attempting to bridge the divide between ancient norms and contemporary insights so that we can be at one as a religious community.

As part of a strategic planning process, JTS reorganized its administrative structure. I became dean of a new unit called the Division of Religious Leadership, which includes the rabbinical school, the H.L. Miller Cantorial School, the Center for Pastoral Education, as well as programs such as our summer Nishma Beit

Midrash. This structure has allowed for greater integration between our schools, and has made it easier to require students to study and build Jewish community together.

JTS is an accredited academic institution and as such, is responsive to the requirements of New York State and also the Federal Government. Like schools everywhere, we have been challenged to define our learning objectives and then to collect data in order to assess our institutional success in achieving these goals. Like administrators everywhere, I am periodically frustrated by the diversion of scarce resources to data collection and analysis, but it has been constructive for us to debate and define our learning goals more precisely. Recently we, like colleges across the country, were told to expand our faculty contact hours with students quite substantially. While this shift has complicated our schedules, our students will benefit from a more extensive and varied learning environment as a result.

Like non-profit organizations everywhere, JTS is receiving a larger proportion of its financial support in the form of program grants rather than general institutional support. Once again, this is periodically frustrating. Few foundations are interested in paying for faculty and staff compensation, recruiting costs, capital improvements or utilities, yet all of these expenses are essential to maintaining a strong institution. Nevertheless, the challenge to define new needs and to propose new programs has been healthy for our school. In recent years generous grants have allowed us to revise our Israel program and to create a new series of opportunities for students to study rabbinic leadership and receive funding for their own entrepreneurial projects. Even as old structures such as congregations in demographically challenged areas crumble, new structures are emerging, and we are preparing our students to lead the way to a vibrant Jewish future.

The rabbinical school that we are rebuilding at JTS responds to the fragmentation of Jewish identity that I experienced to a small extent in comparison to many of my students. Our ultimate goal is to allow students of Torah to feel at one with themselves, with God and with their community. As we pray on Shabbat afternoon, "You are one, your name is One, and who is One like your people Israel?" We seek to educate the head, to engage the heart, and to instruct the hands, so that our students can emerge as *k'lei kodesh,* conduits of holiness to heal the world. Integration, not fragmentation, is our personal and professional aspiration, and each year we come a little close to this never completed goal.

Danny Nevins is the Pearl Resnick Dean of the Rabbinical School and dean of the Division of Religious Leadership at the Jewish Theological Seminary. After his ordination from JTS, he served as Rabbi of Adat Shalom Synagogue in Farmington Hills, MI for 13 years, before returning to become dean. A member of the Committee on Jewish Law and Standards, he has written responsa in the fields of bioethics, sexuality, technology and ritual. These and other of his writings may be found at his website, rabbinevins.com. Rabbi Nevins lives with his family in New York City.

The ALEPH Program:
An Alternative Path to the Rabbinate

By Rabbi Julie Hilton Danan, PhD

The Path

As the Dean of the ALEPH Rabbinic Program, Rabbi Marcia Prager once told us students, "A rabbi is what you should be when you don't have any choice." For me, those words rang true. I had wandered far only to keep coming back to a girlhood dream of becoming a rabbi, a dream I'd had even before there were women rabbis. Although my Alamo Heights High School sophomore yearbook had messages written in it that began with "Hey Rabbi," in the year that I did both my belated bat mitzvah and Confirmation at Temple Beth-El in San Antonio, it would take another two decades until I began to study for the rabbinate. In the meantime I married a Sephardic Israeli, lived in Israel for several years, spent a decade in the Modern Orthodox world, had five children, worked in a variety of positions in Jewish education and communal service, and began leading a Reconstructionist congregation back in my hometown.

Through a long and winding path I returned to my original dream, the dream so compelling that I had no choice. By then, I had published a book for Jewish parents, spoke fluent Hebrew and had a strong background in Jewish studies, but my husband and I also had five young children, jobs we needed to keep, a lack of discretionary income, and an address in San Antonio, far from the few metropolitan areas in North America that are home to non-

Orthodox rabbinic seminaries. I had already interviewed and been accepted to the Reconstructionist Rabbinical College (RRC), but with my growing family was unable to relocate in order to attend. I was distraught by the loss of my dream until my late mother Betty Hilton and a visiting leader of the Reconstructionist movement both strongly encouraged me to apply to the ALEPH program.

Getting into the ALEPH program was difficult, even harder than acceptance into the RRC. It was clear that my academic transcripts, essays and an interview were not enough to guarantee admission. I needed to become part of the Jewish Renewal movement, a process that took about a year of acquaintance. As part of that process, I made plans to attend the Elat Chayyim Retreat Center, then in Accord, New York (now associated with Isabella Freedman Jewish Retreat Center), with my two-year-old, Arielle, in tow. When I arrived at Elat Chayyim, I felt like I had dropped onto another planet, one peopled by middle-aged flower children in flowing garments and embroidered *kippot*, who chanted, meditated, drummed, called each other "Reb," and hummed Chasidic *nigunim* while tending the organic garden. But beyond these externals, the first thing I noticed was the eye contact. Everyone looked me right in the eye with great compassion and tenderness, and I felt that I was seeing and being seen and acknowledged in a new way. After two days of feeling completely alien and ridiculously bourgeois in this Aquarian environment, something clicked. Simultaneously, Arielle, who had been grumpy and unhappy with daycare for the first couple of days, was suddenly blissfully contented and never wanted to leave. We had arrived at a new spiritual home, and as the years went by it became clear that I had found my true spiritual *mishpachah*, a community similar in intensity of commitment to what I had once sought in the Orthodox world, but egalitarian, progressive, and dynamically spiritual. Within a week, I felt my heart opening to a greater sense of love and connection: to people, to the environment, to a vibrant experience of God.

I was introduced to the teachings and personality of Rabbi Zalman Schachter-Shalomi, also known as Reb Zalman, the founder and grandfather of the Jewish Renewal movement, who has been described as the Baal Shem Tov of the post-modern era.

Reb Zalman was a visionary spiritual leader who combined a deep grounding in the pre-WWII Hassidic world and traditional Rabbinic and mystical sources with an unprecedented openness to world religious traditions. The first class that I took with him was "Credo of a Modern Kabbalist," a course that opened up a new worldview that was profoundly mystical and broadly scientific at the same time. And the davening! At Elat Chayyim, I found that Jewish prayer could be both contemplative and ecstatic. I wrote in a letter after that first seminar, "I have never davened like I did there with Reb Zalman's leadership. I felt like every davening before that was like a wading pool, and now I was out in the open ocean." Although undeniably a charismatic figure, Reb Zalman displayed no desire to be a figurehead or New Age guru. As he grew older, I watched him deliberately withdraw from active leadership in order to empower the next generation of leaders.[1]

At one class during my first session at Elat Chayyim, Reb Zalman quoted his own daughter, who as a child had asked, "Abba if we're asleep, we can wake up, but if we're awake can we be even more awake?" From my first week of involvement in Jewish Renewal at Elat Chayyim, as I described it in a letter shortly thereafter, I "felt more awake, awakened to a heightened and deepened sense of awareness in body, emotions, mind, and spirit, the Kabbalistic Four Worlds. It was such a transformative experience that I almost divide my life into BEC (Before Elat Chayyim) and ECE (Elat Chayyim Era)." Over time, I came to see Renewal as neo-chasidism, in the sense that it is a pietistic and pneumatic (Spirit-centered) movement grounded in Chasidic and mystical teachings, yet socially and politically progressive. One participant quipped that we were "the Reform branch of chasidism." Each student in our program seemed to gravitate to the particular Renewal teacher who spoke to the root of his or her soul as in the Hassidic courts of old.

---

1   Shortly after I wrote this essay, Reb Zalman passed on, just shy of his ninetieth birthday.

The Process

The ALEPH Rabbinic Program grew out of the old-style private ordinations that Reb Zalman provided to a small circle of students in the 1970-80's. By the time I entered the program in the mid-1990's, it had become an organized, independent seminary without walls. The program's self-description is "a non-denominational, highly decentralized program of learning which offers structured guidance and mentorship in pursuing the rigorous studies and practica which can culminate in rabbinic ordination."

The ALEPH Rabbinic Program was ideal for people like me and my fellow classmates who were mostly middle aged, approaching the rabbinate as a second or third career, and rooted in our local communities. Many of the students had advanced degrees in Jewish studies or counseling and were often leading grassroots congregations when the call grew so loud they had to respond. Many in my cohort were women who had not had the opportunity to attend rabbinical school in their youth. Some chose to complete an ALEPH program concurrently or after graduation from a more conventional rabbinic seminary. I ended up spending five years in the ALEPH program, which seemed to be a fast track, since some students take seven years or more. Currently, about fifty students around the world are in the rabbinic program, with another twenty-five or so studying in the Cantorial and Rabbinic Pastor (Chaplain), and *Hashpaah* (Spiritual Director) programs.

The process by which the ALEPH program turns a call into a rabbinic career continues to develop. I was in the formal program in its infancy, and it continues to become more sophisticated, especially with the Internet facilitating many new online courses. There is now an Academic Vaad of Renewal rabbis from varied backgrounds running the program, all who are accomplished scholars with PhDs. Each student now has a Director of Studies to shepherd her or him through the program, as well as a committee of mentors. While we were instructed to enter therapy and have sessions in spiritual direction, the program has since added a full-blown component of Hashpaah, which includes spiritual and ethical counseling. Although it has become a more formal and organized process, with a curriculum based on four worlds of experience and graduate level coursework in seven subject areas (mystical numbers, of course!), each course of study remains very individualized, its precise formulation depending on the student, his or her background, geographic locale, passions and strengths. This program is geared to students who are self-motivated and resourceful. Similar to a doctoral degree or even conversion to Judaism, it is not a matter of merely fulfilling course requirements, but of demonstrating that you have gone from one status to another, in this case from student to *chaver/ah*, colleague.

The five years that I spent in the ALEPH program were some of the most fulfilling of my life. I loved the process, the learning; I loved and still love being a student. In order to complete the course work, and at the suggestion of the program's leaders, I undertook a graduate degree, completing my MA in Hebrew Studies (focus on Rabbinic and Biblical literature) at the University of Texas at Austin (UT). This program was done in residence, commuting weekly from San Antonio, which was another horizon-broadening step outside my comfort zone. Professor Harold Liebowitz, himself an Orthodox Rabbi in addition to college professor, became my academic advisor, mentor, and role model of scholarship and *menschlichkeit*. At UT, the first class that I took from Dr. Liebowitz was on Maimonides. Although I had a good background in Jewish studies and had taken many courses at Bar-Ilan and Tel-Aviv Universities, here too, I was stepping up to a new level, a new intellectual plane. Maimonides was the key to understanding and unlocking the entire rabbinic tradition before and afterward. Over the next years in graduate school I learned to approach traditional Jewish texts not only with reverence and awe, but with proper methodology and precision. Graduate school became the complementary left-brain counterpart to my more right-brain experience at ALEPH. I subsequently went on to earn my PhD in the same program, writing my dissertation on rabbinic uses of the term *Ruah HaKodesh*, The Holy Spirit.

The academic grounding was and remains extremely important to me, but graduate school is not enough to make a rabbi. There were many other things to learn, from synagogue skills to life-cycle events, halakhah to voice lessons. How could I possibly fulfill all these requirements in San Antonio? As the old Buddhist saying goes, "When the student is ready, the teacher will appear." People in my community came forward, offering to teach me, guide me, or babysit my children while I went to conferences. The Jewish Federation of San Antonio provided generous scholarships for my study, and my synagogue, Congregation Beth Am, set up a fund to contribute. A local Conservative cantor coached my skills as a *sh'lichat tzibbur*, while a Jewish educator and musician trained in Israel generously provided years of private tutoring to teach me the melodies of traditional trope for each text and holiday. An Orthodox rabbi, who might not be able to sign on as a mentor to a female student, gave me use of his vast library for my study. I felt that the entire community rallied around my project of becoming a rabbi.

I was supervised and guided through the program by a committee of outstanding rabbinic mentors from a variety of backgrounds, including Reform, Reconstructionist, Renewal and Orthodox.[2] Each of my mentors, local or national, taught me regularly in private tutorials or coached me in different aspects of my rabbinate, from how to handle my first funeral service to how to lead the Days of Awe. The summer and winter seminars at Elat Chayyim were also an important component of my training. Our teachers were accomplished rabbis and cantors from diverse Jewish backgrounds. Topics ranged from Biblical or Chasidic texts, to halachic issues and life-cycle events. For example, when learning to conduct a wedding, we not only learned the traditional sources and laws, but explored contemporary issues such as same-sex unions. We were not just taught the words to say under the chuppah, but practiced how to stand, to have a presence, to chant liturgy in English as well as Hebrew, to involve a family or a whole congregation in giving a communal blessing. Through these many classes, my mind was open to new ideas and creative modes of prayer, my heart to bringing Torah study and ritual to life, and my soul to mystical knowledge and experience. Experienced Renewal rabbis were happy to answer my phone calls and guide my development. Not everyone in Renewal was a Jewish flower child.

---

2   The mentors on my committee were Rabbis Samuel Stahl and Barry Block, of Reform Temple Beth-El in San Antonio, as well as several Renewal-affiliated Rabbis from with varied backgrounds and ordinations from Reconstructionist to Orthodox: Rabbis Goldie Milgram, Pamela Frydman Baugh, Judith HaLevy, and (for a time) Gershon Winkler. In addition, I studied (and continue to study) with many outstanding teachers of all backgrounds, too numerous to mention by name in the context of this article, but all revered and appreciated.

For example, a U.S. Army Chaplain in the Reserves could relate to my role as a rabbi in a military town with active duty service-people and veterans among my congregation. I attended many phone classes, today offered in greater profusion as online courses. In addition to graduate school courses in Rabbinic Literature, I pursued private Talmud study and attended a Hartman Institute Rabbinic Seminar in Jerusalem and SVARA Talmud seminars in the San Francisco Bay Area. I also completed a two-semester course and supervision at the Ecumenical Center for Religion and Health in San Antonio, where I became a Pastoral Care Specialist of the AAPC (American Association of Pastoral Counselors), learning counseling and skills that were crucial to supporting my congregants through challenges and difficult times. Here I also learned the importance of supervision and of knowing and acknowledging one's own limits and when, where, and how to offer referrals.

When I entered the ALEPH program, like many other students, I was already leading a community, Congregation Beth Am (JRF) of San Antonio. During my time in the ALEPH program, my duties were gradually expanded to include leading the Yamim Noraim and all life-cycle events. I gradually did everything except for conversions, with which I was involved but didn't serve on the *beit din* prior to ordination. To many people in my community, I was already becoming their rabbi. However, I studiously used the term Student Rabbi out of deference to the ordained rabbis in San Antonio.

When I finally did become a rabbi, the *s'michah* ceremony was an appropriately beautiful weekend that included a *Shabbaton* and ordination ritual with laying-on of hands. I felt honored that Rabbi Arthur Waskow of the Shalom Center was the rabbi standing directly in back of me, with his hands on my shoulders as the formula of ordination was read and certificates conferred. I could feel the chain stretching back from him to Reb Zalman to the Sixth Lubavitcher Rebbe, Yosef Yitzchak Schneersohn, and all the way back to Moshe Rabbenu. The ceremony was then held at Elat Chayyim in the summer. Now it is just before the annual OHALAH Conference in January, where it is always a highlight for rabbis, students, families, and friends. I had set out to obtain a professional credential and fulfill a personal dream. In the process I had woken up spiritually and found myself personally transformed.

The Benefits

Something that distinguishes the ALEPH Program is its emphasis on spiritual growth, or what Catholics like to call spiritual formation. While most rabbinic programs now articulate the importance of spirituality, the ALEPH program puts it front and center:

> The foundation and center of the Rabbinic Program is the Mystery we name God. We understand Judaism to be the individual and collective responses of Jews throughout our history, both in thought and deed, to the ongoing manifestations of the Divine. In studying religious texts, Jewish history, and the visions and values of our spiritual leaders, we are concerned with how the Divine has been and is now being revealed through Jewish experience. And we are equally concerned with how we—as individuals and as communities—respond to Divine revelations in our solitude, in our relationships and in our work.[3]

When my children were young, they loved a picture book called Buffalo Woman, based on a Native American story about a young man who falls in love with a woman who is really a buffalo in disguise. In order to join the buffalo nation himself, he undergoes a ritual in which he is placed under a buffalo hide and then pushed and pummeled by the other buffalo until he is transformed into one of them. At some point in my rabbinic studies, I realized that this was a metaphor for my own process. I was continually being spiritually and psychologically pushed and pulled as I was slowly molded into becoming a rabbi. Each time I attended an ALEPH retreat, I felt stretched, my consciousness expanded. After a time back in my routine, I shrank a bit, but not quite where I had been before. I was definitely a different person when I finished the program from when I began: able to lead, to guide, to inspire others, able to direct

---

3   www.aleph.org.

the power of my role for good without confusing my role with my essence.

The ALEPH program is based on a system of mentoring, and rabbis really need mentors to do our work with spiritual, personal, and ethical clarity, and to avoid burnout. When, after ordination, I participated in the late great trans-denominational STAR (Synagogues: Transformation and Renewal) PEER (Professional Education for Excellence in Rabbis) and STAR Good-to-Great programs, I discovered that many rabbinic colleagues from across the denominational spectrum face burnout due to a sense of isolation in their roles. In some denominations, professional competition may be a factor, leaving rabbis afraid to admit weakness or vulnerability. STAR PEER attempted to counter this by assigning us mentors and *chevrutot*. For me, the process was comfortably familiar. In the ALEPH program, I had already come to rely on my mentors, whether the issue at hand was how to conduct a wedding, how to debrief a job interview, or how to handle a conflict with my board. The ALEPH Program now has many more courses in Practical Rabbinics than were offered when I was a student.

No matter how solid the academic and spiritual training one gets in rabbinical school, working in the real-life world of synagogue politics, personalities, and running a non-profit can be very difficult and requires a whole new set of skills. Reb Marcia told us upon ordination that we were beginner rabbis, just like our new converts are reborn as beginner Jews, and we shouldn't expect to be experts from the start, but should continue to receive guidance and supervision. Moreover, she counseled that being a rabbi is not just about loving Torah and spirituality, but it's also about loving Jews, and interacting positively with the members of one's community. If more new rabbis were sent to lead congregations with these guidelines, there would be less burnout for rabbis and damage to communities.

In addition to mentoring, collegiality with my fellow ALEPH ordinees and OHALAH members is a very important benefit of the ALEPH Program. OHALAH (Agudat Harabbanim l'Hithadshut Hayahadut), the Association of Rabbis for Jewish Renewal, now has over 225 members, including graduates of the ALEPH Program and other streams of Judaism, and some rabbinic students. OHALAH brings together rabbis of many backgrounds who want to experience and work for the renewal of Judaism and its role in *tikkun* olam, healing the planet. I truly see my fellow OHALAH members as sisters and brothers whom I can call upon when I have a personal or professional need. I rejoice in their accomplishments and we support one another through difficulties and challenges. When I attend the OHALAH Rabbinic Conference, held in Boulder each January, I am awed by the talents and backgrounds of our incredible chaveirim. I can and do call on them when I need personal or professional advice or support, and our OHALAH listserv has been an invaluable resource for me.

The Challenges

The ALEPH program can be very challenging to complete because it is so decentralized and requires a great deal of personal initiative and commitment. However, these are qualities that will stand the *musmachim* in good stead as they embark on their careers. The Director of Studies is there to make sure the students stay on track. As a working mother of five, I was already resourceful and self-motivated, but the program helped me learn to take advantage of every opportunity that comes my way for study and personal growth.

Translating call into career track can also be a challenge. In ALEPH and OHALAH we learn of employment opportunities through our listserv, but there is no formal placement system as exists in the larger movements. However, there are increasing positions available to rabbis outside the traditional denominational frameworks.

Other challenges result from how the ALEPH program is viewed in the broader Jewish community. For the most part, I see my fellow Renewal rabbis very involved in *K'lal Yisrael*, as I have certainly been. In general, as an ALEPH *musmechet*, I feel fully accepted as a rabbi (as much as any liberal female rabbi feels fully accepted!). When queried about the program, I find it difficult to condense my complex background and training into an elevator speech. I've rarely perceived a bit of a chill when I mentioned my ALEPH ordination, and have sometimes seen the ALEPH program ignored in the Jewish press or else mischaracterized as if it were a kind of simple correspondence school. Fortunately, these kinds of reactions are less frequent as rabbinic education becomes more diverse and the Jewish world grows more trans-denominational. Unfortunately, one denominational rabbinic association turned me down for membership, not because of my personal qualifications, but apparently because of boundary issues. On the positive side, I have been fully accepted by colleagues in my local communities in San Antonio, and later in the Sacramento area, who have warmly welcomed me into informal rabbinic councils. I am a member of the Northern California Board of Rabbis, and OHALAH, of course, as well as a Pastoral Care Specialist of the AAPC.

Conclusion

The ALEPH program fills a real need for committed Jews who want to become rabbis but are not able to relocate to attend a traditional seminary. It also provides a path for those whose calling to the rabbinate focuses on deep spiritual renewal and transformation. Since ordination, I have successfully led two congregations, one Reconstructionist and my current non-denominational post as rabbi of Congregation Beth Israel in Chico, California. I have taught Jewish Studies and Religious Studies as a lecturer at two universities, and been a guest speaker in many religious and academic settings. I have done extensive interfaith work: co-founding a Jewish-Palestinian dialogue group with a Muslim Imam in Texas and a tri-faith Celebration of Abraham group in California, and have served as president of my local Interfaith Council. I am currently constructing a website, Wellsprings of Wisdom.com, that I envision as a Virtual Retreat Center to impart a small taste of experiences that I had at Elat Chayyim in an online format. This career has been made possible largely because of my study in the ALEPH program. If it were not for ALEPH, the Jewish world would be deprived of the talents of many gifted people who feel called to serve. OHALAH (and STAR, while it lasted), are examples of groups providing real support to rabbis in the field, and such mentoring, supervision, and collegiality are crucial if we are to succeed in our challenging roles, nurture our communities, and avoid burnout.

A rapidly changing Jewish world needs new ways to learn, new ways to serve, and new ways to support rabbis.

Rabbi Julie Hilton Danan (rhymes with Moshe Dayan) leads Congregation Beth Israel in Chico, California. She was ordained through the ALEPH Rabbinic Program and holds a Ph.D. in Hebrew Studies from the University of Texas at Austin, specializing in Rabbinic Literature and Culture. Rabbi Danan has been a lecturer at California State University, Chico, and Texas Lutheran University. She is author of The Jewish Parents' Almanac (Jason Aronson) and is constructing a new website, Wellsprings of Wisdom. com, a virtual retreat center flowing with the Torah of mother earth.

Educating Our Future Rabbis

By Richard Kelber

Rabbis have the single largest role in shaping Judaism for the future. Therefore, the education of rabbis should reflect how we view the needs of future Judaism and the rabbi's role in shaping, transmitting, and perpetuating it. The views of the different movements will differ on these issues, but there will be some overlap. My perspective is most heavily influenced by my experiences of the achievements and problems of the Conservative movement, though I have appreciation of some of the views of the other movements as well.

Rabbis have many functions, and if anything, this is more likely to increase than to decrease. They are quintessentially the religious leaders of Jewish congregations and teachers. Congregational rabbis are full-time spiritual leaders at services, weddings, and funerals. They teach from the bimah, in study groups, formal classes, and one-on-one. For congregational rabbis, both past and present, individual counseling is also very important, dealing with all types of life events. This was very true in a functional sense for the traditional *ravs*, even if they would not call their advice counseling, nor use the terms or the techniques of a psychologist. Rabbis serve in congregations, Hebrew schools, Hillel houses, and universities. How do we prepare rabbis for all of these functions? Just to state the issue is to realize that educating all of the students fully for all of those functions is not possible.

Optimally, a rabbi's education begins no later than the undergraduate level. Though courses in Hebrew and Jewish Studies are certainly important, I do not view majors in those areas as sufficient. Significant course work should be encouraged in history, psychology, philosophy, anthropology, education, and communication. In fact, it is hard to think of areas that would not have some bearing. Even organizational leadership courses taught in business schools may be relevant.

Rabbis need broad and deep knowledge in the various aspects of Jewish studies: Hebrew, Jewish history, Bible, Talmud, holidays and observances, and Israel. These are the areas where existing seminaries are already strong. However, knowledge of these areas alone is not sufficient.

Many of our young are intermarrying, and many are not raising their children as Jews. Presumably they would do so if they thought it important to perpetuate Jewish religion and civilization. As a community, we are failing to transmit that message. Rabbis alone cannot fix that problem, but they are an important element.

Many congregants attend services only on holidays and for the life cycle events of family and friends. There are reasons for this beyond the ability of the synagogue to address, but rabbis must address one reason. A great many congregants do not feel inspired by the services. An oft-heard complaint is that services need to be more spiritual. The response most often heard from the Conservative Movement is that this is the fault of the congregants. I view this response as equivalent to a business blaming customers for not buying its product. It is not a helpful response. A business dies without customers, and it is hard to see how future Judaism can thrive unless congregants appreciate what it has to offer. Though some rabbis and congregations have made progress in addressing this issue, many have not, or have made only halting steps. There is also the general failure of the Jewish community to educate its progeny, notwithstanding isolated successes. The results speak for themselves.

Future rabbis must be trained to address dwindling attendance and sense of identity. Where we do not have adequate answers, we minimally need to provide our rabbis with the tools necessary to develop and lead the community to better answers in the future.

The spirituality and meaning of services was to some extent addressed, and to some extent taken for granted by traditional

Judaism. To enable congregational rabbis of the future to respond to congregants' needs, I think there need to be courses covering the following:

1. In what ways did traditional Judaism succeed in being spiritual? The answer to this varied in different places and different times. Which of these methods can succeed with today's congregations?

2. How have other religions addressed these needs in the past? What worked and what did not? What can still work in a modern context?

3. How are other religions addressing these needs now? Viewing the religious services of other denominations could provide helpful ideas. Not all of their approaches will be applicable in a Jewish context, but some may.

4. Music is an important component of spirituality if used effectively. As the composers/conductors of our service, congregational rabbis need to understand how to use and how not to use this important spiritual tool. To many congregants, the aesthetics of services are as important as content. I think that is understood, but it is not being studied or utilized effectively. Many services fall short.

There are congregational rabbis who appear to have addressed these issues with some success. How they have succeeded needs to be studied and disseminated. Other professions focus on the use of best practices. Rabbis need to do so also. There will not be one answer for all congregations, or even one answer for all members of a single congregation. Rabbis need access to different approaches so that they can be adaptable.

Rabbis need to be prepared to explain, from the pulpit and in educational settings, why Jewish religion and civilization are valuable, and therefore worth preserving. Various approaches have been tried. The most common approach has been to teach traditional Jewish texts and hope that the students infer their own positive answers. This succeeds with some students and congregants, but not nearly enough.

An approach that is seldom used is the direct approach. There is value in, and a need for, an explicit explanation of what is unique and valuable in Jewish civilization, and of its many achievements and contributions to the world over the centuries. I suspect that rabbis and educators are not teaching this way because they have not been given this kind of explicit description of Judaism's value in their studies. This might seem like a simple method of teaching, and a simple message to convey, but to reflect on it is to realize that it is not so simple. It is imperative that we teach future rabbis how to persuasively convey that message. Rabbis of the present and of the future are dealing with an increasingly assimilated and diverse group of congregants, and will need to be adaptable in ways that were not nearly so necessary in the more insular past. Again, multiple approaches need to be taught so that the rabbis of the future will be adaptable to differing demands.

I do not know if all existing seminaries will be capable of and willing to address these issues head-on in a timely fashion. If there are institutional obstacles, these needs must be addressed in other ways. One vehicle that comes to mind is continuing rabbinic education. In any event, conveying all of this information to students in their twenties is a tall order. Post-graduate rabbis will have their own experiences and questions, making them more able to contribute to interactive sessions on these topics.

How to ensure that Judaism thrives is a topic too important to leave solely to the rabbinate. While aware of the problem, seminaries and rabbis have met with only partial success in addressing this growing problem over the past several decades. Concerned lay leaders, particularly those who have had the benefit of a solid Jewish education, have a unique role to play in bridging the gap. They need to join in this conversation, and our rabbis need to be open to their input. No one cares more about the future of Judaism than our rabbis. They devote their lives to these issues. They can be our most valuable asset. We need to teach them how to lead us.

Richard Kelber is a lawyer with the law firm of Moss and Barnett in Minneapolis, Minnesota. He obtained his B.A., with a major in Hebrew language from the University of Minnesota in 1972, having studied at the Hebrew University of Jerusalem during his junior year. He graduated from Harvard Law School in 1975. Richard is deeply concerned with the future of the Jewish people both in America and Israel and brings to this topic the perspective of a consumer of rabbinical services.

Addressing Challenges of Rabbinic Identity Formation

By Richard Hirsh

In asking "How well do non-Orthodox rabbinical programs prepare people for their rabbinate?" we need to ask "How well do rabbinical programs help aspiring rabbis to cultivate their own Jewish identity, challenge their assumptions, orient them to the community they will serve, and allow them to be self-reflective about their own rabbinic identity formation?" While admittedly a longer question, the four dimensions really go the core of how our community prepares people to assume the title Rabbi with responsibility, capability and confidence.

Cultivating Jewish Identity

Before they reach rabbinical school, people have a prior Jewish identity. In an earlier time, that identity could be assumed to fall within familiar patterns such as having two Jewish parents, a strong and vibrant Jewish home life, some substantial Jewish education, likely an Israel experience as well as Jewish youth group and summer camp, and having one's Jewishness as a core piece, even the core piece, of one's identity. Those were most often, if not exclusively, the kinds of Jews who thought about becoming rabbis throughout the mid-to-late 20th Century.

Twenty-first century rabbinic students sometimes resemble this description, but less often. They are increasingly products of families that identify as interfaith (one parent is and remains non-

Jewish) or conversionary (one parent was not born Jewish but converted to Judaism). Increasing numbers of rabbinic students are themselves converts. Irrespective of family of origin, significant Jewish identification by contemporary rabbinic students may be a fairly recent development in their own lives. Their formal or informal Jewish education may be minimal. Israel may be a source of solidarity and pride, but can also be a source of tension or contention, and these are not mutually exclusive. Youth group or Jewish summer camp, especially camp, seems to still play some significant role for many.

The economics of rabbinic school admissions—too many schools, too few students—have seminary admissions committees continually revising their image of an ideal rabbinic candidate. While rabbinical programs might want to hold out for applicants with rich, deep and literate Jewish backgrounds that are expressed through rich, deep and literate patterns of Jewish living, abstract standards or expectations are increasingly in tension with the individual narratives, ways of identifying, and personal Jewish journeys of 21st Century rabbinical school candidates.

Given the diverse and generally less-deep Jewish backgrounds of rabbinic students, one key task of rabbinic school education in the 21st Century is to assure that along with teaching students to be rabbis, seminaries are attending to the cultivation of their Jewish identities as well. This represents a significant addition to the already-crowded agenda of curricula and practicums, but an addition that is critical for the next generation of rabbis to be successful.

In the academic atmosphere of post-modernism, defining core essential Jewish competencies and convictions is a politically charged problem. Today's rabbinic students emerge from a Jewish population that Steven Cohen and Arnold Eisen characterize as embodying "the sovereign self," a population that takes personal choice for granted and often chafes at the idea of a collective norm, standard or expectation. Helping rabbinic students differentiate between the responsibility to master rabbinic fundamentals while also allowing for individual experimentation with their Jewish expression requires sensitivity and nuance. In order to navigate this set of challenges, rabbinic school faculties will need to cultivate not only academic expertise but pastoral and mentoring skills to guide as well as to teach.

The Jews (and increasingly the non-Jews to whom they are married) that rabbis will serve are coming to Jewish life with interest and commitment but often without the tools they need to create vibrant Jewish living. These are people who rabbis will be privileged to guide through the journey into discovery of Jewish resources, discernment about which will and what will not serve individual spiritual growth, experimentation with ritual, and study of classical and contemporary sources. If during their time as rabbinical students these future rabbis can engage those same issues, they will be better prepared to lead others on the path to Jewish life.

Challenging Assumptions

Most academically accredited rabbinic programs in North America are five years long. If a student comes in and goes out without having changed her or his mind about anything, or adapted her or his Jewish ritual practice, or become less certain about some belief or non-belief, and more certain about others, something is wrong.

It is not surprising that to the degree that younger rabbinic students come from a millennial profile, they often reflect a preference for boundary-breaking, norm-challenging, role-bending, and radical autonomy. These sorts of fundamental and foundational challenges can be valuable stimulants towards reimagining and re-visioning what Judaism and the Jewish community may look like in the future. They can serve as provocative but also productive challenges to faculty. But such challenges need to be two-directional, with rabbinic students being gently but firmly challenged about assumptions, ideologies and assertions.

As Mordecai Kaplan noted over eighty years ago in *Judaism as a Civilization*, in (North) America, Jewish identity emerges and exists in the larger context of the majority culture. As American social, political and ideological discourse continues on a path to polarization, it should not be surprising that American Jewish discourse often proceeds on a parallel path. Our Jewish community has been slow to come to terms with the diffusion of formally assumed core consensus and the consequent need to shape a discourse that allows for difference. While debate about Israel is the current prime example, one can find similar problems in addressing areas like religious practice and belief and outreach to interfaith families.

Seminaries need to be preparing future rabbis for the reality that in an era of transition, certitude is a posture that ill-serves both rabbis and the communities in which they will work. How will rabbinic school faculties probe and prod students to rethink their own often rigid ideological assumptions? What can rabbinic schools learn from the tensions on contemporary university campuses between open discussion and the shutting down of open discussion that ideological posturing often creates?

Seminaries can model how other Jews, and other rabbis, may hold very different positions that are just that—different. They are not inferior, or in error, or benighted, or to be dismissed. The goal in generating such dialogue is not to get endorsement or agreement, but to gain understanding as to the fundamental ideas, values and beliefs that lead rabbis to hold divergent opinions.

For a tradition like Judaism that is premised on debate, discussion and challenge, the homogenization of content and the avoidance of difficult issues are particularly ill-suited. It is not a neat world into which rabbis are emerging, not a neat Jewish world and not a neat general society in which Jews are embedded. A seminary that shields students in a cocoon of consensus (real or presumed) does no one a favor, and poorly prepares future rabbis for the community in which they will serve. What seminaries *can* do in a way that other institutions cannot is teach the wisdom Jewish tradition offers about *how* to have difficult conversations. The exegetical traditions on the verse "you shall surely reprove your neighbor"[1] and the wise insights of *Pirkei Avot*[2] are good starting places for that task.

Becoming Oriented to the Community

The early 21st Century is a difficult time to become a rabbi. We are living in a time analogous to that of the rabbis of the Mishnah.[3]

---

1   Leviticus 19:17.
2   "The Insights of the Ancestors."
3   "Paradigms for Contemporary Reconstructionism," *The Reconstructionist* (Spring 2006).

The task of that hour was to help organize a productive conversation through which a fragmented community unsure of its norms could begin both to consolidate and to create.

We are living in a period when the presumptions, processes and principles of the Jewish community in which the older generation of rabbis served no longer seem obvious, and that community itself is increasingly diverse. The traditional denominational paradigms of Orthodox, Reform, Conservative, Reconstructionist and Renewal no longer exclusively frame Jewish spiritual engagement.

Even while noting this diversity, we can still point to some consistent centers of concern and consensus in the Jewish community, even if specific refractions and prior assumptions are no longer as universal as once assumed. One task of rabbinic schools is to help sensitize students to the multi-generational assumptions about Jewish identity, Jewish norms, and Jewish belief and practice that they will encounter.

In his 1986 study *Sacred Survival*, Jonathan Woocher identified seven principles of what he called "civil Judaism," areas where he argued there was a general consensus in the Jewish community. While it would be harder to find the consensus on content that Woocher observed nearly thrity years ago, most if not all of the broad categories he identified remain central to the agenda of the Jewish community.

Woocher's 1986 list included the following core ideas as recurring in those who identified as Jews and connected to the Jewish community: the unity and distinctiveness of the Jewish people; mutual responsibility of Jews for each other; Jewish survival was endangered; support for Israel; affirmation of Jewish tradition (if not always personal practice of that tradition); *tzedakah*; and that integration into American society rather than segregation from that society could be accomplished while simultaneously maintaining identity, individual and communal. The debates within each of those areas has expanded, consensus may have diminished, but the Jewish community in which rabbinical students will work as rabbis still reflects many of these core concepts.

It is a challenge to orient rabbinic students to the community in which they will work. Rabbinic schools often fail to recruit to their faculties rabbis who have had extensive professional experience in synagogues, Hillels, agencies, chaplaincies or other such places—precisely the kinds of places where rabbinical students will seek employment. A few guest lectures or occasional visits by rabbis from the field do not substitute for the day-to-day experience with teachers who have both academic expertise and practical experience in the Jewish community.

Five-year programs of study almost inevitably lead, to one degree or another, to a culture of insularity. That insularity is not only a challenge for students, but for faculty and administration as well. Teaching in a seminary is unlike teaching in a college or graduate school, just as being a seminary student is different than being a graduate school student. The insularity of the rabbinic school experience can easily if unintentionally produce rabbis for whom awareness and understanding of the Jewish community in which they will work, and the mainstream assumptions, sympathies and beliefs of the multiple generations of Jews in that community, may come as a challenging surprise.

The rabbinic custodians of a tradition that holds each person to be created *b'tzelem Elohim*, in the divine image, need to be open to engagement with the full range of opinion and diversity in the Jewish community, not just the viewpoints with which they already agree. Challenging the assumptions within the seminary system, whether of faculty or of students, should be a constant concern.

Being Self-Reflective About Rabbinic Identity Formation

One of the most significant changes in American culture and by extension in American Jewish culture over the past several decades is the recognition that identity is fluid, evolving and changing, not static, stable and fixed. As applied to Jewish identity, this has yielded a series of insights and metaphors, with "journey" and "path" being among the most common. People no longer have an identity, they are on a journey towards one; becoming has replaced being.

If this is true about Jewish identity, then it is all the more so for rabbinic identity. Just as "Jewish" does not fit neatly into a given category of ethnicity, religion, or culture, neither does "rabbi" fall easily into a professional profile. Rabbis are, with some exceptions, not as academically accomplished as a PhD in Jewish Studies might be. But rabbis are more than Jewish social workers with a rabbi's manual. What is rabbinic identity, and how is it formed?

Gil Rendle of the Alban Institute quotes corporate consultants Jagdish Sheth and Andrew Sobel who use the term "deep generalist" to refer to "someone who has a core expertise onto which he or she layers knowledge of related and unrelated fields." Rendle suggests this is an appropriate term for clergy, and adds: "a deep generalist has a very deep knowledge of one's own truth but also…sufficient insight, maturity, experience and wisdom to be able to maintain an informal, generalized approach to complex situations."[4]

As deep generalists assuming a professional identity, rabbis will need to think self-consciously about their roles, both generic and specific. This goes beyond pulpit rabbi, campus rabbi, or chaplain. This goes to the issue of being mindful-in-the-moment as to what we are being asked to do or feel called to. Are we pastors or *poseks*? Are we priestly, dispensing atonement and forgiveness? Are we prophetic, making moral demands and expressing ethical expectations? Is our role what we bring to the moment or shaped by what the moment demands?

I am not arguing for one model for all rabbis. Any rabbi with even a modicum of experience can narrate the span of roles she or he is called upon to fill, regardless of professional setting. I am arguing for the importance of introducing self-reflection on rabbinic identity formation into every year of seminary training, and teaching techniques by which that self-reflection can continue after ordination.

Just as we now prepare Jews to be aware that the ways in which they express their Jewishness is likely to change over the course of their lifetime, we need to prepare rabbis to expect that their self-understanding, areas of emphasis and expertise, and professional profiles will likely evolve, change, develop and grow over the course of their careers. This is potentially a fruitful intersection where seminaries and rabbinic associations can collaborate.

Conclusion

Rabbinical schools prepare people for their rabbinate adequately but not optimally. To prepare rabbinic students in an optimal way

---

4   Gil Rendle, "The Leadership We Need," *Congregations,* Journal of the Alban Institute Sept-Oct (2001) 6.

requires reflection on what moment in Jewish history we are asking them to become rabbis; what are the characteristics of that moment; what can and cannot be accomplished in such a moment; what roles are rabbis more and less likely to be called upon to fill in that moment; and how they will remain simultaneously rooted in core convictions while being nimble, imaginative and adaptive in responding to an accelerating set of changes and challenges supported by a technological revolution in communication? These are likely to become questions not only of content but of practice, and not only of questions of tradition but of technique.

Rabbi Richard Hirsh was the Executive Director of the Reconstructionist Rabbinical Association and an adjunct faculty member at the Reconstructionist Rabbinical College from 1998-2014. He was the editor of the journal The Reconstructionist *(1996-2006), Executive Director of the Philadelphia Board of Rabbis/Jewish Chaplaincy Service (1988-1993), and has served congregations in Toronto, Chicago, New York and New Jersey. Rabbi Hirsh was chair of the Reconstructionist movement Commission on the Role of the Rabbi, and the author of the report* The Rabbi-Congregation Relationship: A Vision for the 21st Century *(2001).*

Teaching to the Head and Heart:
The Power of Weeping

By Dr. Lynne Heller

Most every *motze'ei Shabbat*, my father-in-law of blessed memory, Rabbi A. M. Heller, would compare sermon notes with my late husband, Rabbi Zachary Heller, *z"l*.

"What did you speak about?" the senior Heller asked.

"About twenty minutes," my husband would playfully quip.

After exchanging ideas, invariably, my father-in-law would query, "So, Zachary, did you hit them in the gut?"

My father-in-law understood, as did my husband, that intellectual insights on that week's *parsahah*, however brilliant and incisive, did not suffice in a sermon. The congregation wanted to be touched in the heart as well as engaged in the mind. Often there was a disconnect for pulpit rabbis between the head—the academic learning they had acquired in the ivory towers of rabbinical school and their subsequent role as scholar/teacher—and the heart—the practical applications to real life situations so necessary to their role as pastor/emotional and spiritual caregiver. To be sure, they had mastered the texts in class; however, to paraphrase Professor Abraham Joshua Heschel, they didn't quite know how to take the Torah to the streets, to the pews of the synagogue, and to the hearts of their congregants. Not all rabbis know how to hit congregants in the gut. Are the rabbis remiss or had their teachers, perhaps, failed to teach to the minds *and* the hearts of their rabbinical students.

A ubiquitous theme of head versus heart courses through world literature, suggesting a dichotomy of either/or. I suggest, when we approach teaching the biblical text in rabbinic training and in adult learning, that we do not have the dichotomy of either/or, but a dialectic of both/and, of head *and* heart, with both elements co-existing in dynamic partnership, one infusing the other with meaning. This dialectic between head and heart has shaped and continues to shape my life as a Jew in the pew, a senior educator, and teacher of future rabbis.

A verse from *Mishnah Avot* captures the essence of my life: "*Kol ya'mai gu'dalti bein hahachamim* (All my life, I grew up/have been raised amongst the sages/rabbis)."[1] My father had served several terms as synagogue president; consequently, I grew up surrounded by rabbis when I went to synagogue and when they frequented my home. I married a seventh generation rabbi, and we were surrounded by my husband's historical, illustrious rabbinic lineage as well as the respective living generations of rabbinic friends and colleagues of my father-in-law and my husband.

A few years ago, this verse assumed another layer of meaning for me. The hassidic masters famously tweaked the text, hyper-reading it in order to extract new and sometimes provocative meaning. Reb Nachman of Breslov interpreted the word *bein* in the *Avot* text to mean not *among* the scholars, but *in between* the scholars. Shortly after my husband passed away, I joined a second synagogue, while still retaining my membership in the original synagogue my husband and I had attended together. I began to grow, not among the rabbis, but rather between the two rabbis, drawing strength, inspiration, and knowledge from each of them. I expanded my purview; I began branching out.

Both rabbis, by nature, are sensitive individuals and highly intellectual. Yet, when they each preach, their respective rabbinic styles diverge. One is more academic and scholarly, quoting rabbinic sources and comparing sacred texts; the other, while he builds the sermon on intellectual scaffolding, when getting to the heart of the matter, he hits me in the gut. As an academic, I appreciate the scholarly approach, the opportunity to learn from my Rabbi; yet at the very same time, I seek the emotional component because, as I have come to discover, getting hit in the gut, perhaps even shedding a tear, is a compelling conduit to learning, both for the teacher and for the student.

---

1 *Avot* 1:17.

Borrowing a phrase from *Hamlet*, "by indirection seek direction out," allow me to explain. To be sure, there is an emotional component to adult learning in addition to the intellectual engagement. Several years ago, a fascinating article by Harvard Divinity School professor Kimberly C. Patton appeared in the *Journal of the American Academy of Religion*.[2] In it, she demonstrates how tapping into the emotions, with the resultant weeping on the part of the students, intensifies the learning process and enables students to grasp the subject on a multi-dimensional level. Education is a matter of mind and heart.

Implementing Professor Patton's reflections, I have since worked weeping into my Bible syllabi for *Me'ah* and rabbinical school classes by interspersing several readings throughout the semester, which I know can trigger tears. We read the selections together, usually at the conclusion of the class, and invariably at least one of the students begins to weep. I admit the selection and placement of these readings is somewhat contrived; yet, sometimes, I am blindsided and do not anticipate the weeping.

I was teaching the story of the exodus from Egypt in *sh'mot* and contrasting Israelite religion as a mountain culture (Mt. Moriah, Mt. Sinai, Har Zion) with Egyptian religion as a tower culture (the pyramids). To capture and summarize the essence of the discussion, I introduced the text of the famous poem *Ozymandias*, written in 1817 by the English romantic poet Shelley:

> I met a traveler from an ancient land
> Who said: Two vast and trunkless legs of stone
> Stand in the desert. Near them, on the sand,
> Half sunk, a shattered visage lies, whose frown
> And wrinkled lip, and sneer of cold command,
> Tell that its sculptor well those passions read
> Which yet survive, stamped on these lifeless things,
> The hand that mocked them and the heart that fed.
> And on the pedestal these words appear:
> "My name is Ozymandias, king of kings;

---

2   Kimberly C. Patton, "Stumbling Along Between the Immensities: Reflections on Teaching in the Study of Religion," *Journal of the American Academy of Religion*. Vol.65, No.4, Winter (1997) 831-849.

Look on my works, ye Mighty, and despair!"
Nothing beside remains. Round the decay
Of that colossal wreck, boundless and bare,
The lone and level sands stretch far away.

I asked for a student to volunteer to read the poem. One woman, her eyes welling with tears, raised her hand, explaining excitedly, "My father always had us read this poem at our seders! He died two years ago on the second day of *Pesach*. I need to read this poem."

As she read the poem, I explained how the image of the broken statue was an ironic commentary (a poetic midrash, you might say) on the tower culture that Egypt represented. I included this poem in the lesson because, according to a passage in Diodorus Sicilus, a Greek historian of the first century BCE, the largest statue in Egypt bore the inscription "I am Ozymandias, king of kings." Ozymandias was another name for Rameses II, the Pharaoh of the exodus!

Now my student was weeping. She spoke just above a whisper. "I never drew the connections with our tradition. I'm not sure my father drew the connections, either, but you connected all the dots for me." The new intellectual insights were now forged in the smithy of her soul and became the scaffolding for her emotional memories. Head and heart were interlaced with her tears. "I wasn't going to come today," she continued. "I just had minor surgery and was tempted to stay home and rest. I never would have forgiven myself if I had missed this class. It changed my life."

The class ended in dead silence. Not a paper was rustling as the students quietly filed out, one by one, each trying to process what had just happened, each engrossed in the personal drama of this profound educational moment.

Transposing Professor Patton's concept of weeping into the realm of Torah, it is the difference between Moses as lawgiver—*Mattan Torah*—and Moses as charismatic teacher—*Kabbalat Torah*. Kimberly Patton writes, "The weeping episode was not the extraneous emotional by-product of one class. Rather, their tears had catalyzed intellectual integration, running like a conduit stream between levels of knowing [*Mattan Torah*] and enabling [*Kabbalat Torah*]."[3]

---

3   Ibid, 833.

According to Rashi, when Moses comes down the mountain in Exodus 34, he lifts the veil in order to reveal himself to the people. On the one hand, he is revealed in all his glory—*karan or panav*—still bathed in the aura of his direct encounter with God. And, on the other hand, he is revealed in all his vulnerabilities—his humanity and humility—as he conveys the power of Divine *dibbur* to the people. In that unobstructed encounter, there is an interchange between Moses as teacher and *B'nai Yisrael* that transcends pure intellect and touches the heart. This is *Kabbalat Torah* in the truest sense.

In the summer of 2013, I participated in the Rabbinic Torah Study Seminar (RTS) at the Hartman Institute in Jerusalem. My educational journey came full circle in the compelling, moving, and transformative capstone to my RTS experience. I wept.

That final morning in the *beit midrash*, Dr. Donniel Hartman taught to the head and the heart, punctuating his academic teaching of texts with moving illustrations from the life work of his father, Rabbi David Hartman, *z"l*. Donniel was teaching a roomful of rabbis. Masterfully, Donniel integrated knowing and enabling.[4] He combined critical scholarship *(Mattan Torah)* with tender vignettes of his *Abba* as the *chevruta* (study/learning partner) to the Rambam *(Kabbalat Torah)*.

When he concluded his *shiur*, suddenly and unaccountably, tears welled up in my eyes. There I was, the accomplished master teacher, respected member of the Hebrew College faculty—astonishingly transformed into a student weeping.

Weeping for the very first time, I was experiencing directly what heretofore I had only witnessed and experienced indirectly in my students. The veil had been lifted; I was at once the student and the teacher! *Mattan Torah* and *Kabbalat Torah* were ineluctably linked. I returned home energized and empowered, rendered a far more effective teacher for having experienced for myself the power of weeping. Weeping enabled me to translate the ancient Hebrew texts into the language of the heart.

A dermatologist friend often recounts stories of patients declaring "I am giving myself a gift. I'm getting a facelift." In experiencing the power of weeping, I gave myself the gift of a mind lift.

---

4   The concepts coined by Kimberly Patton.

A mind lift suggests to me a change in orientation—a shift in how we think and how we see the world.

One of my rabbinical students would come into the classroom and routinely stand on her head before class would begin. "I love to get the blood from my heart rushing to my brain," she explained, totally unaware of the prescient message embodied in her exercise. For, it is no coincidence that in the Bible and our tradition, the heart is the seat of the intellect and the emotions as well as the center for one's commitment to God. *Rachmanah libei baei*—God desires the heart. Indeed, the image of the blood rushing from the heart to the brain is a pointedly graphic representation in physiological terms of how head and heart are to be spiritually commingled.

Standing on one's head, one sees the world from a vastly different perspective which can astonish while it awakens new meanings and suggests new ways of approaching the heart of the text.

Standing on one's head demands great discipline and balance—the balance between head and heart, between *Mattan Torah* and *Kabbalat Torah*, between knowing and enabling, and ultimately, a balance between rabbi as lawgiver/*mara d'atra* and rabbi as charismatic teacher/pastor.

If we expect our rabbis to preach and teach to the head and the heart and thus experience the power of weeping, then *we*, the educators, must first teach to *their* heads and hearts. This educational challenge may require that we stand on our heads once in awhile—if not physically, then figuratively and pedagogically.

Dr. Lynne Heller, who holds a Ph.D. in English and Comparative Literature, combines her passion for the biblical text with her academic background in Jewish Studies and Comparative Literature. She is a respected member of the Me'ah Bible faculty at Hebrew College and has taught Bible in their Rabbinical School. She lends new definition to the term "sandwich generation" as the daughter-in-law of a rabbi, wife of a rabbi, and currently the mother of an eighth-generation rabbi.

Keeping Faith in Rabbis:
Expanding the Conversation

By Rabbi Hayim Herring, PhD & Ellie Roscher

"We both came to believe that uncertainty is permanent, chaotic times are normal, change is accelerating, and instability will likely characterize the rest of our lives." [1]

The people who brought one God to the world are becoming increasingly more secular. American Jews outside of Orthodoxy feel distant from Judaism as a religion, which raises important questions about the role of the rabbi, rabbinical education and the rabbinate. Courageous conversation is imperative because we need our rabbis now more than ever. Rabbis do the essential work of translating the sacred, facilitating relationships and preserving ritual. Strategically supported rabbis can ignite thriving Jewish communities that have a sense of where we have been and where we are going.

Today, in these uncertain and unstable times, people often talk at one another. True dialogue, filled with active listening, is the way forward in matters as near and dear to us as faith. *Keeping Faith in Rabbis* creates a venue of rich interaction where people talk with one another. Three primary stakeholders in rabbinical education—rabbis, lay leaders and educators of current and future rabbis—expand their conversations with one another, regardless of denominational or seminary label. What emerges is abundant collective wisdom that can lead to creative and authentic approaches to rabbinical education.

---

1 Morten T. Hansen and Jim.Collins, *Great by Choice.* (Random House 2011)193.

Essayists state clearly that rabbinical school must continue to root itself in our rich tradition by teaching knowledge of Jewish texts, traditions and facility in Hebrew. Technology may change how we acquire this knowledge, but an authentic rabbinic persona is rooted in a broad and robust knowledge of Jewish texts across the ages. This rootedness gives a rabbi authority, but authority that must be matched by empathy, openness, and willingness to learn with the community.

Additionally, stakeholders present relevant ideas for reform in both content and structure to fit the needs of our students and communities. Rabbinical education must take seriously Jewish identity formation and spiritual direction of its students. Often, students are entering rabbinical school with recently acquired or thin Jewish identities. Receiving rabbinical ordination does not signify the end of an ongoing relationship with God. In fact, continuing to grow spiritually once rabbis are ordained becomes only more important. Continuing education, spiritual development, the use of pop culture and the arts as sources of inspiration and teaching are intriguing issues ripe for further exploration. Questions of structure remain, and some essayists advocate for alternatives to a five-year academic program that account for the realities of geography, cost, time, family life and part-time rabbinates.

The wise and exciting voices and ideas in this conversation are not confined to these pages. *Keeping Faith in Rabbis* began as a book project, but the conversation had to be expanded to honor the volume of response we received. The range of ideas, the passion of our contributors and their multi-generational perspectives inspired us to facilitate a multi-channel conversation. We created an online home that exists symbiotically with the book where fruitful talking can continue via blogging, social media, video interviews and thoughtful forums and comment sections. We are also taking the conversation to the streets in live presentations around the country. Our hope is that you will react to our essayists here and online and join in our conversation. Come to the expanding table, asking questions that lead toward action. The ongoing conversation can be found on Rabbi Hayim Herring's Facebook page as well as Avenida Books' and Ellie Roscher's media channels.[2]

---

2   www.facebook.com/rabbihayimherring, www.ktfrabbi.avenidabooks.com, www.ellieroscher.com.

Keeping Faith in Rabbis is not a historical or social science project, so we intentionally do not offer conclusions or policy prescriptions here. Questions help us gain deeper insight into the nature of our time and enable experimentation and reflection that ultimately lead to wiser, more enduring responses. What are the barriers inhibiting a richer, multi-vocal dialogue about the state of theological education, regardless of ideology or movement? How can rabbis embrace the agility needed to lead in an increasingly secular and media saturated society? How can rabbis encourage and enhance the quality of Jewish life in America? How do we move from conversation to experimentation so that more Jewish individuals and families are open to the beauty of the spiritual dimensions of Jewish living?

As the Jewish conversation expands, it's helpful to keep in mind that we are not alone. The Pew Study reports similar trends of secularization in the American Protestant community.[3] Worshipping communities are shrinking, membership is down, and the number of people born Christian who do not claim religious affiliation is on the rise. *Keeping the Faith in Seminary*, a prior volume in this series, also explores questions and challenges in Protestant theological education in light of our changing religious landscape.[4] Seminaries, like rabbinical schools, offer priceless training in translating sacred text and creating ritual. Can that training, however, continue to be long programs on static campuses that require families to uproot and take on significant debt? Do pastors need more training in things like business, finance and entrepreneurship? In short, is the content and structure of seminary still working? It may be time for Jews and Christians to ask hard questions together and learn with each other. We hope these two books can be a launching pad for that powerful and productive interfaith dialogue.

The future quality of Jewish spiritual life is unclear. We can choose to see the change, instability and uncertainty as a crisis beyond our control or an opportunity waiting to be shaped. The passion, honesty, creativity and thought presented here and Keeping Faith in Rabbis Online inspire us with optimism. It's time to seize the opportunity.

---

3   "U.S. Religious Landscape Survey: Religious Affiliation," *Pew Research Religious & Public Life Project*, February 1 (2008) www.pewforum.org, Acquired August 25, 2014.

4   Roscher, Ellie (Ed.). *Keeping the Faith in Seminary* (Avenida Books, Minneapolis: 2012).

Religious communities in America need to be a wellspring for finding personal meaning and contributing collective good. The national conversation needs to support educators to cultivate and sustain rabbis. Locally, dedicated rabbis need to support and be supported by one another, other Jewish professionals and caring lay people. We all must cross human made boundaries to grow together. Join us in doing hard work, asking stimulating questions, talking with all stakeholders, and moving toward creative action.

An ancient rabbinic commentary questions where the Biblical Israelites found acacia wood in the desert to build the tabernacle that God commanded them to construct.[5] One suggestion is that our Biblical ancestor, Jacob, brought trees with him on his journey from Canaan to Egypt. Abraham, his grandfather, had planted these trees in Beersheva. The Israelites would take these trees with them when they were liberated from Egyptian slavery. Did Jacob know his descendants would be commanded to build a wooden ark? Not likely! Rather, we learn that each generation must consider the needs of future generations. We must offer enough of our strong raw materials for them to shape into forms that they need in their time. We have been through transitions before, and by drawing on our understandings of God and Jewish experience, we have faith in our future.

---

5   Exodus 25:10.

CPSIA information can be obtained at www.ICGtesting.com
Printed in the USA
BVOW03s1257061214

377384BV00005B/18/P